STRANGE TOOLS

ALSO BY ALVA NOË

Varieties of Presence

Out of Our Heads: Why You Are Not Your Brain,
and Other Lessons from the Biology of Consciousness

Action in Perception

STRANGE
TOOLS

Art and
Human Nature

ALVA NOË

Hill and Wang

A division of Farrar, Straus and Giroux

New York

Hill and Wang
A division of Farrar, Straus and Giroux
18 West 18th Street, New York 10011

Library of Congress Cataloging-in-Publication Data
Noë, Alva.
    Strange tools : art and human nature / Alva Noë. — First edition.
        pages   cm
    Includes bibliographical references and index.
    ISBN 978-0-8090-8917-8 (hardcover) — ISBN 978-1-4299-4525-7 (ebook)
    1. Art—Psychology.   I. Title.

N71.N64 2015
700.1—dc23
                                                                    2015005199

Designed by Jonathan D. Lippincott

Our books may be purchased in bulk for promotional, educational, or
business use. Please contact your local bookseller or the Macmillan
Corporate and Premium Sales Department at 1-800-221-7945, extension
5442, or by e-mail at MacmillanSpecialMarkets@macmillan.com.

www.fsgbooks.com
www.twitter.com/fsgbooks • www.facebook.com/fsgbooks

1   3   5   7   9   10   8   6   4   2

For Hans Noë and Judith Baldwin Noë

By one of the ironic perversities that often attend the course of affairs, the existence of the works of art upon which formation of an esthetic theory depends has become an obstruction to theory about them. —John Dewey

Contents

Preface

Some years ago I was talking with an artist. He asked me about the science of visual perception. I explained that vision scientists seek to understand how it is we see so much—the colorful and detailed world of objects spread out around us in space—when what we are given are tiny distorted upside-down images in the eyes. How do we see so much on the basis of so little?

I was startled by the artist's reply. Nonsense! he scoffed. That's not the question we should ask. The important question is this: Why are we so blind, why do we see so little, when there is so much around us to see?

This exchange took place when I was a graduate student. The artist's remark stayed with me. It brings out sharply the opposition between two different ways of thinking about visual experience.

In one way, the scientist's way, seeing happens in the brain, thanks to the way the brain manages to make sense of information available on the retina.

In the other way, the artist's way, seeing isn't something that happens automatically, or for free; we are too liable not to see even what is there. Seeing is an achievement, *our* achievement, the achievement of making contact with what there is. We can fail to see.

I have spent the last two decades studying perception and perceptual consciousness. I have sought to develop a new way of understanding perception. Seeing, according to the enactive or actionist position that I have been working out, is not something that happens in our brains, or anywhere else, for that matter; it is something we do, or make, or achieve. And like everything else we achieve, we do so only against the background of our skills, knowledge, situation, and environment, including our social environment.

It dawned on me only recently that my research these last years has aimed at vindicating precisely the perspective of the artist in my anecdote. He had it right all along. The brain is necessary for experience, to be sure. But it is not the whole story. The scientist's conception is impoverished, and it gets in the way of our appreciating that it is not brains that perceive, but active animals or people. Seeing, I have come to realize, and so I've been urging in my writing, is more like climbing a tree, or reading a book, than it is like digesting what you've eaten.

But this anecdote suggests something more. *The artist was right.* Science and philosophy, to the extent that they concern themselves with art, tend to do so from on high. They seek to *explain* art, to treat art as a phenomenon to be analyzed. Maybe we've been overlooking the possibility that art can be our teacher, or at least our collaborator. Not because art is cryptoscience, but because it is its own manner of investigation and its own legitimate source of knowledge. This is what is suggested to me as I think back on this conversation with the artist.

This is a puzzling if attractive possibility. It's attractive, for it offers, right off the bat, some clue to why art is so important. But it's puzzling, too, because art looks very different from science, which is explicitly concerned with the production of knowledge and understanding. What might the character of the knowledge at which art aims be?

Here's part of the answer: art provides us an opportunity to catch ourselves in the act of achieving our conscious lives, of bringing the world into focus for perceptual (and other forms of) consciousness. And so art is a field in which we can take seriously the artist's question posed above: not, how do we manage to see so much? but rather, why do we see so little? Even as it also gives us an opportunity to move from not seeing to seeing, or from seeing to seeing more or seeing differently.

·

This book is animated by three ideas.

First, art is not a technological practice; however, it presupposes such practices. Works of art are *strange tools*. Technology is not just something we use or apply to achieve a goal, although this is right as a first approximation. Technologies organize our lives in ways that make it impossible to conceive of our lives in their absence; they make us what we are. Art, really, is an engagement with the ways our practices, techniques, and technologies organize us, and it is, finally, a way to understand our organization and, inevitably, to reorganize ourselves.

The job of art, its true work, is philosophical. This is the second animating idea. Art is a philosophical practice. And philosophy—artists will like this, I'm not so sure about philosophers—is an artistic practice. This is because both art and philosophy—superficially so different—are really species of a common genus whose preoccupation is with the ways we are organized and with the possibility of reorganizing ourselves. I don't mean that this is what artists think or say they are doing (although some will). I mean that this is what they are and have always been doing. And this is what philosophy does.

The third and final animating idea is one that will itself acquire meaning only after we have advanced considerably: art and philosophy are practices, as I put it, bent on the invention of writing.

PART I

To be part of something one doesn't in the least understand is, I think, one of the most intriguing things about life.   —Agatha Christie

1

Getting Organized

Western art abounds with depictions of the nursing mother. The display of the Mother and Child is central to Christian religious thinking, so this isn't surprising. But it may be that pictures of the suckling infant are important to us for reasons that go beyond our interest in the life of Jesus. Breast-feeding, after all, is basic to our mammalian biology; it is also, for the vast majority of us, our first opportunity for nurturing love. In fact, or so at least I propose, breast-feeding is also a key to understanding the very nature of art; the fact that pictures of nursing mothers are so common may point to one of art's abiding features: art is always concerned with itself.

The connection between breast-feeding and the nature of art is not immediately apparent. This may just show how far we need to go to get a clear understanding of art and its origins in our biology.

When it comes to breast-feeding, the striking thing about human beings is that, alone among the mammals, we do it very badly. It's not just that breast-feeding can be difficult for us—many babies need to learn to latch on, and this can get stressful for both mother and child as the need for food is urgent and dramatic. Our frailty as feeders is more far-reaching than that. With all other mammals, once the infant has latched on, it stays put and sucks until the job is done, until it is sated, or until some external factor (a competitive sibling, for example) drives it away.

But not so the human baby. Our babies are liable to wander during the task. They get distracted by noises. Or they blissfully fall asleep.

Or they indulge in the pleasures of biting and chewing to the neglect of the main business at hand, which is drinking. Isn't it? Actually,
so inefficient is human breast-feeding that some anthropologists and
psychologists have speculated that its primary evolutionary value in
humans may not consist in feeding at all, but may lie elsewhere. Perhaps we've got it backward. We don't suckle to feed; we feed at the
breast, so that we can touch and hold and embrace. Physical contact
induces neurochemical events (such as the release of oxytocin) that
are beneficial and necessary. And then there is the fact, perhaps
not unrelated to the neurochemistry, that physical contact cements
the attachment of mother and infant.

•

Let's explore this issue more fully by taking a concrete look at the
activity of breast-feeding itself. Notice, it has a characteristic shape.
Mother cradles infant, placing the breast—or a bottle, for my purposes
this difference doesn't matter—to the infant's mouth. Baby sucks; then,
let us imagine, it nods off. Mothers respond by gently jiggling the infant and in this way drawing it back to the task; this is a spontaneous
reaction of mothers, not something they learn or are taught. Baby re-
sumes sucking. A movement or sound or noise startles the baby. It
stops sucking. Mama jiggles. Baby starts sucking again. Soon it nods
off. Mama jiggles. And the cycle continues. As the baby grows older,
and stronger, and as the mother gains more confidence, the process
gets smoother and more efficient. But the basic issue—getting the
baby to eat enough before it falls asleep—is something that requires
attention and negotiation.

Now, consider this activity of breast-feeding carefully and notice
that it exhibits six distinct features.

First, it is primitive. It is basic. It is biological. Breast-feeding is not
the achievement of high culture but surely something whose roots lie
deep in our mammalian origins. It is *natural*.

Second, despite being basic, and primitive, it is also obviously an
activity that requires the exercise of delicate and evolving cognitive
skills on the part of both mother and infant. Doing and undergoing,
paying attention and losing focus, feeling, listening, responding to
the action or the inaction of the other—the activity of breast-feeding

is made up of all these elements. Not to mention conflict—the baby has fallen asleep before it has had enough to eat! The baby won't stop sucking, but it doesn't seem to be drawing milk!

Third—and this is obvious—the whole activity has a structure; it is organized in time. Indeed, it has something like the structure of turn taking. Baby acts. Mama listens. Mama acts. Baby listens and responds. This is probably the first example of turn taking in our developmental lives; perhaps it is even the first instance of turn taking in the animal world. Notice that the temporal dynamics of breast-feeding make it a lot like a primitive conversation. It is striking that we alone, the linguistic species, act out this complicated turn-taking, conversationlike transaction.

Fourth, neither mother nor infant orchestrates or directs breast-feeding. Sure, Mama is more powerful than the baby; she has more control. She's the one worried about outcomes and seeking the help of friends and midwives. But the activity itself, with its delicate interplay of listening and acting, doing and feeling, and with its distinctive turn-taking temporal dynamics, just sort of happens; the demands of the activity as a whole control, that is, they downward entrain, the behavior of the individuals caught up in it.

Fifth, the whole activity has a function. Exactly what the function is, as we have seen, remains somewhat ambiguous. But it must have something to do with feeding and with creating a relationship of attachment between mother and child. Breast-feeding seems to be a relationship-building exercise.

Finally, although breast-feeding, as we have noticed, is an almost worklike source of conflict, a negotiation, it is also, at least potentially, a source of pleasure for both mother and child.

•

These six features point to ways breast-feeding *organizes* us. The task itself shapes, enables, and constrains us; we find ourselves put together and made up in the setting of the activity. I'd like to introduce the term "organized activity." Breast-feeding is an organized activity. By organized activity I mean any activity, such as breast-feeding, that is marked by the six features I have enumerated. Organized activities, as I would like to use this familiar phrase, are primitive and "natural";

they are arenas for the exercise of attention, looking, listening, doing, undergoing; they exhibit structure in time; they are emergent and are not governed by the deliberate control of any individual; they have a function, whether social or biological or personal. And they are (at least potentially) pleasurable.

Organization, importantly, is a *biological* concept. Living beings are organisms—organized wholes—and the central conceptual puzzle life throws up for science is that of understanding how mere matter, and the order characteristic of physics, gets taken up, integrated, and *organ*-ized in the self-making, world-creating manner of life.

Companies have organizational charts and good bureaucrats may strive to serve the organization (to be "organization men and women"); "organization" may be a term of art in the business school. But organization, fundamentally, is our biological condition, our existential condition. To be alive is to be organized, and insofar as we are not only organisms but are also persons, we find ourselves organized, or integrated, in a still larger range of ways that tie us to the environment, each other, and our social worlds. People find themselves organized by such shared activities as breast-feeding.

It is one of the important ideas of this book that art and its problems have their origin in this vicinity.

•

Here is another example of an organized activity: conversation. At one level, at the level of consciousness, we might say, when two people talk, they express ideas and pay attention to each other. But it is a remarkable fact that conversation puts together, integrates, and organizes what we do at a much more basic level as well. Two people talking tend to take up the same posture, they adjust their volumes to an appropriate level, they look at each other and at objects in their immediate environment in highly controlled ways and, of course, in doing so, they participate in a complicated activity of listening, thinking, paying attention, doing and undergoing, most of which happens spontaneously, without deliberate control. Conversation is obviously natural for human beings—it is basic; we can't imagine human life without it—even if it is also, obviously, a domain for exquisitely refined cognitive attunement to self and other. Conversation has a function, or rather functions, purposes, both locally—whatever interests motivate the transaction between people—and at the species level: conversation is a fundamental mechanism of relationship building and joint living and problem solving. And conversation can be a source of pleasure; it can be fascinating, engaging, challenging, and so on.

I mentioned that breast-feeding may be a sort of primitive conversation. But maybe it would be better to say that conversation is an elaborate or elaborated form of breast-feeding. The same basic organizing structure is in place, however modulated, amplified, and so altered by different skills, interests, and situations.

This example of conversation offers some insight, by the way, into why it is so dangerous to talk on the phone and drive at the same time. Driving is an organized activity; it involves acting and paying attention, responding to what others are doing, and participating in a set of behaviors with its own very specific temporal pattern. When you drive, you aren't just driving, you are locking into and getting organized in relation to a whole space of relationships with others around you and your immediate environment, not only the environment of the car's interior but also that of the roadway. Talking on the phone makes precisely analogous but conflicting demands. You get caught up in a whole different organized activity, with different attentional landmarks and different temporality. Not so when you and I talk to each other as we drive together, or as we walk down the street, for then our conversational activity is embedded in a joint attunement to the single shared space of salience and interest. But when we talk on the phone—that is, when we speak with someone who is at a remote location—we participate in and give rise to a different spatially distributed environment; we use different methods and cues to guide attention. The point is, we dislodge ourselves, crucially, from the setting in which we find ourselves.

The cases of driving, conversation, and walking show that there is no tension between the natural and the learned when it comes to the ways we find ourselves embedded in patterns of organization. Against the different background of acquired skills and novel settings, our ability to carry on and be organized by the activity at hand, to— if you like—lose ourselves in the flow, is natural for us. It is our nature to acquire second natures. From the standpoint of the theory of organized activities, driving, walking, talking are expressions of the same basic human nature that unfolds in suckling.

•

Another important feature of organized activities is that they are habitual. Habit is grounded, in this way, in biology. I don't mean merely that we walk, talk, drive *habitually*, that is, as a matter of routine, although of course that can be true. I mean rather that to participate in these activities, and to do so well, that is to say, with skill or expertise, we need to relax into habits. Watch an experienced mother suckle her older infant. Each of them just sort of collapses into the familiar, almost ritualized activity. By now the mother may be talking on the phone while, with the other hand, she releases her breast and positions the child who now, like falling off a log, latches on. The whole activity—which is in some ways the very model of joint attention, communication, and, indeed, intimacy, of mindfulness—unfolds almost automatically and without effort.

It is worth noticing that you can't understand organized activities—activities that are structured by habit in this way—by considering these phenomena only in relation to what is happening in the nervous system of the participants. Which is of course not to say that you couldn't modify or disrupt the organization of the activity by intervening, if you knew how, in the nervous system of one of the actors. The point is that the level at which activities are organized is not the level of the nervous system, any more than it is the level of the atom. But neither is it the level of conscious, deliberate action. We are organized at an intermediate level, at what the roboticist Dana Ballard has called the "embodiment level." This critical level is not *sub*personal—it is not the level of things happening inside us, however we model these. What interests us, after all, is precisely what *the person* does, what she looks at, what she pays attention to, etc. But it is not the *personal* level itself either, the level at which the person knowingly and authoritatively decides. The driver doesn't decide to brake or downshift; the pedestrian doesn't choose to shift her weight as she walks. The baby doesn't start sucking again *on purpose*.

•

It is not a requirement that organized activities be social. Sometimes the environment itself organizes us individually. Perception is such a case. We need to be careful here because perception can be many things. Just as there isn't only one thing that is conversation—we fight, we exchange information, we whisper sweet nothings, we conduct a business deal, etc.—so there isn't one thing that is seeing (for example). We use our eyes to guide our driving behavior, to cook dinner, to take a shower, to read a book. Even when we watch TV, which seems so passive, so much a matter of just staring at the box (or rather the screen), our attention is to a world put on display that we take an interest in and that we think about. Perceiving is typically caught up with acting. (I examine different ways of thinking about perception, and their significance for our subject matter, art, in chapter 5.)

But now let's look at seeing at what I've been calling, after Ballard, the embodiment level. Every time you move your eyes or your hands, you produce sensory changes. And as you move around in relation to the environment, how things look changes steadily. We aren't conscious of any of this, for the most part. That is, we don't have the impression that the colors of the clothes we wear change when we go outdoors, even though, in a perfectly straightforward sense, they do. (After all, how they look, with respect to color, is different in bright sunlight!) And things don't seem to swell up in size as we approach them. Psychologists call this perceptual constancy.

What is striking is that we certainly are sensitive to these changes in the apparent size and shape and color of things around us as we move about; indeed, it is our very fluent mastery of them, our familiarity with them, that makes it possible in the first place for us to use this pattern of variability as a means of locking on to a stable world around us. Notice, we don't sit still and contemplate the world visually the way we might contemplate images on a movie screen. We continuously move about and squint and adjust ourselves to, if you like, bring and maintain the world in focus.

Seeing, if this approach is right, is a temporally extended, dynamic exchange with the world around us, one that is guided by principles of timing, thoughtfulness, movement, spontaneity, function, and pleasure, like those we see in operation when we drive or walk or breast-feed, but that are also governed by all manner of learned understandings and expectations and engagements with this or that task (watch repair, typing, driving home, etc.).

Seeing, so long as we pick it out at the right level of description, is an organized activity. It is basic and natural yet cognitively complex.

It is temporally organized, but its organization is not the result of our deliberate control or determination. And certainly it serves vital functions, whether for us individually, or for our projects and relationships, or for our species.

In *Action in Perception*, I argued that seeing is a special kind of activity of exploring the world. In particular, I argued that it is a way of exploring the world making use of implicit practical understanding of the ways our own movements produce and control sensory events. What I would now say, drawing on the ideas presented here, is that seeing (and all kinds of perception) is the *organized activity* of achieving access to the world around us.

•

The point, thus far, is this: We are organized. We get organized. We are organisms! Our lives are structured by organized activities, in the large, in the small. Our lives are one big complex nesting of organized activities at different levels and scales. Talking, walking, eating, perceiving, driving. We are always captured by structures of organization. This is our natural, indeed our biological, condition. It is the basic fact about us.

And crucially, these structures of organization are not of our own making. We don't direct or orchestrate or invent the dynamic patterns that organize us when we walk, look, listen, breast-feed, or talk. We are not exactly slave to them—for our participation in such practices is, in many ways, precisely the exercise of our agency. It's how we make friends, find mates, get from point A to point B, recognize people in the crowd.

But we are, or are at least liable to get, lost in the complex patterns of organization that make up our lives.

What does all this have to do with art?

The answer, whose real meaning will become clear only gradually as we progress, is simple: we make art out of organized activities.

2

Reorganizing Ourselves

In the previous chapter I introduced a way of thinking about organization and explained that we are organized. We get organized by our habitual activities. We follow no script, even if, in a way, so much of our organized living is scripted. We act out of habit, but we frequently lack much in the way of understanding of how we act. For example, people are surprised to learn how dangerous it is to drive and talk on the phone because they are not aware, as a rule, of the way they are taken up by and absorbed within the activities that organize them.

I would like to suggest, now, that art has its origins in this basic fact about us—that we are organized, integrated, pulled together by activities such as breast-feeding, walking, talking, and perceiving.

We can take a step toward explaining this hypothesis by turning our attention to dancing.

•

Dancing, surely, is an organized activity if anything is.

Dancing is natural for us. It is a spontaneous physical response to rhythm, or to music, or to movement. Dancing is also a masterful exercise of powers of attention and perceptual discrimination. We display our sensitivity to what we hear, or to what our partner is doing, or to what we are doing or have done in our movements. Dancing shows understanding and awareness of oneself, and one's relation to another, and the music. Dancing is exquisitely complex cognitively and perceptually, but for all that it is also basic, natural, and spontaneous.

It goes without saying that dancing is organized in space and time and that its structures may be as complex as they are undeniable. A dance may have rhythmic organization; indeed, it may have the organization of turn taking, as with conversation and breast-feeding.

People dance on purpose, but they don't decide how to dance, at least not at the level of the way their movements are swept up into and organized by the dancing. The dancing just happens. One dancer may "lead," but this is just a special way of letting oneself be caught up in the dance. A good dancer is in the flow. When two people dance, their movements and actions and thoughts and perceptions are entrained by the larger organization, the dancing itself.

Dancing has a point. Some people dance to meet girls or boys. Sometimes we dance—at a wedding, say, or, in some cultures, at funerals—because this is demanded of the situation. We might dance to express our feelings, or to establish ourselves as having a peer-group identity.

Recall the character of Tony Manero, played by John Travolta, in John Badham's 1977 movie *Saturday Night Fever*. Tony Manero danced for the most important, if personal, reasons. He felt most alive on the dance floor, most truly himself, most liberated from the otherwise challenging and even degrading features of his domestic life. Dancing served an important function for him personally. Indeed, it is worth emphasizing, it served a function for Tony that has nothing essentially to do with dancing, although it did have to do with individuality, and excellence, and creativity, and puffery. The same functions might have been served by athletic prowess, or being an effective business person. Dancing served the function. But the functions served are autonomous of dancing. Dancing, we have seen already, is an organized activity. It is a pleasurable activity that is at once basic and spontaneous while also cognitively sophisticated; it has a definite pattern of temporal organization as well as a definite function. And it is emergent. Dancing happens; dancers get caught up in the dance.

We get caught up in dancing the way, as infants, we get caught up in suckling. You don't choose to suckle, just as, in a way, you don't choose to read the sign on the wall. If you can read, you will read. The sign reads you, we might almost say.

We are caught up in the activities that structure our lives—looking, reading, walking, talking, dancing. Our lives are structured by activity in this way. We are organized. We don't organize ourselves. And so we are easily lost. We have no guide.

•

Now, against this background, let's ask: What about *choreography*? What is the relation between dancing and choreography?

I hope it will be granted that whatever we want to say about choreography, it should be clear that it is not just a way of dancing, a way of participating in that organized activity we call dancing.

Why not? you might ask. Don't choreographers *make* dances? No. Dances are organized activities. You *can't* make them. We participate in them. We get caught up in them. Dancing happens. Situations produce them. People dance. They decide to dance. But the ability to dance is precisely an ability to let go, to let oneself be danced (as we might say).

•

Okay, so choreographers don't make dances. What do they do? A natural thing to say is that they *stage* dances. What does it mean, though, to stage a dance?

Suppose a real estate agent shows us a model unit in an apartment building. It is a real unit. It might be sold or rented itself. But it's kept vacant to serve as a model of what is available. It is kept vacant so that it can be shown. It really is an apartment—a place where someone might live—but it is used differently. It is used to demonstrate what living in the building would be like. And of course, in the parlance of real estate people, it is also *staged*, that is, outfitted with furnishings, flowers, place settings, and the like, so that it looks as if it were inhabited, even though it is not. The difference between the model unit and the other units in the building is not a difference in the apartment itself, in the way it is built, or how it looks, or anything like that. It's a difference in what we are doing with the unit.

And so with staged dancing. When a choreographer stages a dance, he is representing dancing. That is, he puts dancing itself on display. Choreography shows us dancing, and so, really, it displays us, we human beings, as dancers; choreography shows us dancing; choreography exhibits the place dancing has, or can have, in our lives. Choreography puts the fact that we are organized by dancing on display.

This is not to deny that sometimes dancing happens during works of choreography. Nor is it to deny that sometimes performers are truly dancing for us, strutting their stuff, showing their moves. Just as the model apartment can be materially identical to an actual lived-in home, without actually being a home, so the dance can be just like dancing without, really, being just dancing. Like the model unit, staged dancing is a display model, an exhibit. It's about the showing— and affording the audience the opportunity to look and see, or to look and try to see—not the dancing as such. Performed dance is never just a party on a stage!

This also explains why dance, that is, choreography, can sometimes look so very different from what regular people do when they dance. The aims of choreographers such as George Balanchine, or William Forsythe, or Jérôme Bel are not our aims, or those of Tony Manero. They are totally different. They are in the business of putting dancing and what it means for us on display.

•

If choreography has value, then its value must be distinct from that which attaches to dancing. Tony Manero dances to realize himself. Someone else dances to celebrate the engagement, or to seduce that person, or because it feels good. The value of choreography is not commensurate with these values. For dance—not *dancing*, but dance, that is, choreography—is not itself just a way of dancing and so it is not just a way of achieving the sorts of ends for which we dance.

Choreography is important—I take this for granted—not so much because dancing is important in itself, but because *we are dancers* and that is a deep and important fact about us, about the way we are organized. To stage a dance is to put into view this organized activity within which we are, by nature, embedded but within which we are, as we tend to be, lost. Choreography casts light on one of the ways we are organized, that we are organized by dancing. The value of dancing is one thing, and the value of choreography another, but the source of the importance of choreography in our lives is precisely the importance not so much of dancing itself but of the fact that we are, by nature, dancers.

This conclusion has important ramifications.

•

Choreography is tied to biology. Choreography gets its start from something about our nature. It is grounded in our biology. Not because dancing is best thought of as a neurological phenomenon. And not because watching a performance is a perceptual activity that depends on our neurological equipment, although obviously that is true. No, choreography is biological in a different and more direct way. Choreography is concerned with the ways we are organized by dancing. Crucially, dancing is natural for us. It is our nature to be absorbed into organized activities, and dancing is an organized activity; it is one of the activities that absorb us. Choreography is a practice for investigating our absorption.

We are unknowing dancers by nature; choreography gives us an opportunity to encounter this aspect of ourselves. Choreography, as we have seen, is not dancing, it is an engagement with dancing as a phenomenon. But the phenomenon—the organized activity—is a natural and basic one, a primitive one. Which is of course not to say that it is not also a cultural and a learned one. *That* distinction, between the natural and the cultural, loses its significance from the standpoint of the biology of human organization. Choreography makes a contribution to the biology of human organization.

The links between biology and organization go beyond the idea of organized activity and are exhibited in the fact that we are organisms. Organization, as I indicated earlier, is one of life's hallmarks. Living matter is organized toward its own self-maintenance and self-production in the face of the physical processes that enfold and threaten to dissolve it. It is the distinctive feature of the cell, perhaps the minimum form of life, that it takes in energy from its surroundings and uses it not only to power itself, as an artifact takes energy from a battery, but quite literally to make itself, to produce itself and to establish and maintain the boundary (the cell wall) separating itself from the world around it. This idea that life is tied to autopoiesis, to use Humberto Maturana and Francisco Varela's apt term, points back to Kant. Kant appreciated that although Newtonian mechanics gives you the principles you need to describe and predict the movements of the smallest particles as well as whole planets, physics as such can make no sense of life. Living processes—metabolism, growth, death—are not *merely* physical processes even if, of course, they are physical processes. Living beings are physical systems whose life consists in the distinctive manner of their organization; it consists, as Kant appreciated, in the fact of their self-organization.

For my purposes here the important point is this: choreography, and all the arts—choreography is chosen as a stand-in, as an example—seek to bring out and exhibit, to disclose and to illuminate, aspects of the way we find ourselves organized. Choreography, and all the arts, are organizational, or rather, as we shall see, reorganizational practices. Their value derives directly from the fundamental importance of organization in shaping human, and indeed all, life.

Choreography is philosophy. What the choreographer does, if this analysis is right, is find a way of bringing into the open, to use an image from Heidegger, something that is concealed, hidden, implicit, or left in the background, namely, the place of dancing in our lives, or our place in the activity, the self-organized complex that is dancing. The choreographer exhibits all that and opens for us the place of dancing in our lives. Choreography makes manifest something about ourselves that is hidden from view because it is the spontaneous structure of our engaged activity.

This is a paradigmatically philosophical activity. Recall the philosophical practice of Socrates as we know it in the writings of Plato. These dialogues have a familiar structure. The participants try to say what they know and come up against the blunt fact that they can't say what they know and that, therefore, in a sense, they don't have the knowledge they think they have. Of course, in the meantime, through the investigation, the dialogue—through bringing what they think, or are inclined to say, or what they want to say, or what they feel compelled to say, into the open—they acquire, or at least are in a position to acquire, something like a sense of how their mere opinions hang together and are organized. Gaining knowledge is recollecting, Plato said. And what this statement means, here, is that it is not a matter of gathering new data; it's a matter of seeing how the data you already have—your own experiences, observations, beliefs, etc.—hang together. Plato puts our thinking, asking, arguing—the fact that we are lost in the complexity of our own activities of thinking—on display and in doing so offers us a way to find ourselves, a way to get found where we were lost. The result isn't positive knowledge, or settled agreement, as such. Rather, the result is something like *understanding*, where this means, roughly, knowing your way around.

Wittgenstein wrote that a philosophical problem has the form *I don't know my way around*. Roughly, *I'm lost*. His method in philosophy was, in effect, to create usable maps ("perspicuous representations") to enable one to find one's way around.

If I am right, this is exactly the project of choreography—to fashion for us a representation of ourselves as dancers; to make clear what is otherwise concealed and only poorly understood. The work of choreography—the work of art—is philosophical.

Or better, both philosophy and choreography aim at the same thing—a kind of understanding that, in Wittgenstein's phrase, consists in having a perspicuous representation—but they do it, so to speak, in different neighborhoods of our existence. Philosophy is the choreography of ideas and concepts and beliefs. For these, too, exist only in the organized activity of our thought and talk. Choreography, in turn, is the philosophy of dancing (or of movement). Both philosophy and choreography take their start from the fact that we are organized but we are not the authors of our organization. Instead of thinking of choreography as a philosophical practice, or philosophy as a choreographic one, we would do better to appreciate that both choreography and philosophy are species of a single genus that, for want of a better name, I will refer to as the study of our organization; philosophy and choreography are organizational and reorganizational practices. They are *practices* (not activities)—methods of research—aiming at illuminating the ways we find ourselves organized and so, also, the ways we might reorganize ourselves.

•

You might object: surely this can't be right! Choreography is hot and sweaty; it is bodily and musical. It is emotional. Choreography is not cool and intellectual the way philosophy is. Even if choreography has intellectual concerns, surely there's all the difference in the world between the work and concerns of dance and those of philosophy!

But here lurks a double misunderstanding. First, as we will have occasion to discuss further in chapter 11, philosophy is not so cool as you may be tempted to think, even if it is intellectual. It begins in puzzlement. It works with argument and aims at persuasion. Philosophy runs hot. And choreography, for its part, can be very cool.

Second, my claim is not that choreography and philosophy are qualitatively the same, or that it is the impulse to philosophize that moves the choreographer, or an impulse to dance that moves the philosopher. No, philosophy and choreography are as different from each other as painting is from music, or writing poetry from making sculpture. And yet they all do basically the same job: they expose the concealed ways we are organized by the things we do.

3

Designers by Nature

A striking thing about the arts is that they busy themselves with manufacture. They aim at making things—paintings, sculptures, buildings, installations. Arts seem to participate in crafts and technologies. They are tied to the manual and the constructive. Even performing arts—like music and dance—are bound up in the practical. Musicians wield their instruments as craftspeople wield their tools. Dancers and singers dazzle us with their training, their skill, their strength and fitness. Are painters and sculptors special kinds of craftspeople or technicians? What is the relation of art to technology, craft, expert performance? And how does this relate to the idea of art as an organizational practice? Surely an account of art has to give pride of place to the fact that most artists are more like tinkerers or mad scientists, or like athletes and circus clowns, than they are like philosophers. And what of the fact that art arises out of a creative impulse? We begin on these questions now.

Here's the short and partial answer. There is an intimate link between technology and organized activities. Roughly, a tool (such as a hammer or a computer) is the hub of an organized activity. Technology is not mere stuff. It is the equipment with which we carry on our organized activities. Technologies organize us; properly understood, they are *evolving patterns of organization*. Once this link is clearly appreciated—that technologies are patterns of organization—then we can begin to appreciate that breast-feeding, really, is a kind of primitive technology; dancing, likewise, is a technological activity; developed technologies are domains for organizing ourselves in ever more complicated ways. But the basic principles of organization are the same.

Art is not a technological practice any more than choreography is a way of dancing. But art presupposes technology and can be understood only against that background. Just as choreography is preoccupied with the fact that we are organized by dancing, so painting (say) responds to the fact that we are organized by pictures (or by techniques of picture making and picture using). Pictures, crucially, *are* a technology, and picture making and picture using are organized activities. And so these are raw materials for art. The painter may make pictures (although not all paintings are pictures in the sense of being depictions of anything at all, accurate or inaccurate, realistic or not). But this does not mean that he or she is, as it were, in the business of making better pictures, just as the choreographer is not in the business of dancing. Sometimes the art of the painter or dancer consists in what gets revealed by failing to make a picture or in not being able to move the way a dancer is supposed to be able move. Failure is one of art's most important channels of investigation, something that would make no sense at all if artists were simply technologists, if they were just makers.

A lot needs to be laid out before these points are clear or persuasive. In this chapter I explore further the nature of technology. In the next chapter I explore the shape of my basic argument in more detail. Later, in part III, I show how this account helps us understand pictorial art and music.

·

One of the striking things about technology—this is not a novel idea, but it deserves to be repeated—is that technologies are natural for us. People use tools naturally, in something like the way bees build hives and birds make nests. We are designers by nature. This conclusion is strongly supported by the archaeological record. For more than a million years, our ancestors made no significant technological breakthroughs. There is evidence that they used very simple stones for cutting and pounding but no evidence of any kind of refinement or development in these simple technologies as hundreds of thousands of years passed. About fifty to seventy-five thousand years ago, there appears to have been an explosive revolution in our tool-using capacities. We now find remnants of highly refined tools with specialized functions, even tools for making tools. At this same time period we began wearing clothes and using graphical technologies (the famous cave paintings). And this is probably when we began talking as we do now.

Modern people, behaviorally and cognitively modern *Homo sapiens*, came on the scene about fifty thousand years ago, and this emergence is coeval with the unleashing of powers of technological development.

What explains this extraordinary burst of creative energy and socially transforming invention? One possibility is that we got smarter. There was a brainy mutation, as it has been put. But there is at least one reason to doubt that this is so. Our uninventive ancestors seem to have been just like us physically, at least insofar as we can judge from their remains. It is widely believed that anatomically modern humans existed at least fifty to a hundred thousand years *before* this great technological leap forward.

There is an alternative explanation. Demographic changes might help us understand what happened. Maybe we were clever inventors all along, or at least long before our innovations took hold. Perhaps none of these innovations caught on and got passed along because we lived in isolated bands and had, in effect, no one to build on our achievements. Maybe none of my kids, or the kids in my band, were able to learn to do what I can do. Anyway, there are limits to how much innovating anyone can do if we have to do our work on the move and with only the resources we can ourselves produce. A small increase in density of populations would change the rules of the game. In larger groups with more contact with other groups, it would be possible for trade and specialization to emerge. If you provide me the supplies I need, I can devote myself full time to the task of improving tools. And if I have more people around me, it becomes far more likely that one of these others will be my apprentice and will learn to do what I can do, and, eventually, to improve on it. And indeed, there is evidence of trade between relatively distant groups around this time.

All this is speculation. But there are several important morals to be taken home from these thoughts. First, rather than supposing that we made technology because we got smart, maybe what enabled us collectively to get smarter were new forms of social organization. (This is obviously a very delicate question. One might argue, after all, that our tool use is different from that found among the animals, even the nest builders. One way to appreciate this alternative view is by realizing that, as the neuroscientist John Krakauer put it to me in a conversation, attach a human hand to a chimp's body and it still won't be able to accomplish with its hands what we can do with ours. It isn't only that we use tools; we *think* with them. It just isn't clear whether other animals do the same.)

Second, these new forms of social organization, these new ways of living and working together, form the field of play within which technologies are introduced and develop. Put this way, the technologies themselves can be thought of, as I have already said, as evolving patterns of organization.

And this makes good sense. Consider an instrument like the door handle. We cannot understand such a device except against the background of a whole way of living. Door handles are useful only for people who live in dwellings and have need of doors to keep out the cold, strangers, or predators, and to protect their possessions and keep them safe in the night. Going a step further, it is clear that door handles presuppose, also, that we have bodies of a very specific sort, bodies with hands capable of handling the handles, and that we have the stature and strength to reach the handles and to shift the weight of the door itself.

For an invention such as a door handle even to come on the scene, a whole cultural and biological stage needs to be set. But once the handle does appear, the practice of using doors with handles itself recedes into the background stage setting of our lives. We rarely if ever need to stop and ask questions about door handles. Unless we are designers, we don't think about them very often. Our attention is fixed on getting into or out of the room, on what we are doing and where we are going. Manipulating doors by their handles becomes second nature. Indeed, the handle becomes the hub of a whole little organized activity of getting around in the houses we build and the places we live. We get organized by door handles, spontaneously reaching for them, gripping them appropriately.

•

It is tempting to think of the person here, with his or her finitely enu-
merable problems and needs, and tools and devices available for getting things done over there. But to see what's wrong with such an
idea, consider this. You are in midflight across the Atlantic Ocean
somewhere. Sure, in some sense, you are doing something that
human beings have done since the dawn of history: traveling from
one place to another. From that point of view, a plane is no different
from a train, an automobile, a horse and buggy, or our feet. It's just a
means of getting us from point A to point B. But we need also to appreciate that insofar as we are now *flying* through the air five miles
above the surface of the earth, we are doing something entirely new.
We couldn't do *that* without the technology. The crucial point is
this: subtract the technology—the planes themselves and the vast
information-complex digitized system that supports commercial air
travel—and you don't get people who fly differently. You get people
who don't fly. And insofar as we are fliers, and insofar as that way of
getting around and being in touch with each other is necessary for us
now, given our economies and our ways of communicating, then we
wouldn't be us without the technologies necessary to fly. Our mode of
being—how our lives are organized—is constituted in part by the
technology. Take away the technology and you are left not with us,
but with, at most, something like distant cousins of ourselves.

Consider, as a different example, the modern corporate work
environment. Just as the telephone made it possible to talk to colleagues in different places, so email transformed the ease of communication, not just one to one, but one to many and many to
many. Workplace communications systems today—for example, in-
house social-networking software—make it possible for companies
to acquire whole new styles of organization. Facebook lets people establish links to other people. Status updates concern individuals and
their interests. But in-house social-networking systems, like Chatter,
enable networks to be organized based not so much on people but
on topics. Topics cross the boundary not only of office space and project teams; they can be relevant to widely disparate groups across a
company. Now suppose you are working on a problem in a company
with ten thousand employees. You can search the past chatter about

a topic, essentially gaining access to the knowledge of the whole company. And if you still have a question, you can figure out exactly whom to contact. It may be someone you've never met. It may be someone in a different part of the world.

Now imagine this company but minus the software technology that organizes the way people do business. You can't. The company minus the organizing technology is a different organization.

Technologies don't just fill antecedently existing needs and they don't do so merely by amplifying what we can do. They let us do new things, not only to solve old problems but also to frame new ones.

•

The deep and exciting point that emerges from these reflections—forgive me for repeating myself—is that technologies are themselves evolving patterns of organization. Technologies organize us, and in doing so, they make us the kind of creatures we are.

Technology comes from the Greek word *technē*, which means skill or craft. When we think of technology, we tend to think of instruments, implements, built-up networks, and infrastructures. We think of Silicon Valley and bioengineering. But at its root, technology is skillful activity; it is the expression of expertise, intelligence, understanding, thoughtfulness.

Technē is at work in that original organized activity of suckling. We see there, already, the transition from trying to do something, struggling with it, to fluency and expertise. Or think of the way we learn a second language. Painstaking memorization of vocabulary and rules of grammar. We spend energy thinking about words and rules and pronunciation and manners. At some point, all that tends to fall away, and we find ourselves simply using the language, no longer thinking about how to use it. At that moment the language becomes not something mediating our relation to the world around us, to other people, but rather a modality of direct access to others and to what is going on around us.

This insight brings out the sense in which technologies are natural, that is to say basic. Technologies are activities organized by skill. Breast-feeding, talking, dancing—the organized activities of the previous chapter—are, thought of this way, technological practices.

•

Have you ever tried to talk on the phone to young kids? They can't do it. One reason they have difficulty is that talking on a phone is different from talking face-to-face. You have to speak more clearly. You have to be sensitive to the different quality of the exchange. And then of course there's the fact that you need to be alert to the different ways you communicate your meanings to another person when you can't see each other, and when you can't jointly attend to things or papers or events in your shared space.

But there is a further, more pervasive reason. Children younger than, say, ten, don't have conversations in the way grown-ups do. Talking is a way of being close and sharing oneself; it is like dancing or snuggling or arguing. It's more than just a way of sharing information or solving a problem. But whereas some kids are good at snuggling, and they can certainly enjoy music and dance to it, kids don't typically know how to dance with another person in the grown-up manner, and they don't know how to converse. Compare what happens with teenagers, for whom the need self-consciously to cultivate relationships comes on strong. For them—at least when I was a teenager!—the phone becomes important and the idea that one might spend time on the phone with someone idly talking about nothing in particular takes on great meaning.

The point of this example is that technologies are coordinate with who and what we are, with what we know how to do.

•

Technologies are organized ways of doing things. But this equivalence has a startling upshot, one that has been noticed before. Technologies carry a deep cognitive load. Technologies enable us to do things we couldn't do without them—fly, work in a modern office place—but they also enable us to think thoughts and understand ideas that we couldn't think or understand without them.

This is true in both a modest and a radical sense. Modestly, technologies provide solutions to problems, but they also provide new problems requiring solutions. The quest for a better mousetrap. Improvements to the internal combustion engine. The unceasing and inexhaustible development of computer operating systems. Even the humble door handle. Technologies are not static. They both invite and incite refinement and improvement. To be an engineer today is to jump right into the middle of an evolutionary process, taking up where others have left off. Engineers, whether working on software or building roads and bridges, don't need to think about the evolutionary history of their practices, but everything they do think about—the problems that interest them and are important—is determined by this history. So the point runs deep. The problems that technology throws up are really problems about how to live—how more effectively to do what we need to do (fly, drive, use computers, etc.). But these are problems that wouldn't even come into focus for us if we were not already at sea in the ocean of technology. We live life always in midstream, in the midstream of life itself.

But there is a more radical sense in which technology makes it possible to think new thoughts. I can perform complex calculations—find the solution to quadratic equations, figure out how much tax I owe, or determine how much each of us should contribute to the check in the restaurant—but only thanks to the fact that I have access to and know how to use arithmetical notation. Arithmetical notation is a tool for thinking thoughts that I (at least) couldn't think without it.

Initially, arithmetical notation arose as a way of keeping track. We moved from keeping track of how many sheep we have by keeping that many pebbles in a purse to making that many notches in a piece of wood or marks on the ground. But once we have the notation, it becomes possible to use the notation to think new kinds of arithmetical thought. That's what we learn at school today. We're taught how to write the numbers down so that by performing simple operations on written symbols we can reach very complicated results.

Basic quantitative reasoning is possible without notation. Infants and animals show some aptitude for it. But could we even conceive of real numbers, or primes, or the transfinite, or groups, or topographies without ways of representing these in writing and diagrams? No. But we need to be careful, as this observation invites a silly misunderstanding. The fact that mathematics requires notation for its practice does not mean that mathematicians study systems of symbols (although there are branches of mathematics that do just this). We're not thinking *about* numerals when we calculate, any more than we were thinking about pebbles when we were figuring out how many sheep there are; we use pebbles and numerals to think about how many sheep we have.

The point can be expanded beyond mere notation to language itself. One way to think about something is to look at it and pay attention to it, to hold it in your hand and inspect it. But how can you think about things that are far away in space and time? How can you think about Julius Caesar, or what you will have for breakfast in seventeen days, or the center of gravity of the solar system, or the big bang, or the lives of your unborn descendants? We need ways to reach these things in thought. We use language, and writing, to do this.

•

Now consider this: Where does your thinking take place? You might as well say that it takes place in your hand, on the paper, or on a keyboard as that it takes place in your head. For even if you believe, as many cognitive scientists do, that our ability to perform arithmetic depends on our brain's ability to represent value, quantities, and suchlike, it is clear that it also depends on our ability to use external symbols, the kind we write on paper or put up on the blackboard.

In this way we can appreciate that technology extends not only what we can do. It also extends what we are. Our minds bleed out of our heads, onto the paper, into the world. The philosophers Andy Clark and David Chalmers (of the University of Edinburgh and New York University, respectively) frame the issue this way: Where do you stop and where does the rest of the world begin? There doesn't seem to be any principled reason to think the stuff going on inside our heads is privileged in comparison with the stuff we write on paper. Both are necessary for the kinds of thoughts we have, for the kinds of thinking and problems that interest us.

Thinking is more like bridge building or dancing than it is like digestion. We ourselves are creatures of technology through to our most intimate cores. And this is so because thinking, no less than dancing, traveling, and talking, is an organized activity. And technologies are evolving patterns of organization.

•

Back to the main argument: art, I am proposing, takes its impetus from the fact that we are organized but are lost in the nesting, massively complicated patterns of our organization. Art—and philosophy, too—are practices for investigating the modes of our organization, or rather, the manner of our embedding in different modes of organization. Art is not just more organization.

Given this fact, and given the basic, biological, necessary place of technology in our lives, it should not be surprising that art is concerned with making things—paintings, sculptures, buildings, etc. Painting as an art, sculpture, and architecture are precisely investigations of the ways our lives are organized by the technologies of picture making and the other relevant technologies of manufacture. Art happens in the neighborhood of depiction and manufacture not because artists are interested in making a better mousetrap or a more realistic picture, but because depiction, manufacture, etc., are profoundly important organized activities and thus are vital aspects of our nature as culturally embedded persons.

4

Art Loops and
the Garden of Eden

The basic argument of this book is this:

Our lives are structured by organization. Art is a practice for bring-ing our organization into view; in doing this, art reorganizes us.

Painters, insofar as they are artists, are not really in the business of making pictures. And choreographers, as we have been consider-ing, aren't really dancing.

We can think, then, of there being two levels. *Level 1* is the level of the organized activity or the technology. *Level 2* is the level where the nature of the organization at the lower level gets put on display and investigated.

At level 1, we have activities like talking, moving, dancing, making pictures, singing, etc. The defining feature of level-1 activities is that they are basic and involuntary modes of our organization. They are things we do by nature or second nature. This is true even though many of the activities at this level—talking, dancing, making pic-tures, etc.—are socially shared and culturally shaped.

Correspondingly, at level 2, we have the different arts: poetry and fiction, choreography, painting and photography, music, and so on. Level-2 practices play with and reshape level-1 activities.

A running theme of this book—I take it up directly in chap-ter 11—is that philosophy is a level-2 reorganizational practice that stands to our level-1 cognitive undertakings—reasoning, argument, belief formation, and, crucially, the work of science—in the same kind of relation that, say, choreography stands to movement and dancing, or painting as an art stands to picture-making activities as these flourish in our lives.

Let us consider tools again. A tool has significance only in the context of its embedding. Remove it from its context and it becomes nothing more than a thing. And so, as I will argue in a later chapter, with pictures. Deprive the picture of its context—remove its caption, say, or its place in the family album—and it loses its significance as a picture. It ceases to depict.

Art is interested in removing tools (in my extended sense) from their settings and thus in making them strange and, in making them strange, bringing out the ways and textures of the embedding that had been taken for granted. A work of art is a strange tool, an alien implement. We make strange tools to investigate ourselves.

Now this way of putting things is only a first approximation. We bring out something important about choreography, for example, when we stress that it is, properly, an investigation of dancing rather than a participation in dancing. But the idea that choreography is, in this way, *meta*dancing, or that art practices are, as I have been suggesting, metalevel, is too simple.

So let's make things more complicated.

Consider, first, that although art and philosophy are practices of investigation of the ways we find ourselves habitually organized, it is critical that these second-order activities *arise out of* the first level. Art is like mapmaking, in this respect. And crucially, people don't make maps just for the heck of it; no, they make maps because they get lost without them. The task of generating a representation of the lay of the land has its source in a real need, or a felt anxiety.

And so for art (and philosophy). The first-order activities that organize us—walking, talking, singing, thinking, making and deploying pictures for this task or that—structure the landscape in which we find ourselves. But we may lack a sense of the lay of the land; we may be lost; we undertake art and philosophy so that, within this or that region of our lives, we can be found. Art, and philosophy, are organizational or reorganizational practices, practices for making sense of the ways we are organized. And they exist as the result of a genuine and important need.

It is here, in this fact about the depth of the need, that we can understand why art is so bound up with feeling and emotion. Being lost and retrieving your bearings. It doesn't get more felt than that.

So the first point to appreciate by way of bringing out the ways things get more complicated than merely first-order versus second-order is that the second-order reorganizational practice arises out of the first-order organized activity. It is not a view of that activity from on high; rather, it is an attempt *from within the activity* to make sense of where we find ourselves. And so there is a basic and real, an existentially vital, link between arts and the domains of living, the organized activities, from which they source.

But there is a second source of complexity: reorganizational practices loop back and change first-order activities.

Take the case of dancing. We dance; it is our nature to do so. Choreography puts this fact about us on display, for us to witness and understand. But the existence of choreographies—their image, their power to coalesce and stand forth as models of how the activity could or should be done—loops back down and shapes how we think about dancing, and thus how we dance, even when we are by ourselves or in our most intimate settings. In a world in which dance has been *represented*, it is not generally possible to dance in a way that is insulated from dance's image, that is, from choreography's model of ourselves as dancing. Watch people dance, and you see them perform; they cite and sample the postures, attitudes, steps, and styles that they have consumed. It is as if their spontaneous, free, untutored forays into dancing are shaped by a culturally shared motion bank.

Our most inspired, most fun-spirited, most playful dancing is itself organized, cliché-like, by what are choreographic representations of ourselves dancing. Choreography loops down and alters the first-order activity that is its source. In the process, new material for the choreographic imagination—new ways in which we are humans who are organized as dancers—comes to light.

One consequence of this process is that the difference between dancing and choreography gets obscured, since the fingerprints of choreography are always present when we dance. Another consequence of this—and now we come to a critical point that we've mentioned repeatedly but not explained or justified—is that our dancing gets *reorganized* by choreography. This, then, finally, is the manner in which art reorganizes. It reorganizes because it gets consumed and digested and reworked at the first order.

Nothing more beautifully illustrates this looping structure of art and its place in our lives than writing.

It is widely believed that writing is a fairly recent invention—only a few thousand years old, ten thousand at most—whereas spoken language is ancient and has its origins in our beginnings as a species. Spoken language belongs to our biological inheritance, whereas writing is conventional, a product of culture. Whether this distinction is right or not (a bit later I'll suggest that it can't be quite right), it is a safe bet that our *concept* of language is shaped by writing and the place of writing in our linguistic lives. Writing, for us, is the *image* of language; it reveals its likeness, we suppose. We think of language as writable through and through. Writing may not be the mirror of language, but it mirrors language's self-image.

Our very thought about and experience of language, both as human beings and as scientists, is shaped by our prior grasp on writing as a method of representing language. We experience language as it shows up in the context of the technology—and the ideology—of writing. And we easily lose track of this fact. The fact that writing shapes our conception of language, and so how we experience linguistic phenomena, is easily obscured.

To see what I mean, consider this example. It is taken from an introductory textbook on linguistics. The author seeks to introduce the concept of linguistic structure.

> If sound sequences had only *linear* structure (whereby one sound precedes the next), then sentences would be written as a continuous sequence of sounds—e.g.

> (3) thisboywillspeakveryslowlytothatgirl

> But sentences aren't unstructured sequences of sounds: any native speakers of English can tell you that the sounds in (3) are grouped into *words*, and can tell you what the word-divisions are. We'd all agree, for example, that the word-divisions in (3) are those in (4) below:

(4) This boy will speak very slowly to that girl

And not those in (5) below:

(5) Th isb oywillsp eakv erys lowlytot hatg irl
    T his boyw ills peak ver ysl owly toth atgi rl

But although the English spelling system provides a sys-
tematic representation of the way the sounds are structured
into words, it generally only provides a very inadequate, inconsistent and sporadic representation of the way in which
words are structured into phrases. For instance, we'd all agree
that in (4) *very* "goes with" or "modifies" *slowly*, and not e.g.
speak—and yet our spelling system provides no representation
of this fact. One way in which we could represent this type of
structural relation diagrammatically is by grouping the two
words together into a single set, e.g. as follows:

(6) This boy will speak [very slowly] to that girl

Likewise, we'd all agree that *that* in (4) "goes with" *girl*,
not with e.g. *to*. Once again, we could represent this intuition
by grouping the two words together into a single set as follows:

(7) This boy will speak [very slowly] to [that girl]

And in much the same way, we all share the intuition
that *this* "goes with" *boy*—a fact which we can represent as:

(8) [This boy] will speak [very slowly] to [that girl]

It is impossible not to share the linguist's "intuitions" about which
words "go with" which other words to form structural units. But what
is remarkable in this presentation is how dimly the author seems to
appreciate that the intuitions in question are precisely intuitions about
how we ought to write language and not about speech as if it were insulated from writing's shaping influence. We are asked to think of words

as graphical items that can and ought to be written together. Notice that the author takes the categories of *word, sentence, phrase* for granted, but these already represent a remarkable and highly culturally embedded ontology of what language is made up out of. You don't find words and phrases in the fluid play of sound and action in actual speech. Or rather, you *do* find them there, for this is precisely the ontology that is set up for us as speakers when we set up a system of writing as a method of representing, and so of normalizing, speech. You don't find words and phrases in the underlying physics of sound.

"We'd all agree." Yes, but we all live in the language world. Just as baseball fans find it natural to talk about home runs and base hits, even though they have no existence outside the confines of the play of baseball, so talk of words, sentences, and phrases, and of which words *go with* other words makes sense only in the setting of our language play. But this language play in question is already a play that is framed in terms of a way of representing the moves of the game. And the way we do this, in the language world, is with writing.

Writing doesn't represent language from outside, modeling sounds and structures. We write "cat" CAT and we think that CAT spells out the word by spelling out its sounds, how we say "cat." But we don't have any grip on the sounds apart from or prior to our model of how to represent them (in writing). That's why we can write only those sounds that are already words. You can't write down the door's actual squeakiness or the floor's actual creak. We don't represent sound in writing; we represent speech, or language. And these representations are not sound as a physicist might think of them. These are words as we might write them on the board. These are things that have spellings necessarily. We don't step outside language to write them; writing itself is one of the standard things we do with language.

So the idea that spoken language predates writing and that writing was invented as a technology for representing speech hardly does justice to the way writing shapes what speaking is for us. We can't step back and factor out *real* speech from culturally sanctioned written language. We may dream of language as it was in the beginning, in Eden, before culture and class and writing exerted their controlling standards and prescriptive demands. In truth, however, the very distinction between language as it truly is, or was, and language as it has been molded through generation after generation of ideologically blinkered language users, and the practice of writing, no longer makes any sense. Speech may seem first order, and writing second order, but we live in a linguistic domain in which it is no longer possible to be a language user who is not also already someone who thinks about language and, indeed, who does so in the idiom of writing. There is no going back to before the Fall. The second order—language's ideology, its self-understanding—is bound up inextricably with language as it lives in conversation and our lives.

Scientific linguistics, as the subject likes to refer to itself, doesn't quite appreciate this point, as we have seen. The evidential basis for linguistic theories—that is, for theories of what it is we know when we know the system of rules that is a language—are the judgments that speakers of a language can make about what sounds right and what sounds wrong, what is grammatical and what isn't. But judgments of grammaticality are not data points that give us insight into the nature of language as a natural—that is to say, noncultural—feature of our biological endowment. These judgments are just exercises in our own self-understanding, a self-understanding that is thoroughly cultural and shaped by ideologies.

It is sometimes objected that writing, with its conventional standards—influenced by media, class, social power, etc.—falsifies speech. There are conventional rules of style governing writing that have no counterpart in the spoken language of "the man on the street" or teenagers on the street after school. No doubt this is true. Let us stipulate that writing privileges norms of speech that may in fact be quite strange and inaccurate or prescribed. But notice that writing, by giving us a resource for thinking about what we are doing when we are talking, also affords us opportunities to think about our talking and so, also, to talk differently. The fact is, by providing a model of our speech, however prescriptive, writing loops back down and transforms how we speak. Our speech is always in the vicinity of text and writing. Just as a kid on the dance floor moves the way he saw Robin Thicke move, and having seen Thicke, it is not possible for him to move in a way that is not sensitive to how Thicke did it, so we speak as we have read people speak, or as we hear people speak written words (for example in theater, in movies, and on television).

What speakers think of as a technology for representing language, more or less adequate, useful for certain purposes, comes then to transform how we think about speech, and so how we think about ourselves when we speak, and so how we speak. Which of course leads in turn to more change in how we write. The looping doesn't stop. The result is a dense, historical, many-layered scriptoral-linguistic structure.

My proposal, then, is that we think of the relation of the arts and philosophy (second-order practices) to their raw material (first-order activities) as analogous to the relation of writing to speech. Writing is invented by speakers to model how they speak, or to represent language to themselves. The availability of this very image of language serves to change and reorganize the way we speak in the first place.

•

Actually, the relation of philosophy and the other arts to writing is not merely one of analogy. I would like to propose that art, and philosophy, are activities *bent on* the invention of writing.

•

One of philosophy's enduring myths about its own origins is that it begins not with the written word but in conversation, in dialogue. After all, Socrates, Plato's teacher and one of the first philosophers, never wrote a word; we know Socrates only in Plato's texts, Plato's reconstructions of remembered or imagined dialogues.

In fact, Socrates' philosophic work is anything but conversational, whether he was a writer or not. A Socratic dialogue begins not with conversation but with the interruption of conversation, with the disruption of the engaged, ordinary thought and talk practices of his friends and colleagues. This is why he made them so angry, and it may be why he was perceived by his contemporaries to be such a threat. Socrates was telling them that their talk was not good enough.

For example, Euthyphro tells Socrates why he is on his way to court. Instead of pursuing conversation or discussion with Euthyphro, Socrates challenges him to give reasons and justifications for his action. He urges him to try to make explicit that which he has never before bothered to make explicit and that which he does not know how to make explicit. Euthyphro, and Socrates, too, lack the means, the tools, to make explicit that which governs their thoughts and actions. They don't have a clear view, an *Überblick*, of their conceptual activities.

Far from being an exercise in conversation, Socratic dialogue is an interrogation (or refutation, in Greek: *elenchos*). And the aim of the interrogation is to call conversation itself into question, to exhibit its limits, to bring what we take for granted—what we mean by the words we use, for example—into focus as a problem. Socrates stands on the back of conversation and our engaged thinking about what we do, and he provokes us to try to bring all this, all that we take for granted, into view.

A Socratic dialogue is staged. It is a *model* of a conversation. It is not a conversation. It is *philosophy*. Or, we could say, it is art.

Socrates may not have written anything down, but that is not because he was content with orality, with mere conversation. Socrates occupies a vantage point from which we can first seriously try to invent a way of representing to ourselves our practice of talking and thinking. And so Socrates takes the first step toward the invention of the writing that he at least, as a true philosopher, feels we need.

Plato famously attacked poetry and the arts in the *Republic*. He thought they were poisonous, deadly for the soul and for society. Can we take seriously the idea that philosophy and art are one if Plato himself saw poetry and the other arts as so inimical to the very aims of philosophy?

We can, once we realize that Plato's target was not poetry as such, but precisely rather the oral, preliterate culture that found its strongest expression in Homer and Hesiod. Homeric poetry is not the poetry of the written word; Homeric poetry fails to make *words* its material but takes words for granted, and with words, also the habits of thought and living that are expressed in words. The *Iliad* and the *Odyssey*, for Plato, were like pop tunes whose composition was designed to aid their easy memorization and so to allow them to play an uncritical role in perpetuating Greek ways and values.

Plato hated poetry because it was mere song, mere talk, mere *orality*. Athenian aristocracy hated Socrates—they sentenced him to death—for his refusal merely to talk.

For Plato there is no art in Homeric poetry, precisely because there is no philosophy. And there is no philosophy because Homer's poetry amounts to an essentially preliterate mode of thinking.

Choreography knows itself to be, at least in part, a quest for a not yet discovered method of notation. This self-conception is in the very word "choreography" (literally dance + write) itself. It is the hallmark of choreography that it strives for and always fails at making adequate scores.

If I am right, this feature is the hallmark of all the arts, and philosophy, too.

•

To get clear about this, let's return, once again, to writing in the case of written language. We can gain insight if we consider what might seem like a fringe and esoteric graphical practice, score keeping in baseball.

A baseball game lasts about three hours and consists of a messy and complicated stream of activity. Players move about on the field; others warm up on the sidelines. The managers and coaches send signals back and forth to each other and to the players on the field. Given the fact that there are an open-ended number of ways to individuate events, there is a practical infinity of movements, actions, and events that can occur in a baseball game. But there is a special activity known as keeping score. Every baseball game has an official scorekeeper, and fans and enthusiasts may also keep score. Keeping score at the simplest level is keeping track of who's winning. But at a more sophisticated level it means keeping track of what happens more broadly. A half inning is over after three outs. Players bat one after the other, in a specified order, until there are three outs, and then it's the other team's turn. When a batter is at the plate, he faces the pitcher. Some pitches are good to hit; if he doesn't hit them, they are strikes. Others aren't good to hit, and if the batter "takes" them, they are balls, and they count in his favor. Four balls give him a base. Sometimes he hits the ball out of play; this may or may not count as a strike. But other times he puts the ball in play. This will be an out or an opportunity to run. To keep score is to record what happens. A well-kept "scorecard" allows you to know, for every batter, what happened when he was at bat, and for every inning, what took place. It allows you to "replay the game."

Two interesting points immediately come up.

First, it isn't easy to keep a scorecard. You need to understand what is going on and make judgments about, say, whether the runner advanced on a fielder's choice, a stolen base, or whatever. People will disagree how to score a play.

Second, when you score baseball, you can't score *everything* that happens. Most scorekeepers notate every pitch: Is it a ball or a strike? Was it put into play? But I don't think most scorekeepers notate the exact location of every pitch (high and inside? low and down the middle?), nor do they indicate the amount of time between pitches, or whether the pitcher scratched his ear or some other part of his body before throwing. As a result, the score doesn't give you the resources to actually replay the game; it's not like a videotape. It is, rather, a list, a digital encoding, of what happened, relative to a specific taxonomy for thinking about what happened and relative to one's interests. The scorecard will indicate that the runner beat out the second baseman's throw at first base, getting an infield single, but not, say, that the runner slid headfirst into the base. Sliding into first base headfirst for a single is, we might say, not a category that matters when keeping score.

Of course it might matter for certain purposes! You might care very much about the health and safety of the runner; in almost every situation it is foolish to slide headfirst into first coming from home. So if I were the bench coach, I might very well want to note this sort of detail. But for more general purposes, there'd be no need to do this. It doesn't particularly add to your understanding of what happened.

This brings us to a third point: there is no one way to notate the game. How we notate depends on our interests. Some notate pitch locations. Some use colored pencils. Some use one kind of chart, others another. This said, there are shared, communal interests, there are conventions, and so, relative to the shared goals of a community, we can speak of doing a better or worse job.

So now let's ask: What is the point of scoring? What are we doing? What is this all about? One answer—it's a way of recording what happened—is right, but superficial. A better answer is that keeping score is a way of thinking about and organizing our understanding of the play. It is a meaning-making activity. It is a kind of research. We write the game down to think about the game.

With that said, we come to a telling further point.

Keeping score is not, in fact, an activity *external* to the game. Very literally, how a game is scored defines what is going on in the game and so it matters to the players.

Crucially, whether you take the trouble actually to keep score, playing baseball requires that you have a scorekeeper's mentality, that you think of what is going on around you in the same terms as the scorekeeper would. How we score the game affects how a player feels or thinks about what he is doing, what situation he finds himself in, and so on.

Players live in the scorekeeper's reality.

·

Let us think of writing, then, and the role it plays in our lives, along the lines of score keeping in baseball. Books on the history of writing tend to treat writing as a way of encoding speech. And for this reason they tend to think of the alphabet—*our* way of writing—as superior because of its ability to represent speech sounds (rather than, say, ideas).

But our considerations suggest a different possibility. Writing, in the first instance, is not for representing speech at all; it's a technique for thinking about whatever domain it is we are writing about. It is a way of making sense of it. It is a way of (re)organizing it.

In fact, the best theories of the origins of writing suggest it derived, originally, from techniques of marking for the purposes of counting. Writing was literally *scoring* at the beginning. The first writers were bookkeepers and they wrote not to represent their speech or talk about goats or bushels but to keep track of goats and bushels and transactions with them.

Fast-forward to musical notation today. Musical notation is not for reading aloud in French or Korean or English. It's for playing. Of course you *can* read it aloud. But not exclusively in one or another of these languages, but in any of them. We use the notation not to encode ways of talking but rather to encode musical ideas and problems.

Things are exactly this way with mathematical writing. It is inconceivable that there could be higher mathematics as we know it if there were not mathematical notations. The point is not just that we calculate with the notations, as with basic arithmetic. Nor is the point just that the notations are themselves mathematical objects (as for example in model theory). The point is that the notations make it possible to frame problems and think about phenomena in a way that we couldn't do without notation.

These uses of writing are basic. My suggestion is that they are the foundational, the first, the original uses of writing. We do not write to record language. Like language itself, *writing is to think with*. The use of writing to score music, or baseball games, or engage in mathematical proof are not merely specialized applications, they are a glimpse into the fact that writing is precisely *not* ancillary to speech, a subsequent development for the purposes of recording speech. It is rather an autonomous linguistic technology for engaging with the world around us. It is a framework, or a manner, or a style of engagement.

Insofar as you think of writing as a means of recording speech, then it follows ineluctably that speech comes first and writing second. But if you appreciate that writing is a graphical technology for engaging cognitively with the world, like speech itself, then it becomes an open question which comes first. As a matter of historical fact, it is clear that the use of writing for the purposes of recording speech is a recent invention. Yes. But we also know that there are graphical practices—manifest, for example, in the cave paintings of Europe and Africa—that are at least as old as our linguistic capacities (or as old as we have reason to think our linguistic capacities are). So the idea that using graphical means to think about the world and our problems—writing, that is—is as old as language isn't far-fetched at all. Writing, in this sense, is in fact autonomous of language.

But of course, we do use writing to represent language. This is the point with which I began. We use writing to make sense of ourselves as language users. Which brings us to a crucial and truly remarkable point. The need to do this—to help make sense of the way we are organized by language—predates the deployment of graphical means (e.g., drawing) for this purpose.

Consider: the need to make sense of and think about one's talking practice—the need to clarify and make explicit, to adjudicate, explain, and guide—would have been present from the beginning. Language brings with it the possibility of misunderstanding, and there could be no instruction in language without the need to articulate and express a conception of how one ought to speak or what are the correct or preferred or most comprehensible ways of speaking. Think of baseball again: whether or not you score the game, the standpoint or attitude of the scorekeeper—the standpoint that asks: What is happening here? Is this good? Bad? What's the score?—is already in place. This standpoint is part of the game itself. And so with a certain metareflective attitude about language. There could not be language as we know it in the absence of attitudes, values, norms, prescriptions, and ideologies about language. There never was a Garden of Eden, and so there never was a language that we carried out and made use of freely, automatically, always without need for reflection on such basic questions as How to go on? What is right and what is wrong? What does he mean when he says that? Why did he say that? and so on.

For all intents and purposes, then, there can be no speech without the availability, to speakers, of what I'll call the writerly attitude. And this, as we have already noted, is independent of the actual availability of writing as a technology for representing speech. We had been using speaking to model speech long before we started using drawing (that is to say, writing) for this purpose. The application of writing to the modeling of speech was the response to an urgent felt need.

·

The upshot of these reflections on writing is subtle. First, writing is not ancillary to speech. Writing, in the case of baseball, is a tool for thinking about baseball, just like speech is itself. And as such, devising ways of writing baseball reorganizes baseball itself and transforms it.

It is also the case that we can apply this sort of graphical technology to language itself. And as in the case of baseball, so *writing language* organizes and transforms language.

And moreover, we have seen, it is not just that we *can* apply this sort of graphical technology to writing, as we do to baseball, but that we *must*. Here I need to be careful. Granted, it is not the case that we must invent ways of writing language, literally. For much of our history we didn't do this. And there are perfectly good languages spoken today that have never been written. My point is that whether we actually invent a way to write down our speech, we do what is, conceptually, at least, the equivalent. We take up what I am calling the writerly attitude to our own speech activities. There wouldn't be speech without these practices of self-organization. As with baseball. There is no baseball without thinking about baseball. The second order penetrates the first order through and through.

This may be what an ideology is: a way of thinking about an activity that so permeates the activity that we can no longer really differentiate them. Baseball rests on an ideology, and so does language.

Now, when I say that the arts, and philosophy, are bent on the invention of writing, that they aim at or tend to its invention, what I mean, in effect, is that they arise precisely at the juncture where our genuine, full-blooded, first-order engagements become problematic for themselves. Which is to say when they fully become what they are, that is to say, organized activities that are governed by a self-conception of those activities themselves (i.e., by an ideology).

It is sometimes remarked that writing is oppressive. No doubt writing and dictionaries and institutions of language governance are associated with the nation-state. And anyway, it is clear that without writing, what we think of as civilization, government, law, not to mention science, could never have come to be. So from our standpoint, living as we do in a scriptoral-linguistic world, writing is already extant and there is no sense in which art aims at inventing writing or in contributing to its authoritarian rule. Neither art nor philosophy aims at serving reigning ideologies in that way.

Try to put yourself back into the state of mind of a someone trying to invent, for the very first time, a way of writing our speech. What a self-exploratory, self-reorganizing project! And what an apparently impossible task!

But notice, this is *exactly* the position we find ourselves in today with regard to dancing. We have no way of writing how we dance or how we move. Sure, some of our gestures—"she shrugged her shoulders," "he shook his fist at me"—are nameable units. But when it comes to the enormous, vast, fluid stream of the expressive use of movement, posture, the face and the body, we are thoroughly *illiterate* (or, as it were, preliterate). Or rather, we are in the same position as that of our ancestors who were indeed able to take up the writerly attitude to their speech but entirely in the absence of the technology and also the conceptual apparatus necessary to write it down.

What we call dance (choreography) is our method for doing this. And for this reason what we call dance is a way of doing the philosophy of the moving body.

Inventing a way of writing the moving body is transformative and imaginative in precisely the way that the invention of the writing of speech once was but is no longer.

One way to capture the historical transformation that has occurred would be to say: writing, which was once applied to speech as a way of modeling it, has looped down to such a degree that we can now think of writing itself as an instrument of our linguistic organization. It's not that art, and philosophy, need now to resist writing, or turn away from it. It's rather that the need to write ourselves starts all over again. We need to write the way scriptoral-language organizes us.

And this is the work of the literary arts. Literary artists take all the ways we find we must express ourselves, or write down our stories, or articulate our lives, and they make *that* their problem. They try to invent new ways of writing. The task of writing the way we are organized by writing may require a direct engagement, as it were, at a technical level, with writing itself, as when Emily Dickinson treats words as objects to decorate a page, or when James Joyce pushes written language to its imaginative limits, finally producing a language that cannot, in any ordinary sense, be understood at all and that has value for that reason. Writing, so familiar, so dominant, so hegemonic, is made strange.

But other artists look elsewhere, not to writing as such but to storytelling, and so they rewrite, reorganize the very idea of what the telling of a story might be. Here Herman Melville and Thomas Mann come to mind. Narration is something new and strange in their hands, even if, taken sentence by sentence, and word by word, they are not experimenting.

•

What goes for the writerly attitude undoubtedly goes for the painterly attitude as well. The impulse to stand back from the world we encounter with our eyes and to turn our attention to the manner of our visual engagement with that world is not something we need to learn to do. I remember lying in bed at night as a child playing with my eyes and the lights from outside. By opening and closing my eyes one after the other, I could make the streetlamp jump about, and by squinting I could make its light turn into shooting rays. And who hasn't marveled that it is possible to blot out whole buildings, or even the moon, with one's own thumb! So it seems plausible to me that, from the beginning, two very different avenues have been open to us as visual artists. We can depict the world, and in doing so, regiment the world for our understanding, description, and thought (Byzantine art, for example). Or we can regiment our visual experience itself (art in the Renaissance, Impressionism). Both impulses probably operate at all times but sometimes one or the other takes precedence. There is a familiar way of thinking about the history of painting according to which painters aimed at the discovery of appearances, at the achievement of the unbiased eye. This concern can find expression in works of great naturalism but also in works of Impressionism. And there is no doubt that just as the invention of ways of writing our words down was once a liberating achievement of artistic creation, so it was once similarly transformative and emancipating to find ways of writing down what we see in painting. And similarly, just as conventional systems of writing are authorities that can threaten to limit artistic invention and strangle thought and individual expression, so exactly the same has been true for a slavish devotion to realistic depiction either of what we see or of how things look. Just as Dickinson or Joyce might rebel against inherited and prescribed ways of relying on words and phrases, so painters like Cézanne, Matisse, and Picasso were able to reorganize the ways we take for granted what it is to depict the world precisely by refusing even to try to draw things as they are seen to be (or alternatively, to reconceive what it is to see things at all).

And of course many other visual artists turn their attention away from problems about *visual* perception altogether and find the impulse to reveal and reorganize elsewhere. Just as Thomas Mann turned from language to narrative, some painters either stopped making pictures altogether (Barnett Newman, Mark Rothko, Robert Irwin) or deployed naturalism (that is to say a concern with effective depiction) in totally new ways (Gerhard Richter, David Hockney, Lucian Freud, for example).

My point is a simple one: in contrast to the designers of catalogs trying to flog retail wares, picture makers who are artists are putting picture making itself, or vision itself, in the frame for inspection. If pictures are the result, then they are pictures that don't only show you something but also invite you to wonder what you could possibly see in or with or thanks to a picture.

Painting as an art, like poetry and fiction, is in the business of writing us, or writing us again or anew. And what gives these undertakings their importance, at least in part, is the fact that, if I am right, it is truly our nature to deploy graphical technologies—writing, making pictures, taking up the painterly and the writerly attitude.

•

Choreography aims at writing the dancing and moving body, just as philosophy strives to bring out—to set forth—what ordinary thought and talk take for granted. And painting is grappling with the existence of the graphical practices that we have inherited from our prehistoric ancestors.

But the art form that seems to have come closest to mastering itself in a graphical medium is music. Here alone, it would seem, the mesh between score and practice has achieved the closeness of fit that we find with writing and speech. Just as you can read off the spoken language from the written page, so it seems some people can read off the music from the score. Musical scores dominate musical practice, and their advent marks the birth of music as an art.

This is too big a topic for me to investigate thoroughly here. But a few points will serve to keep us oriented.

First, it is an illusion that a score determines the way the music is played. Scores are instruments for playing and they capture the work, they capture the music itself, only in the setting of a practice of making, teaching, training, using, and criticizing the use of scores in performance.

It is also an illusion to think that, as a general rule, the written text determines how we are to read it aloud. There are so many subtle distortions and confusions in the vicinity of this idea. (1) Not all scripts record speech. Nothing in a baseball score dictates whether it is to be read aloud in English or Spanish. (2) In the case of alphabetic writing systems, we do in fact have settled practices of reading aloud. But notice, a Glaswegian, a New Yorker, and a child will all read the same text very differently, even if each reads it correctly. And the text, that is to say, the score, leaves lots open to interpretation (volume, emphasis, impersonations, pauses, etc.). (3) We also forget that whereas there are settled practices for reading some kinds of writing aloud—for example, short stories, poetry—this is not so for other kinds. Is there one way to read a web page aloud? Or the back of a book jacket, as the linguist Christopher M. Hutton has asked (in conversation)? Or road signs? Or advertisements in the subway? And even when you are reading the story, are you supposed to read aloud everything on the page? For example, are you supposed to read the page numbers and other header material? (4) And similar points go in reverse as well. A Mandarin and a Cantonese can both read the same text aloud even though, in a sense, the text no more determines how it *sounds* than mathematical notion does.

What is true is that there are ways of using texts to govern, guide, or inform performance. And the same surely goes for musical scores. But not because the score captures and determines the music, as it were, all on its own. One might just as well have said: the music captures the score.

The point is deep. Beethoven heavily annotated his scores. Are these instructions part of the score, or are they notes on how to read the score? Could one write a score that answered every question that one might have about how to play it? No. No text is self-interpreting.

What is true is that at a certain point in history, musicians devised a way to model their musical activity in writing—their melodies and scales and instruments—and this in turn looped back down into the practice of allowing musicians to rethink their activity in new ways. Scoring reorganized.

But what is striking is that the strength of confidence that the score uniquely fixes the musical work is in direct proportion to the degree to which the musical work confines itself to what is, in effect, a limited range of precataloged musical possibilities. You can't write down the blues, or jazz, or electronic music. And after the twentieth century, it has been necessary for composers to invent new ways of writing what they are doing, and their struggles are comparable to those of choreographers. If the musical work is tied to the score, then the musical work is concerned with a problem: how to write itself.

I don't think it is a far-fetched idea that music is bent on the problem of writing itself.

I once asked a composer friend of mine, a student, who his favorite composer was. Thomas Adès, he replied. And he explained: for sheer putting of notes on paper, no one compares!

What a remarkable utterance! You might have thought, naïvely, that music was concerned with, well, music, and that notations are, well, just that, notations. But my friend's sense of Adès's genius turned essentially on Adès's achievement in writing, in creating a text, a score.

And so, I suggest, for all the arts. Art, and philosophy, aim at the invention of writing. Sometimes this takes the form of resisting conventionalized ways of drawing, writing, notating, scoring. And other times it takes the form of weaving methods of representing ourselves to ourselves from scratch.

5

Art, Evolution,
and the Puzzle of Puzzles

Plato remarked that it is easy to make a picture. Anyone can do it. You just hold up a mirror to whatever you are interested in, and *presto!* you have its picture.

Plato was mistaken. A reflection is no more a picture than a footprint is a sculpture. We make pictures for this or that purpose; reflections, in contrast, just happen, we stumble upon them. Moreover, I see the car in the rearview mirror, but I do not, in the same sense, see my grandfather, long since deceased, when I look at his photograph.

In another sense, perhaps not quite intended, though, Plato may have been exactly right.

Mirror images may not be pictures, but we use them, sometimes, as if they were. This is because we think of ourselves, and of others—of how we look—on the model of how we show up, or might show up, in a picture. The picture, in the words of the art historian Anne Hollander, "is the standard by which the direct view is assessed—including the direct view of the self in the mirror." And so when we turn to look at ourselves in the bathroom, vestibule, or bedroom mirror, what we take an interest in is a kind of provisional self-portrait. In Hollander's words, "Far from seeing objectively, the mirror gazer is engaged in creating a posed studio portrait of himself, not even a candid shot." Mirror images, we might say, are transient or throwaway selfies.

Hollander's idea is far-reaching. Her particular interest was clothing and the idea that our attitude and response to clothing reflect standards and conventions that are most vividly realized in visual art. We measure the dressed people we see, and how we feel about our own visible, clothed bodies, by the standards set up in pictures.

The point is stronger than the mere thought that art influences how we see ourselves—sort of in the way ideologies might shape attitudes of all kinds. She gets at something more surprising and more radical: that our lively and everyday interest in dressing and in the way others are dressed—an interest that is not parochial or contemporary but may very well be one of our defining preoccupations as a species; remember, we've been dressing ourselves for at least thirty thousand years, as we noticed in passing in chapter 3—is in fact also a kind of engagement with art and art's history. When we dress ourselves, we respond to—we sample, cite, and play with—the looks of others, as we have found these recorded in painting and photography. And we do so with an eye to how we ourselves would show up in pictures.

This is an exciting thought. It opens up the possibility that the kid on the street corner with his basketball shoes *just so* and his jeans and jewelry and tattoos *just so*, with his definitive style, is actually doing something *serious*. Well, in a way, this is old news. Ours is a culture that is continuously getting worked over by the style choices of our young people—1950s greasers, 1960s hippies, 1970s punk rockers, 1990s hip-hoppers, and so on. But if Hollander is right, whatever else it is these kids are doing when they make up new ways of dressing themselves, they are also doing something in the vicinity of art. In dressing themselves, they are playing with the stuff of art, with pictures, just as we are when we take up a stance or a pose before the mirror.

In one sense, then, pictures hold us captive, they reign over us. We are captured by them.

But they also supply the resources we need to free ourselves of their control. We don't step outside of pictoriality. That's not possible. But we can dress differently, that is, we can make different pictures. In this way, art emancipates us from the organization and regulation imposed by technologies.

Now there is something hard to believe in all this. Surely, one wants to say, dressing comes first, and the making of pictures of dressed people comes second; our own visual experience of what clothes and the clothed body look like must come before and provide the true standard by which we measure the effectiveness or the value of pictorial representations of what we know in the first instance by direct contact! More generally, the idea that culture could make over vision itself cannot be taken seriously because vision is biological and biology is prior to culture.

But this is exactly what Hollander's considerations allow us to challenge. You may not need pictures to see, strictly speaking, but pictures—at least pictures of dressed people—shape our very conception not only of the look and feel of the dressed body but also even of the look and feel of what it is like to be dressed. Our own experience—visual and bodily but also social—derives from our culturally shaped conception of dress via pictures. This is not to deny that vision is a biological faculty, one we share with animals, and one that can be treated medically and without regard for cultural anthropology. Although it is striking to consider that the way the eye doctor tests your eyes is by asking you to discriminate letters and pictures. Even our medical sense of optimal visual performance, it would seem, is tied to pictures.

Hollander's point can and should be extended. The very idea of seeing as a kind of looking, or contemplation, an act of thoughtful inspection or visual evaluation, is, we might say, one we get from pictures. Pictures, after all, are made to be inspected. No cultural rules stand in the way of close looking, or staring, at a picture. In contrast, we are rarely if ever permitted to stare at a living person the way we might look at her in a picture. It is rude to stare, after all. And if we do stare or gawk or ogle a living person before us, we run the sharp risk of offending or violating her.

Pictures afford the model of what it would be to step back and take a look, to detach and disengage, to contemplate rather than carry on. Pictures gives us what we might call the *aesthetic sense*. Pictures are not so much the result of an applied aesthetic sense as they are its very precondition. In the beginning was the picture.

We can contrast aesthetic, contemplative seeing with what we might call seeing in the wild. Wild seeing is active, embedded, subordinate to task, an openness to our world rather than, if you like, a state of reflection on or contemplation of the world. Most seeing, most of the time, is precisely not contemplative; not, in any sense, aesthetic. It does not rest on deliberate acts of looking and inspection. We drive, we tie our shoes, we prepare dinner and then eat it. And we use our eyes and our other senses when we do all this. Wild seeing is spontaneous and engaged; it is direct and involved. Wild seeing is acting in concert with the stuff around us. Aesthetic seeing, in contrast, is something more like the entertainment of thoughts about what one is looking at.

It would be wrong to say that you can't see without pictures, or that seeing has no biological autonomy from the cultural practice of making and using pictures. The point, rather, is that just as writing shapes our conception of language, as I argued in the last chapter, so pictures shape our conception of seeing. And just as writing loops down and alters our live action in and with language, so pictures loop down and alter the ways we exercise our visual powers. Pictures become an instrument for seeing. Pictures become the standard by which at least a certain variety of direct awareness is assessed.

Pictures transform seeing from a skill that operates in the background, guiding our work and play, to a thoughtful activity of attentive evaluation. But it is not only *seeing* that pictures alter, it is *what we see*, or at least our conception of what we see, that gets transformed. Insofar as seeing is active, embedded, subordinate to task, then what we see is always just the furniture of our living, the equipment, the gear we use to take care of business. And our fundamental relation to that which we see is not that of looking, or contemplation, or curiosity, but rather something like reliance or dependence or the relation of *taking for granted*. We don't contemplate or look at the gearshift, but we do use our eyes to drive. Similarly, we don't visually inspect the ground in order to walk upon it, but we guide our movements with our eyes.

When it comes to pictorial seeing—the exercise of the aesthetic sense—we get something altogether new. Pictorial consciousness gives us not furniture or gear, but rather objects, and so it gives us the idea of a world made up of objects. An object is a freestanding, neutral, physical thing. It has properties. In particular, it has visible properties such as shape and color and size, and it is these, according to the standpoint of pictorial consciousness, that we really see. Pictures give us this way of thinking about seeing, for pictures are, in a way, the very model of what an object is supposed to be. A picture is put there to be inspected, with a cool and discerning eye. Objects show up only when we have stepped back from the field of play, when we have turned away from our engagement itself. The object, in this sense, is the correlate of the act of contemplation; it is a way of thinking about the world that we bring into being when we exercise our consciousness in the pictorial way.

And so we can say, after Hollander: pictures are the standard by which both visual awareness as an act of contemplation and also the objects of such acts are conceptualized.

Now crucially there is something false about picture consciousness. Mommy and Daddy are not objects. The bed is not an object. The ground we play baseball on is not an object. At least they are not objects until we step back, detach ourselves, and think of them in a certain way. Until we look at them as we might look at a picture.

Nevertheless, it is too easy to try to repudiate picture seeing as fake or inauthentic, as "merely cultural," although there is a grain of truth in this. The world is not given to us as pictures are given to us. The world is not made up of objects for us, for our inspection, as pictures are made for us, for our inspection. A truer phenomenology would downgrade the salience and importance not only of contemplation but also of objects themselves.

But as there is no going back to Eden, so there is no going back to a way of seeing that was before pictures. And we need to remember, first, that pictures come *very* early in our history and our prehistory. There is no record of modern humanity prior to the existence not only of sketches and scratches but also a highly evolved picture-making ability. But second, the idea of the object is necessary for physical science or, indeed, for any idea of the world as it is anyhow, independent of us. We can't give that up. Objects are real; it took pictures for us to discover them.

At the same time we need to admit that this power of pictures over us is somehow troubling. Pictures rule over us; in a sense, they hold us captive. Recent evidence shows that even our hominid cousins the Neanderthal were preoccupied with carving shapes with pointed stone implements onto cave walls. And, as we've had occasion to note several times, our own ancestors have been making pictures, stashed away in private cave spaces, for something like as long as we have been around as a species. Today, with the newer digital technologies of making, storing, reproducing, and transmitting pictures, and with the advent of the selfie, pictures have come to occupy an even more energetic place in our experiential lives. We have already been considering the many ways pictures transform how and what we see. There's nothing surprising in this. I am sure we have all had the experience of looking at a sunset and exclaiming: it's so magnificent! it is almost like a picture! Or we say: it is picturesque! What better example of the tendency to view the picture as the standard by which we assess the direct awareness could there be? But the dominion of pictures goes beyond these familiar observations. We don't make pictures to lay down memories; we make pictures, in this epoch of pictorial consciousness, so that we can even have experiences. It is as if, were we to fail to make an image, or, indeed, to concern ourselves with images, nothing would ever really happen. And so lovers hold each other tight on the bench by the sea, but she holds her camera phone out and takes the selfie that authenticates the event as significant.

It's worrying. If every moment is a Kodak moment, then, really, no moment is. I suspect that the compulsion to take pictures of ourselves—not unlike the compulsion to look at ourselves in the shop windows as we walk by—reflects not merely a passing fad or impulse, but a kind of culmination of the way pictures have made us, as it were, in their own image.

•

Some thinkers believe that the aesthetic sense is universal among humans. "Who among us," writes the University of Auckland philosopher Stephen Davies, "has never taken aesthetic delight . . . in a sunset, a rainbow, a kitten's playfulness, a story, a song? And this kind of pleasurable response seems to be characteristic of humans generally across historical periods and cultures."

Davies may be right about this. Pictures belong to our prehistoric technology and so they have truly shaped how we human beings experience vision; it isn't that hard to believe that the pictorial way of thinking about our relation to things around us is sunk deep in our human way of living.

But it would surely be a mistake to argue, as Davies does, that we are "genetically disposed" to take up the aesthetic stance to (for example) animals because doing so led our ancestors to cope effectively with the threats and opportunities that animals may have posed.

No doubt the disposition to take pleasure in one's visual encounters with some animals, or with members of one's own species, or with safe and sustaining environments, would have conferred reproductive advantage on our remote ancestors; it would have been similarly beneficial for them to experience perceptual encounters with predators or inhospitable locales as frightening or unpleasant. But such perceptual encounters in the wild are a long way from aesthetic seeing.

Aesthetic seeing, as we have considered, is a kind of seeing that is detached and contemplative. It is a type of visual evaluation. It is never simply a felt response, no matter how strongly felt. What makes it aesthetic is that it stems precisely from a curiosity and disinterestedness about one's very own inclinations to respond. The aesthetic attitude is thoughtful and inquiring, which doesn't mean that it is not also strongly felt and passionate. But it does mean that we shouldn't expect to find examples of aesthetic sensitivity among creatures lacking the supporting cognitive faculties and shared social practices of evaluating. It also means that it is highly unlikely that aesthetic seeing would confer enhanced fitness on those capable of exercising it. Indeed, just the opposite is more likely to be the case. Contemplation is not a safe response to an attacker, nor is it an effective response to the good things that present themselves in one's environment.

If the aesthetic attitude is natural and universal, we need a different explanation of this fact. Following up on a suggestion of Davies, I think we can offer a conjecture. It is unconvincing to think that an animal such as a peacock could engage with the world aesthetically—and precisely because that would require of it the ability to *disengage* with the world thoughtfully, or to reflect on the world around it as if the world were a picture to be inspected. But by the same token, it is almost impossible to imagine human beings who are *not* capable of taking up this sort of aesthetic attitude. The aesthetic attitude is *normal* for people, and in at least two different ways. First, most people can, as a matter of fact, take up the aesthetic attitude: they spontaneously and naturally talk about how things around them look or seem; people spontaneously engage in critical argument about these matters. And because the aesthetic sense is normal in this statistical sense—most people do have an aesthetic sense—it is also normal in a second, *normative* sense. A person ought to be able to take up the aesthetic stance for the simple reason that almost everyone can. The inability to do so would be a sign that all was not quite right, that one was lacking in some mental respect, perhaps in intelligence, or curiosity, or inventiveness, or in perceptiveness or imagination. It is with the aesthetic sense as with nipples on the human male. They are not good for anything. But the fact that they are universal means that their presence carries valuable information about one's own normalcy (and so one's fitness).

So we can agree with those who argue that the aesthetic sense is an evolved expression of our human nature, even if, as a matter of fact, the aesthetic sense is less a single trait than it is a broad capacity to participate in a whole suite of culturally beholden responses and evaluative attitudes to the things we perceive, and even if, as seems likely, humans alone possess this aesthetic sense.

•

To embrace an evolutionary account of the aesthetic sense, however, is so far to have said nothing about art and its place in our lives. The aesthetic sense, after all, is not an *art* sense. We can take up, we do take up, this attitude to objects of any kind—kittens, sunsets, Boeing 747s, you name it. So we can't move from the biological normalcy of the aesthetic sense to an understanding of art. Aesthetic seeing does not pick out art.

In fact, there may be an even more tantalizing reason why we can't explain art in terms of our aesthetic dispositions. I have been arguing that the aesthetic sense depends on the prior existence of picture-making technologies. But it is precisely *art's work* (and philosophy's), as I argued in the last chapter, to invent these technologies, these means of writing ourselves down.

We need art, if this is right, to invent the very technologies whose existence is a precondition for art—for we make art out of our organized activities, our technological practices—and whose existence enables us first to take up the aesthetic sense necessary not only for the appreciation of but also for the making of art or technology (or science!), in the first place.

However far back we go in time, where we find ourselves, we also find language and dress and pictures and technology. And we find art.

•

But isn't it possible to explain art itself, this complicated cluster of behaviors, in evolutionary terms? Isn't it possible to give a biological explanation of how it all got started?

Some thinkers feel this must be possible. For example, the independent scholar Ellen Dissanayake argues that art is so widespread, so passionately engaged, so important to us, and its pleasures so physical, so sensual, that we must recognize that it has an evolutionary biological origin. We love art and its behaviors the way we love sex or the way we love eating. And when a love or passion is so direct, so unmediated by the demands of civilization and "high culture," it must surely have its sources in what is good for us, in what we like because we need it, as animals.

She illustrates her point with lines from Walt Whitman's *Song of Myself* that give expression to the sexual, physical character of the pleasures we may take in art.

> I hear the trained soprano . . . she convulses me like the
>   climax of my love-grip;
> The orchestra whirls me wider than Uranus flies,
> It wrenches unnamable ardors from my breast,
> It throbs me to gulps of the farthest down horror,
> It sails me . . . I dab with bare feet . . . they are licked by the
>   indolent waves,
> I am exposed . . . cut by bitter and poisoned hail,
> Steeped amid honeyed morphine . . . my windpipe squeezed
>   in the fakes of death,
> Let up again to feel the puzzle of puzzles,
> And that we call Being.

It is the fact of this sort of extreme, bodily, passionate response to art that requires explanation, she says, and only an evolutionary, only a truly *species* perspective, one that takes into account reaches of time on evolutionary scales, can provide the needed explanation.

If the argument of this book is right, then Dissanayake gets things exactly backward. Art's effects are not immediate. And they are never simple or unproblematic or direct in the way that the pleasures of food and sex are (or can be) simple and unproblematic and direct. Art's responses are always perturbable by criticism, by questioning, by context, and by reflection. They are magnificently and necessarily cultural.

If there is any exception to this, it might seem to be music. Music exerts a power and an immediacy that seem to make it special. You *look* at pictures. You *inspect* sculptures or buildings. All very cool, detached. But music *attacks*; it engulfs you in a wash of physical energy. And you don't need any special training to feel its effects. Music soothes the savage breast, after all, or so they say. Its force on humans is *psychiatric*; music operates, or so it seems, according to a *neurologic*.

None of this is true. Yes, music affects us. But so does an insult hurled our way. Just as our response to the insult is at once spontaneous and entirely unmediated, but for all that grounded on the learned and practiced knowledge of language, so our musical responses always occur against a background of shared musical knowledge and culture. Beethoven will do nothing to the musically uninitiated. Indeed, to a musical outsider, Beethoven wouldn't even be recognizable. When I look at the portico of the Taj Mahal, I am unable to distinguish the letters of classical Arabic from the ornamental squiggles beside them. A musical stranger would be exactly that successful in picking out Ludwig van Beethoven from Johannes Brahms, Wolfgang Amadeus Mozart, or George Frideric Handel, even Charles Mingus. Sure, if you sit people down and get them to focus on the music, they'll find that there is something there for them to take an interest in. But the act of sitting down and listening is already a move within our musical culture, not simply the exercise of acoustic competence. (Listening is not the same thing as hearing.)

Do you think it is a coincidence that we tend to have a special attachment to the music of our own time, or perhaps of the time just preceding our own? One exception to this tendency to like the contemporary, or the comparatively contemporary, is the special importance we attach, as a culture, to Bach, Mozart, and Beethoven, and a few others. Could it be that these are simply the best composers ever so that people around the world today measure musical accomplishment in connection to them? Or might it be that we built our shared musical culture on the foundation of their achievements? Are they internal, then, to our very notion of what music is supposed to sound and feel like?

Anyway, the point of this digression is simply that music, painting, and all the arts are products of a culture, and they have meaning only against the background of that culture. But, and this is the crucial point, this in no way implies that our responses to works of art are not genuinely felt.

Dissanayake, it seems to me, takes for granted not only a simple-minded opposition of nature and culture, but also a more subtle but, I think, equally confused idea that passions and emotions are physical and that these are opposed to thought, intellect, understanding, as if the latter are always linguistic, and deliberative, and, indeed, grounded in society's conventions. Art, Dissanayake wants to say, is too passionate to be shaped by understanding or knowledge; it is too animal to be cultural.

Against this I would offer that it is the very hallmark of human existence that it is impossible to factor out thought and feeling, nature and culture, in our lives.

We've already noticed (in chapter 3) that we are designers *by nature*. Technology shapes our lives; it organizes us, and thus it shapes what we are, our very nature. This kind of organization, I have urged, deserves to be thought of as biological.

Cultural formations loop back down and shape not only our minds but also our bodies. Consider: humans are bigger now than we were three hundred years ago. Visit a Shaker Village and you'll be struck by how very small everything is. This is because these houses and chairs and tables were built for smaller people. Body size is physical if anything is. But it is implausible that our increase in size over these last few centuries has anything to do with changes in the genome. What's changed, rather, is culture—agriculture, medicine, hygiene, these are what have changed us.

There are also examples of culture changing the genome. A thousand years ago most humans were unable to digest lactose; the domestication of animals and the concomitant availability of abundant supplies of nutritious milk have created a (cultural) environment in which people who can digest milk have a reproductive advantage. The place of dairy in our lives is at once biological and also cultural.

Or consider the fact that although widespread literacy is a very recent phenomenon, reading seems to be enabled by exquisitely detailed and specialized neural structures. Damage in the parts of the brain responsible for reading brings about specific corresponding deficits in our reading abilities. Those neural structures couldn't have evolved for that purpose. But they have this purpose for us now. Is it the brain that constrains culture here? Or is it the other way around: culture organizing the brain?

The very idea of culture or technology as something that floats entirely free of biology is a nonstarter.

But so is the idea that bodily lusts and sensations and desires and pleasures are disconnected from what we know or understand. If you need proof of this, ask yourself: Doesn't your knowledge of what you are eating, of what its origins are, affect how you experience its flavor? Would the knowledge that the pâté garnished so elegantly before you is dog food affect how it tastes? Or take the case of sex: Do you like to kiss your partner because you like how it feels to kiss him or her, or is it that you like how it feels because of your affection? Thought experiment: imagine that you are making out with someone and you are enjoying it. Would it affect how you feel to discover that the person's gender was different from what you had supposed? (Recall Neil Jordan's film *The Crying Game*.)

Importantly, it isn't prejudice to prefer kissing your partner, even if you might not be able to pick out your partner from a lineup just on the basis of a blind kiss. And so with all forms of valuing. Our likes and dislikes, what we find interesting, repellent, or attractive, are shaped by skill, knowledge, and understanding. This is especially true when it comes to art, where the true aesthetic question is not Do you like this? but rather, *Why* do you like this?

I find that there's something startlingly self-defeating in Dissanayake's appeal to Whitman's poem to document the bodily, visceral, sensual character of our art responses. For one thing, Whitman's poem is, well, it's just that, a work of nineteenth-century literary art. And while its artistic merit is not in question, it does not produce in readers the riot of bodily, erotic excitement that the poem itself describes. So its very existence gives the lie to the idea that physical-sensual response is, if you like, required for art, or what art most truly aims at.

Yet the effectiveness of Whitman's poem demonstrates that cultural know-how and background understanding—literacy, familiarity with and interest in reading—serve as the *vehicle* of artistic creation and aesthetic experience and are not, as it were, some kind of "high-cultural" overlay. The poem exhibits the fact that thought and feeling cleave to each other.

Whitman's poem investigates the encounter not with a woman, or her voice, but precisely with a *trained* soprano, that is, with art. The poem affords us the opportunity to consider the ways that, through such an encounter, we come up against what he, in the penultimate line, calls "the puzzle of puzzles," namely, the inexplicable fact of our being. Whitman's example brings out that physical feeling and emotional response are art's preconditions, its raw materials, rather than something at which art aims. Art aims at much more. For Whitman, as for us, art is a kind of philosophy.

•

The trouble, finally, with evolutionary theories of art is that they tend to be empty. They don't tell us why we make art or why art is valuable for us. They don't bring the art in art into focus. The problem is not that they offer theories of art with which we might, or might not, be in agreement. The problem is that they don't get so far as even to say something substantial about art. (Later we will see the same tends to be true of neurobiological approaches.)

Ellen Dissanayake herself, for example, argues that art serves the function of "making special," and "making special" is crucial for the formation of relations of intimacy and, ultimately, of identity, both individual and group.

This is a plausible idea. But it doesn't give us an explanation of why we make art, or why art is so important to us, for the simple reason that art is not the only way to "make special." Religion makes special, and, I think she would agree, so do play, and ritual, and love, as well as other forms of cultural activity such as sports, war, and trade (all of which are probably prehistoric in origin). If art has any distinct qualities and distinct forms of value—and certainly it does—Dissanayake's theory doesn't tell us why these are selected for. Her account fails to secure its explanandum, which is art, not the much wider domain of activities that serve to "make special."

The University of New Mexico psychologist Geoffrey Miller appeals to sexual selection to explain art's adaptive significance. Art is like the peacock's tail. It is not a first-order adaptation. Long, awkward tails don't enhance fitness; indeed, they are positively counteradaptive. It is just this fact, however, that makes the case that the possession of a long tail by a peacock can be a marker of fitness. For it demonstrates to potential mates that its possessor is so far above the minimum threshold of survival that it can afford such a nonutilitarian and indeed risky display. The peacock's tail acquires adaptive value because peahens choose peacocks with big tails.

And so, Miller argues, with art. The ability to make art, and also the ability to own it, to buy and sell it, to educate oneself about it, are costly achievements that only an affluent and intelligent person can manage. An engagement with or sensitivity to art is thus a desirable thing in a potential mate. Art is selected for thanks to its role in signaling fitness, even though there is nothing directly adaptive, that is to say, fitness enhancing, about art or its behaviors.

The details of this account needn't concern us. In particular, we can pass in silence over the absurdity of the idea that art's significance is exhausted by its deployment in the context of mating. For our purposes the relevant thing to notice is this: a sexual-selection account of art can tell us nothing about art beyond the fact that it is, in relevant respects, like the peacock's tail or flashy cars or extravagant jewelry. But what such a view cannot explain is why art has values that go beyond those it may have in common with other sexual displays of the sort mentioned.

Stephen Davies offers a more promising and more profound account, according to which art, whatever its origins, comes to acquire the status of an adaptation.

Davies notices, to begin with, that art may originate as a non-fitness-enhancing side effect of traits that are adaptive in their own right, such as intelligence, imagination, humor, sociality, emotionality, inventiveness, and curiosity. But it would be wrong, he argues, to suppose that art is, now, for us, a mere "spandrel," that is to say, a nonadaptive side effect of our genuinely adaptive cognitive capacities. For what begins as a spandrel can come to take on adaptive significance. We have already taken note of such facts, as Davies reminds us, that navels and male nipples serve no adaptive function, yet their possession, by dint of their very normalcy, comes to be a signal of just that, normalcy, and so of health and fitness. In the same way, he argues, although art behaviors—making and enjoying pictures and singing and listening to songs—may lack any direct fitness-enhancing value, our ability to undertake them may come to acquire adaptive significance. For the ability to participate in these practices is sufficiently cognitively demanding, and sufficiently widespread in the population, that a disability in this regard would be a marked deficiency. "A person who showed no interest in any form of art would be as unappealing as someone who is without intelligence, humor, social grace, care for others, and a navel." Art behaviors are, therefore, rich signals of fitness. They may have originated as non-fitness-enhancing side effects, but they came to take on the standing of true adaptations.

I made use of Davies's line of reasoning to explain how aesthetic consciousness might come to be selected for, even if, as a matter of fact, it lacks a direct fitness-enhancing benefit. But I don't see how the argument works for art itself.

Once again, the problem is that the account fails to zero in on *art*, and art's distinctive values; it explains art as adaptive only to the degree to which art is a "transmissible human form or behavior that [is] recognized as signifying well-formedness and developmental normalcy." As such it becomes not only "statistically average as it successfully spread[s] through the population," but it comes to be "normative in the evaluative sense, whether it first emerged as an adaptation or as a spandrel."

Here's the snag: on this view, *any* "human form of behavior" that gives broad expression to our cognitive powers and is sufficiently widespread and entrenched must be an adaptation.

One worry is that this casts the net too wide. If art is an adaptation, on this view, then so are reading and writing. A person certainly puts his or her wits on display in reading and writing. And an inability to read or write is, surely, other things being equal, a telling defect. By Davies's lights, then, reading and writing are a rich signal of fitness and are, thus, adaptations, whatever their origins.

We might bite the bullet and admit that reading and writing, like other "transformative technologies" such as fire, and a broad range of other culturally transmitted practices, are in fact adaptations. They acquire their status as adaptations thanks to the same mechanisms that make it the case that art is adaptive.

The problem now is that this view explains art, but does so precisely by viewing it as just another cognitively challenging, widely entrenched technological practice. If art has any sources of value that are particular to it—if art is not merely technology—then, it seems, Davies's view can have nothing to say about this.

In one sense this seems like a good result. It suggests a place where we might want to draw the limits to what biology can help us understand. Evolutionary theory can contribute to our understanding of the place of art in our lives, but only up to the limit of art viewed as a species of technology. Art looks like technology. It is *useless* technology; works of art are *strange tools*. So as a matter of fact art will always tend to be materially indistinguishable from its technological sources. The paintings of an artist-painter may be indistinguishable, regarded materially, from those of someone working in advertising. Whether the one picture is a work of art and the other an ad is not a *material* difference between them. And so, from the point of view I have been developing in this book, there is something fitting about the idea that, viewed through the lens of Darwinian explanation, art and technology should look exactly the same.

But crucially, they are not the same. Technology serves ends. Art questions those very ends. Art affords revelation, transformation, reorganization; art puts into question those values, rules, conventions, and assumptions that make the use of technology possible in the first place.

So if art has sources of significance that outstrip the significance of technology in our lives—and it does—then we need to look beyond evolutionary theory to understand these.

•

The framework of first-order organized activities versus second-order reorganizational practices can help us make this clear. It is, in my extended, social sense, a *biological* fact that we are organized at the first order. And so it is a welcome result that these first-order activities themselves can be explainable using the framework of Darwinian evolution. Davies's discussion gives a better account of how this might go than any other that I am aware of.

But we shouldn't expect the account to apply to second-order reorganizational practices. For these are not, at least they don't seem to be anything like, first-order modes of social/biological organization. They are, rather, modes of investigation and researching and displaying these first-order facts about our condition.

Now, in fact, the theoretical predicament of the evolutionist may be worse off, and for reasons that have to do with the oversimplifications inherent in the contrast between the first and second orders. We have already considered at length—in the previous chapter and in this one—that first-order activities of dancing and talking (and now we appreciate even perceiving) are reorganized thanks to the way second-order investigations of these activities loop down and change them. This means that even our first-order activities like talking and looking and making pictures are always informed by, and so in a sense are also alive to, second-order art and philosophy. Art and philosophy, we might say, are always ready-to-hand.

This means that art coexists with practical life and organized activity. Art and philosophy are always in the offing in human life. Art and philosophy are implicit already in our basic, organized, biologically grounded form of life. And this is just another way of making explicit what, in a sense, everyone really already knows: human beings are animals—we are confined by patterns of activity—but we are more than just animals. We are animals who are never engaged only with the tasks of living but are always, also, concerned with why and how we find ourselves so occupied.

I say this is something everyone already knows. But of course it is also true that this proposition—human beings are animals but not only animals—marks the boundaries of a battlefield. Naturalists of all stripes are committed to the idea that we ought to be able to understand *our* nature as a species of animal nature. This naturalism has been resisted by many. It is resisted by humanists, who insist that the cultural floats free of biology, that there are no facts of human nature that constrain what we are and what we think and what we value. It may also be resisted by those who reject science, whether on religious or perhaps on other grounds.

My sympathies lie with the naturalists. We *are* part of the natural order. And art is tied, in ways that are beginning to emerge in this discussion, to basic facts about human biological nature. But crucially: nothing compels us to say that human being is a species of animal being; we can instead say that human being and animal being are each species of a more encompassing natural being. It is dogmatic and unimaginative to insist that we can explain the human exhaustively in the terms we use to explain the nonhuman animal. Why should we assume that?

It is likewise utterly wrongheaded to suppose that if we can't explain human being in the same terms we use to explain chimpanzee being, or corn being, or bacteria being, then it must be that humans are divine or supernatural beings.

•

I used to play in Washington Square Park growing up. One day—I couldn't have been more than eleven—I came upon an angry protest at the park's entrance at LaGuardia Place. I learned from the placards that New York University had invited a "Nazi" to campus to give a lecture. This was a terrible thing! The crowd was outraged. I remember being frightened. And I can still remember the speaker's name: E. O. Wilson.

Now, E. O. Wilson, the noted Harvard University biologist, neither was, nor is, a Nazi. He did, however, dare to defend "sociobiology." According to sociobiology, some features of human social life, as with the lives of ants, are, or at least could turn out to be, explicable in Darwinian terms. To the political imagination of the mid-1970s, the very idea of biological determinism smacked of race theory, eugenics, and pseudoscience. The mob wanted to silence the discussion.

A few years later I was sitting around a dinner table on the Upper

West Side listening to adult conversation about an important new book called *The Mismeasure of Man*. This book, by another Harvard University scientist, Stephen Jay Gould, argued that prejudice and bad values shaped the so-called science of human intelligence. The moral: there is no place for science when it comes to thinking about value and what makes us human.

Well, things have come pretty much full circle. When Thomas Nagel wrote a book not that long ago daring to raise the question whether contemporary biology was in a position to claim adequately to have comprehended human nature, he was widely denounced as having joined with the religious right and the benighted forces of antiscience. Although his argument is, to all intents and purposes, identical to one he had developed in a paper published in the early 1970s—a paper that made him famous—times had changed, and Nagel was now widely vilified.

When we turn to efforts to understand art using the resources of evolutionary biology—the topic of this chapter—it is worth reminding ourselves of this broader, volatile political context.

•

Proponents of the view that art *must* reduce to neurobiological or evolutionary biological phenomena are not speaking for science, or for reason; they are arguing rather from the standpoint of a fantasy about science and its requirements. They are speaking for scientism, not for science.

Scientism is committed to something like the idea that it is possible to describe the world as it really is in a way that is independent of our particular interests, needs, values, or standpoint. If there were scientists on remote planets, so it is said, there is every reason to expect that their understanding of the world, and that of Earth scientists, would converge on a common account of how things are. The fact that we have bodies, and experience the world through our senses, and at time scales that are intelligible to us—seconds, minutes, hours, days, years—is a limitation, to be sure, but it is precisely this limitation that the scientific method enables us to surmount. Science aims at a "view from nowhere," as Nagel puts it, or, in the words of Bernard Williams, at an "absolute conception of reality."

This seems to have been Descartes's view. We occupy the position of embodied consciousness. Things show up for us as colorful and noisy. But this is all false appearance, a consequence of our particular makeup and local perspective. The qualities of objects we seem to see wouldn't get cataloged in the final description of absolute reality. For they are merely effects, in our minds, of processes that are, in themselves, without color and without sound. The material world, at least for Descartes and Newton and the first scientific revolutionaries, consists of particles moving in accordance with mathematical laws. Everything we know in the world around us—from mountains to ice creams to sunsets to rose petals to the sun and the earth—is made up of physical parts that are made up in their turn of parts that are made up of still smaller parts. It's pure matter, devoid of quality, all the way down.

Scientism, thus described, is tantamount to what is sometimes called reductive materialism—the idea that fundamental reality is material and that everything there is consists of bits of matter combined in different ways. Reductive materialism has the further consequence that the final science will give a unified account *of everything*. It's physics (or maybe physics and chemistry) all the way down, and all the way up, and all the way out.

It is sometimes said that the worldview of natural science is committed to the nonexistence of God. This is not so. Science doesn't have a worldview in this sense.

The standpoint of science is something like that of a person repairing an automobile. The "check engine" light is on and she wants to know why. That light is an explanatory itch and the woman wants to scratch it. Now there may be a potential infinity of possible explanations of why the "check engine" light is on, ranging from "it isn't really on, I'm hallucinating it" to "my guardian angel is protecting me from going out today" to "a North Korean spy has tampered with my car." But these aren't very good explanations. They're unreasonable, which is to say that they don't scratch the explanatory itch. Why not? One reason is that, other things being equal, they are not likely. Given the way things are, it is much more likely that, oh, the alternator is on the fritz. Another reason is that, in part because they are so improbable, these further possibilities seem to raise more questions than they answer. It's like trying to scratch an itch by tickling it with a feather. The true natural attitude of science, it seems to me, is committed to acknowledging that it doesn't work.

Far from its being the case that science is committed to there being no God—as if this is something science has discovered, or learned, or found out, or that it could discover—it would be better to say that for science God is irrelevant. This is bad enough, I suppose, if you are one of the faithful. But it's one thing to make the substantive claim—there is no God—and another to say, roughly, the question of God doesn't come up for natural science. It doesn't come up, that is, *in* natural science.

Some religious thinkers—notably the philosopher Alvin Plantinga—have argued that unless there is a God, we have no reason to trust our own cognitive faculties. The scientific attitude, he claims, is self-defeating. Why? His argument goes like this: according to science, our cognitive faculties have evolved to maximize our fitness, not to represent the world accurately. What is a belief, from the scientific point of view, but a cluster of firing neurons whose job is not to capture the truth—what would that even mean?—but rather to get our bodies where they need to be to avoid predators, to find food, encounter mates, and so on. So science entails that our cognitive faculties are unreliable. But then how can we take science itself seriously as something we might believe? Evidence for its truth would be self-defeating.

This argument is clever, but confused. It turns on thinking of science in the way scientism does, as a kind of monolithic theory of everything.

Importantly, science does not *believe* in the reliability of science or, for that matter, in the reliability of human cognitive faculties. Science is an expression of our rationality, not a belief in it. Consider: rationality is not a lockstep set of rules and regulations stipulating what we may and may not think. It is rather the appreciation of the way our interests, knowledge, evidence, and concerns, our sense of "other things being equal," shape what is likely, what is pertinent, what is useful, and what matters. And the thing about the woman fixing her car is that, if she's rational, she won't trouble herself with guardian angels, hallucinations, or North Korean spies. We don't need

God to be rational and reasonable. Indeed, we couldn't make sense of God, or anything else—we couldn't make sense of "making sense"—if we were not sensitive to reasons and to the difference between good explanations and bad ones. Nor could a scientific theory—the theory of evolution, for example—give us evidence that we were not rational. Rationality, in the relevant sense, is expressed in the way we live; it is not something for which we need to argue, or for which we could argue.

We don't need God to secure our rationality and reasonableness. Plantinga is confused about that.

But it's worth noticing that we don't need science to secure our rationality either. Rationality is not a trait—like the color of the moth's wings—that might change and leave everything else as it is. Rationality is a condition of anything we might call thought or perception or consciousness. And so our rationality—however imperfect or problematic—is presupposed by any investigation we might hope to undertake into its biological underpinnings.

Scientism has shaped not only our culture's approach to questions of mind, consciousness, and human nature but also the nature of art. But to reject the claims of one unified science and reductive materialism is not to turn against science. And to deny that evolutionary biology (or neurobiology) has the resources to frame an account of human nature is not to embrace anything remotely like the standpoint of creationism or mystery mongering. The idea that we need to give up the project of understanding ourselves as part of nature because we cannot understand art, or rationality, or values more generally, in either neurobiological or evolutionary biological terms is silly, for it presupposes that all the phenomena that interest us are evolutionary biological or neurobiological in nature. There is nothing in science, however, that should lead us to embrace such a narrow view. And whatever else we know—my arguments in this chapter and chapter 10 are meant to secure this knowledge—we know that we do not now have anything even remotely like a reductive materialist, or a neurobiological, or an evolutionary biological, explanation of ourselves.

•

We can't reduce art to the natural aesthetic sense. That much is clear. The aesthetic sense operates over a much wider domain than art does.

And moreover, as I have argued, it is impossible to make sense of the existence of the aesthetic sense in the absence of art—for it is art that gives us pictures, and it is pictures that make the aesthetic sense possible.

But what we can say is that we make art—and we've been making art for thousands of years—*for* the aesthetic sense, not so much because we aim to stimulate it as because we aim to understand it. Not because art aims at pleasure, or wonder—as the philosopher Jesse Prinz has argued—or any other feeling state or emotion. Art aims at the disclosure of ourselves to ourselves and so it aims at giving us opportunities to catch ourselves in the act of achieving perceptual consciousness—including aesthetic consciousness—of the world around us. Art investigates the aesthetic. Not because it aims at special "aesthetic" experiences but because the aesthetic marks, as I have been arguing, a crucial aspect of what we are and how we stand in relation to the world around us. If we lacked the capacity to adopt the aesthetic attitude, we'd have little need, or capacity, for art or philosophy.

6

A Short Note on Ecstasy, Sports, and Humor

The philosophical nature of art is no obstacle to the recognition that art offers, sometimes, nothing less than ecstasy. Indeed, it explains it.

Ecstasy means, literally, getting out of one's self, or one's state (*ek* "out" and *stasis* "state or condition"). The characteristic of the ecstatic is that you can't stop, you can't want to stop, but your actions lead, inevitably, to your coming to a stop, to a climax or a fulfillment that is also an escape.

But it is exactly this structure—trapped within, can't stop, breaking out—that, we have been considering, is defining of art and its place in our experience.

Art sets us free, we might say. It lets us break out of the myriad ways our movement, our thought, our conversation, our perception, our consciousness are organized or held captive. It is our nature to be held captive, our biological imperative to be organized. Captivity and organization are, we can say, the animal in us. Drives, instincts, reflexes—these bind us to the environment, to tasks, to objects, to other people.

But we are not only animals. Our captivity puzzles us, it burdens us, it confuses us. We seek release from captivity, or at least some kind of self-understanding of the forms that it takes. Or, to use a different image, and one that captures the kind of emotion we sometimes know: we seek ecstasy.

Let us return to Whitman's verse, discussed in the previous chapter in connection with Dissanayake's evolutionary theory of art.

I hear the trained soprano . . . she convulses me like the
    climax of my love-grip;
The orchestra whirls me wider than Uranus flies,
It wrenches unnamable ardors from my breast,
It throbs me to gulps of the farthest down horror,
It sails me . . . I dab with bare feet . . . they are licked by the
    indolent waves,
I am exposed . . . cut by bitter and poisoned hail,
Steeped amid honeyed morphine . . . my windpipe squeezed
    in the fakes of death,
Let up again to feel the puzzle of puzzles,
And that we call Being.

Whitman describes ecstasy for art: he is captured, throbbed, sailed, dabbed, licked, steeped, squeezed, suffocated, pulled down, held deep. But he is finally "let up again," or set free, or released, or permitted to stop; he is "let up again" to encounter not only Being, but Being as "the puzzle of puzzles." Here we see that it is not only that the music of the trained soprano provokes an ecstatic reaction, as if the latter were just a feeling of great intensity, a special kind of sensation. No, the singer's song affords a kind of engagement, a getting trapped and a finding of release, and it is in that process, that engagement, that we find the art experience.

In my earlier discussion, I pointed out that Whitman's lines, for all their power and artistic merit, do not produce in us the sensual effect he describes in response to the singer. But now we can admit that, in a sense, his poetry does produce a comparable effect in us. Not a physical sensation, to be sure. But just the kind of engagement, the kind of being captured, and the kind of working toward release that is, we can now appreciate, so basic for art because it is tied so intimately to the human condition.

•

I have been arguing in these pages that art is disruptive and destabilizing, and also that it is a mode of investigation, a form of research aiming at transformation and reorganization. Art investigates or exposes by destabilizing. Art, I have urged, is a philosophical practice.

One upshot of this approach is that anything can be art, but nothing, at least by virtue of its intrinsic nature, is guaranteed to be. Art is always relational and contextual.

Art has a point the way jokes have a point. Joke telling is a basic and ready-to-hand form of art. When we tell jokes we do something, or invoke a response, but we can never avoid bringing to the fore the very fact of our having in this way referred to the communicative circumstances, the very setting of the telling, in which we find ourselves.

One of the nice things about humor is that, so to speak, it has a low bar to entry. The joke teller brings the joke, the point, the twist, to you; he delivers it to you where he finds you. He draws on what you already know, and what you know that he knows that you know. The pleasures in comedy—and they are sweet pleasures!—come from the shared getting it and the complicit achievement of it.

Wittgenstein said that you could write a book of philosophy that consisted entirely of jokes. The point is not merely that you can do the work of philosophy with jokes. The point, really, is that every joke occasions moments of knowing appreciation. We catch ourselves in the act of thinking, responding, evaluating, presuming, liking, being turned away or turned off when we enter into a joke. This is philosophical insight.

Comedians—professional joke tellers and funny guys—don't merely tell jokes. They put joke telling itself on display, even as they, at the same time, put themselves on display as performers and so let us catch ourselves in the act of watching and thinking about other people. Comedians make art out of telling, and, like other artists, they make art out of art, and so—like other artists, again—they make art making itself one of their abiding themes.

Not so athletes, who may be performers but are not artists. Sports can be spectacle on a very grand scale. And athletes and their achievements are sometimes beautiful, stirring, valuable, fascinating, and deserving of our thoughtful interest and attention.

But there is never art in sports, and this disjunction of performing sports and performing arts is easy to understand. Sports have specific, understood goals. They aim at winning, or achievement, and always take for granted what winning is or what counts as achievement. Athletes are slaves to preexisting goals and the preset rules of play. Artists, in contrast, do the miraculous: they refuse to play by rules, or rather, they invite you, with them, to make up the rules as you go along. Athletes are slaves; artists are emancipated.

This has nothing to do with innovation. Athletes innovate. Think of the first high jumper who twisted his body so that he went over with his backside down (the famous "Fosbury Flop"), or players who introduce new pitches or strokes, or put to use new equipment and new materials. But what sports greats never do is rewrite the rules of their sports; they don't change the criteria for assessing what counts as "good" or "success." As an example, consider boxing great Muhammad Ali's development of the rope-a-dope—bending over, covering himself, taking blow after blow with the aim of exhausting his opponent. "That's not boxing!" one was perhaps tempted to say. But at the end of the day what made it boxing, and what measured Ali's success, were familiar boxing standards based on rules, points, punches scored, etc.

Sports and art are disjoint categories. But this leaves open the possibility that one can make art out of sports as a raw material. There can be an art of sports, just as there is in fact an art of dancing. But sports art wouldn't be sports, just as choreographers aren't dancers.

An interesting case is the circus, which, in the last few years, has come to understand itself as an art form in very much the same way as dance has conceived itself as one for more than a century. There are now conservatories where artists study handstanding or rope walking and where their aim, as in the broader world of art, is to refuse to take mere technique for granted, mere tricks for granted, and to explore what these circus skills presuppose—in relation to performance, and audience, and the cultural politics of high and low, and in relation to the phenomenology of the performer, who is expert, or who cultivates expertise, and that of the audience, and on and on. Juggling or trapeze work come to be, in this setting, *sites* for the kind of research, the kind of goal-divorced-making practices, the kind of teaching, learning, and conversation, that are characteristic of art-making practices like ballet and painting.

Some Asian martial arts may occupy a similar space to art. Players of tai chi chuan, for example, aren't primarily fighters even if, as with American boxing, fighting is the original aim and governing idea behind what they do. But somewhere along the way the focus shifted from a first-order engagement with fighting and with the body as a weapon to other strange, difficult, and more philosophical questions about the nature of the body and our control over it, the relationship between training and experience, the role of thought and mind in physical activity. Tai chi is a martial art, and it is also a kind of philosophical art, not so much a philosophy of the body as a philosophy with the body. And here, too, as with dance and the other traditional arts, but also as with circus work, the work culture of the practice is organized around the influence and authority of especially charismatic and innovative teachers. Yang Chen Fu and Chen Man Ching, like Balanchine and Forsythe, or like Titian and Matisse, work within and find significance within lineages of influence.

Any region of human activity—typesetting, cooking, dancing, handstanding, fighting, talking—can be a site for art and philosophy. And that's true even though art is a very specialized undertaking.

Someone once asked me: Can't art just be consoling, or entertaining, or knock-your-socks-off gorgeous? Yes, of course it can be. But crucially, there is always more to be said about why art matters and what it accomplishes for us. And this in turn lets us understand not only why art can be so urgent and necessary even when it is none of these things. It also lets us understand why not everything that consoles, entertains, or moves us is art. Mama's lullaby is not art, precisely because it is a lullaby.

Notice, the fact that we do sometimes turn to some art in search of consolation is no counterexample. A poet's or a musician's invocation of the safe is itself a subversion, for it is a defiant decontextualizing of those very values. And anyway, most of the time, it seems to me, when people think of art as safe and pleasurable in this way, they are really confusing art and its power, for the safety of the familiar or the escape that background noise can offer. Listening to Bach cantatas while you clean the kitchen, or plastering your walls with posters from MoMA is, all too often, precisely a way of not engaging with art. It is something else altogether. Not that there is anything wrong with it.

7

Philosophical Objects

When I first started to write this book, I had the idea that it would be wonderful to write it in the style of a DVD commentary. The thing about DVD commentaries is that they don't need to concern themselves with bringing their topic in view. They're talking about whatever they, and you, are seeing on the screen, in real time, as they talk about it. All you need to do is point. That one can't take this approach in a book of this kind turns out to be revealing. You can't point to art; art isn't the sort of thing we can take for granted. But more significantly, bringing our topic—art and its place in our lives—into focus for us, shaping our subject matter, is, really, our main challenge. And this is typical of philosophy. In philosophy the greatest portion of time and effort goes to bringing one's task, one's problem, one's topic into focus so that one can then go on and say something about it.

Anyway, this is my special concern in this chapter: to bring some works of art, some philosophical objects, into focus so that we can have their example in mind as we move on.

•

Richard Serra makes sculptures that get under your skin and change how you feel. It is tempting to credit this to their massive size. There's no doubt about it: in the presence of unnaturally sloping thirteen-foot-tall hull-like sides of steel, you may feel dizzy and slightly off balance.

For some this is a curious and pleasurable state to find yourself in; the encounter with the work is a kind of a psychological demonstration of the way what you see gets shaped by, and is bound up with, your sense of your body and your position on the ground and in space.

For others this can be very unpleasant. I know a woman with vertigo who gets sick in the spaces created by Serra's sculptures. And it isn't surprising that, back in the 1980s, there was a public action to remove Serra's giant *Tilted Arc* from its downtown New York location. Perhaps the work was too visceral and affecting for public art, at least in the minds of some.

But we underdescribe the work Serra's objects do if we confine ourselves to their psychological power to upset us. They are not special effects; and they are not psychology demos. In fact, it is a mistake even to call them *objects*. It would be better to say that they are *worlds* or *cityscapes*.

To encounter these works is to meet up front the fact that you can't see them, you can't locate them as objects with fronts, sides, and backs and clear boundaries. There's no standing back and taking in what you see; there's only stepping in and exploring the lay of the land.

So this is a different way of getting under your skin.

To encounter one of these works is not so much to see something you don't understand as it is to find yourself someplace and not know your way around. But this isn't psychological manipulation; it's not just getting under your skin. It's an invitation to find out where you are by exploring the work. The pieces are worlds, and worlds *afford* opportunities for exploration, investigation, and learning. These works are complicated and compelling, and they really do invite you in. The surfaces of the steel are painterly, smooth, sometimes almost velvet-like and lush. But mere surface properties have almost nothing to do with the pleasures that this sort of encounter can afford. The pleasure is that of the passage from being lost to being found.

I would say that there is also the opportunity for a certain kind of enlightenment. These days we like to understand everything in the key of neuroscience. We think of seeing as something that happens in the head. In fact, seeing is something that whole animals (not just brains) undertake; it is, in Dewey's image, a transaction of doing and undergoing. Seeing, or any other kind of conscious experience, happens not in the private caverns of our minds but out there, with others, in environments that we make and that then in turn surround us and compel.

Serra's work may be psychological; it may be theatrical (in exactly the sense that the art critic and art historian Michael Fried found objectionable). But the real work that it does for us is philosophical. These are philosophical spaces that excite us by letting us remember what it is like to discover the world through active living.

•

The heart of the Abstract Expressionism exhibition at the Museum of Modern Art in New York a few years ago was the Barnett Newman room. Newman's paintings seem new; they are startling and they command attention, and perhaps something like reverence. Even the noisy, shopping-bag-carrying travelers, who make MoMA sometimes feel like an airport terminal, were silenced in the face of these spiritual objects. Or perhaps what was altered was my perception of the presence of those around me. Many of the works on display at MoMA were first shown in 1950 at the Betty Parsons Gallery. Reportedly Newman had then posted a note on the wall of the gallery instructing visitors to view the works from up close; he warned against standing too far back.

This surprised and intrigued me.

In our daily lives we continuously adjust ourselves in relation to what is around us. We vary our distance from text to bring it into focus, and we move our heads and bodies the better to see where things are or what is happening. What is remarkable is that, for the most part, we do all this automatically, unthinkingly. We act spontaneously to keep the world in focus. We move forward, toward. We move back. We peer and squint and draw near. These skillful ways of grappling with the world give expression to motivations and ways of thinking that are otherwise mute.

It's the most natural thing in the world to enter a room and then step back from a large picture on the wall, seeking to take up the optimal vantage point on it, just as we would if we were trying to take in, say, a friend's outfit. Whatever his intentions may have been, Newman, in admonishing us to resist our natural tendency spontaneously to respond to what there is around us by, in this case, moving back so as to get a better overview of the scene, is inviting us to violate our habits as lookers and thinkers, to confound our unconsidered motivations.

Now, it isn't possible to alter our basic perceptual motivations and ways of thinking. But it is possible to alert us to their existence. Perhaps Newman believed, as I do, that one of art's tasks is to afford us just this sort of opportunity to catch ourselves in the act of encountering the world, and so to let us encounter ourselves in a way that we otherwise never can.

•

I find myself interested in Tino Sehgal's live piece installed in one of the main galleries of the Giardini at the 2013 Venice Biennale. If the piece has a title, it isn't posted anywhere. I say "live piece" rather than "performance," because the work itself seems crafted precisely to question the nature of performance. It has no beginning, middle, or end; it is just there, as the pictures hanging on the walls of the gallery are just there.

Two, three, or four people sit or lie on the ground; they improvise their own music with their voices—vaguely electronic sounding, or even human beat box, but sometimes more like droning, or chanting, and always very rhythmic—and they move, evenly, slowly, to this self-generated music. Some movements are dancerly, others less so. Beyond the temporal organization on display in the music and smooth pacing of the movement, there is an obvious organizational structure. The performers—they are performers, after all—pay attention to each other, clearly responding to movements, gestures, or sound. I had the impression that they imitate each other, but not quite directly, always as if going to some basic core quality of a movement or feeling.

When you enter the gallery, the piece hardly jumps out at you. There are people on the floor moving slowly, making noise, but there are dozens of visitors milling around them. The piece is sort of invisible at first, just as it is unclear what, if any, logic or rule governs what is going on. My first response was to find the work uninteresting and to want to move on. Gradually the piece comes into focus, and when I left, about an hour and a half later, I felt that I had gotten to know something definite and particular, a thing, this art thing.

The performers are made into objects in this piece. You feel no inclination to applaud them when they stop or compliment them on their work. This is because their actions—though freely their own, it seems, and often quite virtuosic—seem somehow governed by a task or instruction.

Moreover, this artwork doesn't play the "attention" game that is basic in the performing arts. It doesn't try to capture your attention, or direct it, or organize it. The work is just there, like a picture on the wall, and the actors might as well be battery-operated machines as people.

But of course they are not automata, they are people, and they are lovely each in his or her own way, and they are obviously (or so it seems) making choices about what to do and how to interpret whatever task it is that they have been given as a team and as artists. On the surface at least, though, they are indifferent to you and are entirely turned in on themselves and the demands of their task. Only one performer, in the course of the ninety minutes I watched, directed her gaze to me and to other people in the gallery.

Because they were on the floor, moving and singing, and because the gallery was full of people, you actually had a very vivid sense of the spatial boundaries of the piece. You also, of course, had a somewhat anxious feeling about how fragile those boundaries are. The actors colonized space on the floor, but occasionally someone—a child, for example—would walk through their grouping. Sometimes people were standing nearby talking loudly, or telephoning, as if not noticing they were intruding, or entering into the territory of the piece and disrupting it—or perhaps activating it—for those around them.

Sehgal prohibits the documentation of his work. This meant that the performers in today's installation had two jobs. They were either on the floor "in" the work; or they were out in the gallery policing the room. Every time someone with a press badge started to take pictures, the actors, like undercover cops, pounced.

This patrolling of the boundaries of the piece belongs to the work itself. What we have is a piece within a piece, and we ourselves are folded into the act.

The play within a play is an object for us to contemplate. But the play itself, the one in which we find ourselves, is anxious; its boundaries are undefined, its subject matter open-ended; it is an object of contention.

Art doesn't activate us, as psychologists and neuroscientists like to think. Rather, it gives us an opportunity to activate it, to switch it on and make it happen.

•

The first thing I discover when I look at one of Robert Lazzarini's sculpture guns is that I can't bring them into focus, no matter how I move or adjust or squint; the guns resist the normal adjustments whereby we achieve access to the world around us. Lazzarini's sculpture-gun is somehow beyond my sensory-motor machinations. Skill and knowledge fail me; I have no access.

The experience is an odd one. I find myself wondering whether there is something wrong with my eyes. Or perhaps this is a kind of temporary neurological breakdown, a sort of optic ataxia, an inability to reach out and take hold of what I see—the world of solid realities is transformed into absences! In normal life, there are two ways of going blind. One way is for the sensory mechanism (e.g., the retina, or visual structures in the brain) to get damaged. The other way is to retain sensitivity but find oneself unable to make any sense of what stimulates the eyes, either because of some additional neurological breakdown or because one lacks the skills or knowledge needed to make sense of it. This is what happens, for example, if you put on left-right or up-down inverting goggles. You can't negotiate your ocular relation to the things around you. Although they are there, and although they stimulate your eyes, they are lost to perceptual consciousness; things lose their presence when we lose our grip on their sensory-motor significance.

And so here. Lazzarini's work induces something like this sort of blindness; he creates artifacts that defy us, that deny us the possibility of getting a grip on them. Lazzarini undermines our fluent access to the world around us. His achievement consists in the fact that in doing this—in undermining our fluent access to the world around us—he brings into view the unnoticed ways our access to things depends on background skill and context.

This kind of art, at least, is more than instructive; it constitutes a research practice. Lazzarini gives us an artifact we cannot resolve or bring into focus, and so he delineates for us, as it were, the limits of what we can do, or of what we need to do in order to bring the world into focus. Lazzarini enables us to catch ourselves in the act of trying to achieve access to the world.

This is the work of philosophy. And so I propose that we think of Lazzarini's artifacts—of art objects in general—as philosophical objects, and of his art as a philosophical practice. The work of art is philosophical.

•

I was moved, stunned really, by Sarah Michelson's work *Devotion Study #1*, which was performed during the Whitney Museum of American Art's 2012 Biennial. She's saddled with the weighty history of dance in New York, with dance's special collaborations with art and music, with the art world, and with the anxieties of being a maker who takes what she does seriously now, at a place and time, where serious can seem ridiculous and play is judged by the standards of cruel wit and also by the demands of creating performance for audiences who may not know what they are looking for and how to tell when they've found it.

One critic described the work as slit-your-wrists dull. I suppose it is boring, in the way that a religious ritual can seem boring, or even in the way that love, hate, greed, sexual fantasy, ambivalence—so familiar, so humdrum—can be boring. But this work, like these other things, is also an opportunity.

The drive engine of the piece is a metronomic musical score. The set is a floor painting that resembles an architectural blueprint. The movements are steady, simple, laborious, repetitive, and animal. The dancers work hard, always moving, spinning backward, arms held aloft. The dancers sweat. The whole is a sort of saga of their sweat. One dancer's costume first darkens beneath her bosom. For another, it is the naked chest and the small of the back, then the pelvis area that first glisten, like the moisture on the coat of a working animal. At the end they are all black with wet.

The dancers work, and they also always perform. Erect posture, head held high, they display themselves for us as ballerinas should, with elegant composure and knowing eyes. They are not work animals. But nor are they ballerinas. They are more like hardworking angels who range over human creation. These angels of ambivalence, and maybe of love and greed and hate and lust, are devoted to us. And we find ourselves devoted to them.

These performers took no bows. This didn't surprise me. We don't applaud artists in art galleries, and clapping after performances is a strange custom anyway. But it also made sense. Sarah Michelson made something happen in that performance space, during those ninety minutes. What happened? The cool of controlled movement became the hot of sweaty work. The anxious struggle to make art as a dancer became an opportunity to see our angels sweeping over us.

•

The elements of Robert Irwin's installation at the Whitney are named in the work's title, *Scrim veil—Black rectangle—Natural light*. There's no mystery. No magical ingredient. A large rectangular room divided lengthwise by a taut curtain of thin fabric (the scrim) hanging down to about head height; the fabric is translucent, from some angles invisibly transparent, from others impossible to see through; the fabric has a thick black border; there is a thick black line painted on the walls, bisecting them horizontally; light coming through a single large window at the end of the corridor.

And yet you could practically hear people gasp as they entered the room on the Whitney's fourth floor (the same room, by the way, where Michelson's performance had taken place). Somehow the combined effect of the elements was not only gorgeous but also astonishing.

Yes, there was an optical trick. You could not always quite see the scrim, and because of the black line of its border, and the similar line on the wall behind, you had a sense that the two lines were one, and so you lost a sense of their location in space.

But the fascination of the piece doesn't come down to mere optical play. I wish I understood what it does come down to.

One remarkable feature of the installation is that it has no focus. You're in it, for one thing, so you can't look at it. And there isn't any one thing for you to look at or contemplate anyway. Or rather, everything—the window, the scrim, its border, the floor, the wall, the other people in the gallery—commands attention equally.

Compare with James Turrell's thematically kindred exhibition at the Guggenheim just uptown. With Turrell you know just what to look at; there is something to inspect. (I recall one piece: a dark room, on the facing wall a blue rectangle. At one point it may dawn on you that the rectangle is a windowlike opening into a space bathed in blue light.)

Or compare with the Richard Serra. Serra's works disorient you and compel exploration. You can't just stand there. You need to do something.

But not so with Irwin. There is nothing to do here. Or, I suppose, there is everything to do. The installation is just a place. A place to be. It is a pure place. Space. And light. Could this be why it feels so good to be there?

•

Sometimes art leaves things as they are and gives you an opportunity to notice; this was the case with Robert Irwin's show at the Whitney. And sometimes art bangs you over the head with new experiences. Richard Serra's work, for example.

But sometimes it does both at the same time. This is the case with Anri Sala's strong, loud, but at the same time cool and understated installation up in the French Pavilion at the 2013 Venice Biennale.

In the first room you encounter a film of a woman; the shot is close and you can see only her face. She appears to be making music, which we can hear; or is she only listening to music? From her face, and head, you can tell that she is engaged with her whole body with the music, which is Ravel's piano concerto for the left hand. She *can't* be performing it. It doesn't feel like there's an orchestra present. But from her upper body it looks like she could be playing piano. And then the music occasionally speeds up, or slows down, as if a DJ were maneuvering the turntable. This first room of the exhibit is puzzling.

Room 2 is loud and thrilling. Two films are projected on the wall. Each shows the (hairy, manly, big) left hand of a pianist as he performs the Ravel concerto live with an orchestra. But each film shows a different soloist. Even though the musical score is the same—indeed, the two recordings were made with the same orchestra and conductor—the soloists make different choices, have different timings. The result is a luscious cacophony, layers of dissonance, and the occasional, delightful, coming together of the two versions. As the art critic Blake Gopnik has remarked, it is surprising how good it sounds to hear the Ravel played twice differently at the same time.

But there is another element as well: as we had seen a close-up of the woman's face in the first room, now what we see are close-ups of the two left hands as they play. I was reminded of an old *Sesame Street* routine from my childhood in which a hand is treated as a puppet; sometimes the hand looked sad, but it could also look cheerful or satisfied. I loved that routine. And so here: you felt, watching the two left hands racing along the keyboards, as if you were watching two complete beings, two whole intelligences.

Which brings us to the historical point that Ravel wrote this piece for Paul Wittgenstein, a noted pianist who had lost his right arm in the First World War. The piece is composed for a person with an incomplete body. But here the left hands show up, no less than the face of the woman in the first room, as complete, as whole, as expressions of the complete and whole person.

Which brings us to the philosophical point that Paul Wittgenstein happens to have been the brother of Ludwig Wittgenstein, one of the most inventive and important philosophers of the twentieth century. A central theme in Wittgenstein's writing is the connection between our "inner" lives of feeling and thought and our "outer" lives of movement and the body. These are not two distinct domains, thought Wittgenstein. A person is not a mind trapped in a body, but rather a living human being.

Rooms 1 and 2 have been about Ravel *unraveled*—the show is called *Ravel Ravel Unravel*. Room 3 is about putting it back together. In the film here, we now have a proper view of the woman from Room 1. She is stationed at a mixing table with two turntables; she is mixing the two separate recordings, blending them, as best she can, into one. She slows one turntable down, races another forward. She orchestrates. She creates. The sun behind her blasts into the clean white room—the films were made in this very gallery where the films are now shown in Venice—and as the music soars, she herself glows with creative presence.

Art making: the power to make song, or to make art about the making of song. But what's going on here is more than that. Sala has contrived to have a two-armed woman take two gorgeous renderings by big-handed men with hairy knuckles of music for a one-armed brother of a philosopher by a romantic French composer and ravel them together into a new piece of music.

Technology, or the passage from the hand to the piano keyboard to the laptop and the mixing deck, is the final abiding theme in this work of art. Technology extends us; it extends what we can do and so it extends what we are. Technology had taken the lady at the turntables, two keyboardists, an orchestra, Ravel, and all of us sitting there in Venice in rapt attention, and made us into something altogether new.

•

I watched *Rosemary's Baby* by Roman Polanski again the other night. It is a monster movie. And like the best movies in this genre, you could call it a skepticism movie. It is philosophical. And remarkably, it is terrifying because it is philosophical.

Things aren't going right with young Rosemary. Her husband is distant, removed, self-centered; he is unkind and even brutal; he spends his free time with their new next-door neighbors, an odd, elderly couple. Rosemary's pregnancy is difficult; she has pains continually and is losing weight; neither her doctor nor her husband seems to be interested in helping. Rosemary is in a stupor, as if she were under the influence of drugs. She has their new apartment painted to lighten it up, but this does little to dispel the dark in its halls and rooms. The only bright spot in this dim scenario is that her husband, Guy, who is an actor, has had a turn of good luck at work. His rival woke up blind and Guy got the big part. Professional success is around the corner.

Rosemary's Baby is a story about coming to recognize that something is wrong. At first Rosemary resists this conclusion. What *could* be wrong? Occasionally pregnancies are painful. Husbands get caught up with pressures and demands at work. Life isn't supposed to play out like a fairy tale. She resolves herself to be a better wife, to reach out to Guy and help him be more open in their relationship.

Now the character of the movie's skepticism shifts to one of philosophy's enduring concerns: the very possibility of knowing other people and what they think and feel. Philosophers have long noticed that there is room for doubt in this domain: all we ever really know, when it comes to others, is what they say and do. We can't get inside their heads to learn directly what they actually think and feel. We are always at a remove from the other. It is also clear, to philosophy, and to us all, that this intellectual worry can be safely set aside in the course of our ordinary lives. Questions about what those around us are thinking and feeling and doing, let alone questions about whether they have inner lives at all, don't seriously arise. Which itself raises a philosophical question: If the basis of our knowledge is so slight, why is our confidence in other minds so robust?

Sometimes these sorts of theoretical worries achieve practical prominence in the setting of neurological trauma when we are confronted by, for example, a persistent vegetative state and must make decisions about what is going on inside the mind of a badly injured person.

But *Rosemary's Baby* addresses these questions in, if possible, an even more terrifying way. It gradually becomes clear, to Rosemary, and to us, the audience, that we can no longer trust Guy, or the neighbors, or the doctor, or just about anyone else in Rosemary's life. Skepticism about the thoughts and feelings of those around Rosemary is now a hypothesis that must be taken seriously. Her life, and that of her baby, depend on it. She is the victim, it seems, of an elaborate plot. And (almost) everyone, even those most close to her, is in on it.

But is this not madness? It certainly has that look and feel. How could *everyone* be in on it? This, then, ratchets the movie's skeptical theme up a notch: Could it be that she is hallucinating or confabulating the whole thing? Could this be some sort of prepartum hysteria? Can she, do we, know what is real?

Rosemary's Baby is not just a psychological thriller. It is a monster movie. And what makes Rosemary's predicament so very difficult is the fact that what is really going on, what is really driving events in this film, is so unlikely, so impossible, so unthinkable as to rule out the possibility of anything like a straightforward "figuring out" of what's happening. Satan himself has come to earth and raped Rosemary, with the assistance of her husband. This is too far-fetched to be true. It is too far-fetched to even be thinkable.

The distinctive charms and fascinations of horror films arise at this kind of juncture, according to the noted philosopher of art Noël Carroll. It is the hallmark of all narrative forms that they offer us cognitive delights. Plot intrigues; we are curious; curiosity motivates us to follow the story, to figure out what's going on, to understand how forces at play in a situation drive the action inexorably forward. Plot is cognitive, and the pleasure of story arises from the achievement of getting it.

I think Carroll is right about this. The basic idea was anticipated in Aristotle's treatment of tragedy. Plot, Aristotle argued, is the life and soul of tragedy. And plot is concerned not with mere event, not with one thing happening after another, but with human action. So to tell a good story, or to enjoy one in the audience, you need to be sensitive to what makes an action significant in the setting of a human life. You need to be a student of human nature and experience. It is because the meaning and importance of a work of dramatic fiction such as a tragedy unfold here, in the exploration of ideas about human experience, that it is possible to enjoy a play just by reading it. It isn't spectacle that moves us; for Aristotle, it's understanding. Which doesn't mean that one does not also enjoy *felt* or *emotional* responses to the story. A tragedy, Aristotle thought, always aims to arouse fear and pity. But it doesn't aim to produce emotion the way a ride on a roller coaster produces a sense of danger. Fear is not merely an effect on us or in us, for Aristotle. It is an expression of our sensitivity to what is playing out in the story and so it is itself an achievement of understanding and insight.

Now, the distinctive difference between horror and other genres— this is Carroll's argument—is that at the heart of the horror genre is a monstrous phenomenon that actually, truly, makes no sense. Monsters are unfathomable. They are unknowable. They are betwixt and between. Neither alive nor dead, neither human nor animal, neither natural nor, really, unnatural. They are, as Carroll puts it, interstitial. The point is that there is no understanding of the monstrous. There is no genuine satisfaction of our curiosity. A good horror movie, I would say, then, is a kind of paradox in itself. It engages us in a mystery whose intrinsic character rules out, or threatens to rule out, its resolution. And it is the distinct feature of art horror that it affords the opportunity for this distinctive kind of unresolvable philosophical engagement. From this point of view, the fact that we find the monster scary is secondary. We like horror movies not because we enjoy feeling negative emotions. It is rather that the negative emotions horror movies provoke in us are outweighed by the philosophical delights.

I'm not sure whether this account does justice to *Rosemary's Baby*. Perhaps its real fright stems from the possibility that the philosopher's unresolved skeptical puzzles about the limits of doubt and knowledge actually point us to the possibility of total, absolute, abject, terrifying isolation. But is that something we take pleasure in discovering?

PART II

The purpose of art is to lay bare the questions that have been occluded by the answers.

—attributed to James Baldwin

8

See Me if You Can!

What is art? Why does it matter to us? What does it tell us about ourselves?

Stop! you might say. If you know the answer to these questions, don't tell us! We don't want to know. Don't spoil it for us!

This reminds me of what they say about jokes: you can't explain a joke; you ruin it if you try. In a way this is right. If you need an explanation, it's too late, you've already failed to get it. And the explanation won't make you laugh.

But in a way this is quite mistaken. When it comes to jokes, there is always something to get, and so there is always something to explain. The question *Why is this funny?* is always appropriate, even if it can be difficult to answer adequately. And even if comprehending such an explanation is no substitute for the spontaneous achievement of the understanding in which getting a joke consists. The point is, the explaining, the talking, the laying out of the logic of the joke is not in direct competition with getting it and laughing. You don't make someone laugh through explanation. And so, for these reasons, you can't ruin a joke by talking about it.

And so with art. To understand art and its place in our lives is not to explain it away. You can't break the spell of art by thinking about it.

These days, as a matter of fact, there is a strong tendency to at least try to explain art away—along with humor and everything else. It is widely supposed that questions like those posed above—What is art? Why do we value it? What does it tell us about ourselves?—can and should be answered in the key of neuroscience. We think that everything about us that matters is fixed by our brains and that by turning our focus inward we can discover our true nature. And so it seems right, when we face the task of making sense of art, to look to neuroscience.

I take a different approach. Not because there's anything wrong with trying to understand art in relation to our biology; indeed, this is an exciting and important aspiration. But rather because neuroscience has yet to frame an adequate conception of our biology. We can't take neuroscience for granted as an intellectual readymade.

Semir Zeki, a neuroscientist at University College London, likes to say that art is governed by the laws of the brain. It is brains, he says, that see art and it is brains that make art.

This idea that a person is a functioning assembly of brain cells and associated molecules is not something neuroscience has discovered. It is not even something that it asserts. It is something it takes for granted. *You are your brain.* Francis Crick called this "the astonishing hypothesis," because, he claimed, it is so remote from the way most people think about themselves. But what is really astonishing about this supposedly astonishing hypothesis, as I have remarked before, is how astonishing it is not! The idea that there is a thing inside us that thinks and feels and that we are that thing is an old one. Descartes thought that the thinking thing inside had to be immaterial; he couldn't conceive how flesh could perform the job. Scientists today suppose that it is the brain that is the thing inside us that thinks and feels. But the basic idea is the same. And this is not an idle point. However surprising it may seem, the fact is we don't actually have a better understanding of how the brain produces consciousness than Descartes did of how the immaterial soul accomplishes this feat. After all, at present we lack even the rudimentary outlines of a neural theory of consciousness.

What we do know is that a healthy brain is necessary for normal mental life, indeed, for any life at all. But of course much else is necessary for mental life. We need roughly normal bodies and a roughly normal environment and we need the presence and availability of other people if we are to have anything like the sorts of lives that we know and value. So we really ought to say that it is the normally embodied, environmentally and socially situated human animal that thinks and feels and decides and is conscious. But once we say this, it would be simpler, and more accurate, to allow that it is *people* who think and feel and decide, and not their brains. It is people, not their brains, that make and enjoy art. You are not your brain, you are a living human being.

We need finally to break with the dogma that you are something inside of you—whether we think of this as the brain or an immaterial soul—and we need finally to take seriously the possibility that the conscious mind is achieved by persons and other animals thanks to their dynamic exchange with the world around them (a dynamic exchange that no doubt depends on the brain, *among other things*). Importantly, to break with the Cartesian dogmas of contemporary neuroscience would not be to cave in and give up a commitment to understanding ourselves as natural. It would be rather to rethink what a biologically adequate conception of our nature would be.

There is a second obstacle to progress in what is sometimes called neuroaesthetics. Neural approaches to art have not yet been able to find a way to bring *art* into focus in the laboratory. As mentioned, theorists in this field like to say that art is constrained by the laws of the brain. But in practice what this is usually taken to come down to is the humble fact that the brain constrains the experience of art because, after all, it constrains *all* experience. Visual artists, for example, don't work with ultraviolet light, as Zeki reminds us, because we can't see ultraviolet light. They do work with shape and form and color because we can see these.

Now it is doubtless correct that visual artists confine themselves to materials and effects that are, well, visible. And likewise, it seems right that our perception of works of art, like our perception of anything at all, depends on the nature of our perceptual capacities, capacities which, in their turn, are constrained by the brain.

These sorts of facts about how the brain constrains our ability to perceive, however, have no greater claim to explaining our ability to perceive *art* than they have to explaining how we perceive sports, or how we perceive the man across from us on the subway.

Some might wonder whether the relevant question is how we

perceive works of art, anyway. What we ought to be asking is: Why do we value some works as art? Why do they move us or touch us or speak to us in this distinctive way? And here again, the closest neural scientists or psychologists come to saying anything about this kind of aesthetic evaluation is to say something about *preference*. But the class of things we like, or that we prefer as compared to other things, is much wider than the class of things we value as art. And the sorts of reasons we have for valuing one artwork over another are not the same kinds of reasons we would give for liking one house or one flavor more than another. And it is no help to appeal to *beauty* here. Beauty is both too wide and too narrow. Not all artworks are beautiful (or pleasing, for that matter, even if many are), and not everything we find beautiful (a person, say, or a sunset) is a work of art. And anyway, it is not as though the nature of beauty is something we can take for granted; nor is it likely that our grip on beauty is independent of prior engagement with art and its questions.

Again we find not that neuroaesthetics takes aim at our target and misses, but that it fails even to bring the target, art, into focus.

Yet it's early. Neuroaesthetics, like the neuroscience of consciousness itself, is still in its infancy. Is there any reason to doubt that progress will be made as we move beyond the pathbreaking work of these first-generation pioneers of neural approaches to art? Is there any principled reason to be skeptical that there can be a valuable study of art making use of the methods and tools of neuroscience?

It's a terrible thing to be negative. I don't want to stop investigation or shut down the conversation. But there are reasons to be skeptical of the prospects for an empirical neuroscience of art.

One reason is that it is a mistake to think that our responses to works of art are ever only mere responses. They are more like *judgments*, and, like judgments in general, they are thoughtful. Also, they are shaped by our knowledge and background and experience and the larger culture and shared attitudes and the ongoing dialogue among artists and experts and the rest of us. The idea that there is an aesthetic response whose neurological underpinnings could be usefully exhumed strikes me as something that could be seriously advanced only by people who are quite removed from art and the ways it matters.

A work of art is not merely a trigger for a feeling or a perceptual response or anything else. In that sense, it is not merely a thing. It is a *work*. Art is a topic.

Actually, it is a mistake to think of seeing (or perception) in general according to the trigger-experience conception. As if things just cause the lighting up of experiences inside our heads. This may be a traditional way to think and talk; it's the British way. But it's a straitjacket. The world acts on us and changes our brains. But we act right back on the world, and so we change what there is changing us. We do so just by moving, not to mention by making, doing, taking hold. John Dewey offers an alternative to the trigger theory: perception is an activity of doing and undergoing, a *transaction* with the world around us. Or, as the psychologist James J. Gibson claims, seeing doesn't happen in the eye-brain system, it happens in the eye-brain-head-body-ground-environment system. It is something we do, not something that happens inside us. And like everything we do, it depends on more than just what is going on at a time inside the skull.

A work of art is less like a rock, a pair of pajamas, or a pencil than it is like a joke. And a joke is more than a thing or a stimulus. A joke is an act of communication; it is a response, a transaction, a move. And getting a joke is not just reacting or being affected. As we have already considered, it is an accomplishment.

So, for example:

Two Irishmen walk out of a bar.
Yes, this *can* happen.

Think of how much you need to know to get this joke, and not only about people and culture, drinking and stereotypes, but also about jokes themselves, and their genres, expected shapes, and rhythms.

But if artworks are in a similar way acts of communication, transactions in a community, moves in a landscape of shared ideas and understanding—as I hope to convince you that they are—then it is misguided to think that we can study them, or why they matter to us, by looking at what goes on inside us—that is, inside our brains—when we engage with art. To do so is to look for the art in the wrong place. It's like looking for the value of money in the paper it is printed on. Or, to choose a better analogy, like looking for baseball and its

values in the brains of individual baseball players, or, indeed, specta-
tors at a baseball game. You can study what is happening in these
brains, but you won't be learning about baseball; at best you'll be
learning about its neurological concomitants.

And so with the study of art. Neuroaesthetics gets it wrong at
both ends. A work of art is not merely a thing, and the source of an
artwork's value is not merely its effect on the nervous system. This is
not to deny that works of art, or jokes, or even rocks do produce
effects on the nervous system. Of course they do. Everything does. If
you want to understand how artworks differ from rocks and sunsets,
though, you need to look elsewhere.

Neuroscience is too individualistic and too internal to be a suitable science for the study of art. Indeed, if I am right, it may be too
individualistic and too internal to be a suitable science for the study
of experience itself. Experience—the showing up of the world for us—
is not something that happens inside us; it is something we achieve,
with others. Experience is more like baseball than it is like digestion.

•

This is a book about art.

Again, I ask: What is art? Why does it matter to us? What does it
tell us about ourselves?

To understand art, I propose, we need to look at it against the
background of technology. Artists make stuff, after all: pictures, sculptures, performances, songs. And art has always been bound up with
manufacture and craft, with tinkering and artifice.

Art, however, is not itself one of our technologies; art presupposes
technology in something like the way irony presupposes straight
talk. Technology—practices of making, the harnessing of knowledge
for this purpose—is no contribution to art; it is its precondition.

A work of art is a strange tool; it is an implement or instrument
that has been denuded of its function. Art is the enemy of function,
it is the perversion of technology. This is why architecture has a
problematic standing among the arts; it is not an accident that great
architects make houses with leaky roofs. And this is why, although
much art concerns itself with love and erotic feeling, there is no pornographic art. Pornography has a function; it aims at something. Art,
in contrast, is always the subversion of function.

Which is not to deny that there are works of art that may as a matter of fact serve this or that function. Just as something can be a hammer and a paperweight, so something can be, literally, a urinal and a work of art, or a doorknob and an item of sculptural interest. To say that art is one thing and technology is another is not to preclude the same physical object falling into both of these categories. Indeed, it is an important fact that this is possible, for it shows that the relevant differences are not differences in the intrinsic makeup of pictures, urinals, doorknobs, or whatever. What matters is how we use them.

To appreciate this proposal that works of art are strange tools, it is helpful to review four facts about technology and its place in our lives and culture that I have already discussed back in chapter 3.

First, technology is natural for us. We are technological animals. We are designers by nature. Knives, tools, dwellings—these all belong to our way of living in something like (but not exactly like) the way nest building belongs to that of birds. For nearly a million years our ancestors settled for blunt stones; technological progress and improvement are entirely absent in the archaeological record. And then, fifty to eighty thousand years ago, there was an explosion of technological innovation. We can date sewn clothing to this period (using new methods of population genetics), and also the proliferation of specialized stone instruments of great refinement. It is this revolutionary transformation—perhaps best explained by changing demographics such as increased population densities, opportunities for trade, and suchlike, rather than by, say, the occurrence of a "brainy" mutation—that signals the emergence of the modern human (and *thereafter* the modern brain).

One important upshot of the idea that technology is natural for us is that we need to frame a conception of our biology that is adequate to explain technology and its place in our lives. Such a newly framed biology will appreciate our social nature.

Second, the scope of technology is broader than clothing, utensils, and dwellings. Language and picture making are also technologies (or technical practices). The cave paintings of Europe and Africa date from just this same period of revolutionary innovation that witnesses our birth as a species, and it is plausible that language arrived on the scene at this time as well. Language, in this view, is itself an expression of the technological revolution that gave rise to us.

Third, tools help us solve problems, and they also enable us to frame new problems. Tools such as rakes and hammers extend our bodies, whereas other tools—language and pictures, for example—extend our minds, enabling us to have experiences and think thoughts that would be impossible without these means. Some technologies—such as writing (a comparatively recent invention)—extend both the body and mind; writing enables me to communicate my thoughts to someone out of the range of my voice.

Fourth, tools are useful only against the background of our needs and capacities. Let's return to the doorknob. A simple bit of technology, yes, but one that presupposes a vast and remarkable social background. Doorknobs exist in the context of a whole form of life, a whole biology—the existence of doors, and buildings, and passages, the human body, the hand, and so on. A designer of doorknobs makes a simple artifact, but does so with an eye to its mesh with this larger cognitive and anthropological framework.

When you walk up to a door, you don't stop to inspect the doorknob; you just turn it and go right through. Doorknobs don't puzzle us. They do not puzzle us just to the degree that we are able to take everything that they presuppose—the whole background practice—for granted. If that cultural practice were strange to us, if we didn't understand the human body or the fact that human beings live in buildings, if we were aliens from another planet, doorknobs would seem very strange and very puzzling indeed.

Exactly the same thing can be said about pictures. The pictures in the daily newspaper or the family album strike us as self-evident and natural. It seems to us as if they are like transparencies through which we see the world. In fact, pictures, like the words of our native language, are moves or gestures in a familiar communication game. We are at home in the game and so the game seems natural. But pictures, like doorknobs, are natural only in the way that all good design is natural. Design wears the guise of nature.

This brings us to art. Design stops and art begins when we lose the possibility of taking the background of our familiar technologies for granted, when we can no longer take for granted what is, in fact, a precondition of the very natural-seeming intelligibility of such things as doorknobs and pictures. Art starts when things get strange.

Design organizes and enables; art subverts. It does this by abrogating the background that needs to be in place for things to have their functions. You never ask, when confronted with a doorknob, *What is this?* For the question even to come up is for the doorknob's utility already to have been undermined. If you even notice the knob, it's potentially bad design.

But art is bad design on purpose. It calls attention to itself. It begins precisely with this ungroundedness or absence of utility, this free fall. When you stand before a work of art, you are bound to ask, *What is this?* And crucially, when we are dealing with art, although there are many answers we can give to this question, there is no one answer that we can take for granted at the outset. We say what the doorknob is when we say that it is a doorknob. But we haven't said what an artwork is if we say that it is, for example, a picture. When we ask of a work of art *What is this? What is this for?* we need to come up with our own answer. And so we need to take a stand, a stand, critically, on our relation to the background, on our relation to that which we normally take for granted.

Artists make strange tools because tools, in the broad sense I have been urging, are critical for human beings. They organize our lives and, in part, make us what we are. Works of art put our making practices and our tendency to rely on what we make, and so also our practices of thinking and talking and making pictures, on display. Art puts us on display. Art unveils us to ourselves.

•

Writing in the *Tractatus Logico-Philosophicus*, Wittgenstein claimed that propositions have a general form. *This is how things stand. This is how things are. Such and such is the case.* What you are doing when you say anything at all—whether about love, economics, or the color of roses—is asserting: this is how things are. A proposition represents a possible state of affairs.

There is something dubious about the idea that our thought and talk, despite their apparent variety, have one underlying propositional form, as Wittgenstein himself came to insist in his later writing. Nevertheless, throwing caution to the wind, and in the spirit of the younger Wittgenstein, I want now to assert that the work of art has a general form.

The general form of the work of art is: *See me if you can!* The work of art dares you to try, to look hard enough so that you can.

Let me explain. Every work of art (whether dance, song, poetry, film, whatever) challenges you to *see* it, or to *get* it. The work of art (not the artist, not the performer) says, *Bring me into focus, if you can!* Crucially, you usually can't, at least not right away.

Consider: you go to a gallery and are confronted by an array of unfamiliar works. At first it's just a sea of undistinguished stuff. But you look harder. You notice similarities and differences among the works. Gradually something happens: the works come into focus in something like the way individual faces begin to come into focus at a party. At first it's a sea of people. Then it is particular people with particular personalities.

Art is in the business of affording us the opportunity for just this kind of transformation from not seeing to seeing. In this way, art recapitulates a basic feature of our perceptual experience, to wit: that our consciousness of, perception of, access to the world around us do not come for free. We achieve them, by thoughtful and active looking.

Tony Manero in *Saturday Night Fever* was not an artist, from this perspective, and his dancing, however charming, was not art. Tony was in the business of showing off. His motto was: Look at *me*! Check *me* out! I am sexy! I am a man! I am powerful! I am dominant! He danced to achieve something. His dance was the dance of power and seduction. He danced to affirm himself, to realize the fact that he was not just a hardware store clerk but a dancing, proud, lively, energetic man. Dancing, for Tony, however inspired, however passionate, however personal, was, in effect, a technique, a technique in the service of achieving his particular ends. He might just as well have been a fighter as a dancer (as his friends in the movie were).

The motto of the work of art is never: Check me out! (As I discuss later, pop music might seem to be a counterexample, but it isn't really.) The artist, rather, shows you something that you can't see, or says something you can't understand. And the artist gives you the opportunity to catch yourself in the act of trying to get your bearings. The artist says: Get me, make sense of me, bring me into focus, see me, if you can! This is his or her motto. And so the artist affords you the opportunity to transform yourself and to discover the ways you or we manage to bring the world into focus for ourselves.

The case of Tony Manero brings something else to the surface: the art of dance (choreography) isn't just more dancing (as we know it from parties, night clubs, weddings, etc.). In a way, however strange this sounds, it has nothing to do with dancing. At best the art of dance uses the familiar conventions, aims, interests, styles, attitudes, and feelings connected to dancing as a social activity and manipulates and obscures these; it makes art out of these. Choreography, in a sense, is the interruption (or subversion) of dancing. Just as, we shall see, painting is the interruption of picture making.

•

At this point you may be tempted to object. Sure, you may be thinking, all this makes good sense when it comes to modern or contemporary art. The idea that works of art are strange tools, that they are always ironic, that they challenge us to see them seems tailor-made for art after Marcel Duchamp or after Paul Cézanne. But can it seriously be maintained that it finds application more generally to *all* art, always and everywhere?

It has been argued that art, as we understand it today, is a recent invention, not older than the eighteenth century. Before then, the very idea of art, as a distinct taxon, as something separate from other forms of skillful production and work, would have seemed unnatural. Our distinction between arts and crafts, on the one hand, and art proper, on the other, is itself a cultural artifact. But doesn't this entail that there is something wrongheaded in any theory of art, such as the one I offer here, that takes the distinction between art and nonart craft for granted as if it were given in the nature of things? Art, in the sense that seems to be inevitable and so salient to us now, is a shadow cast by our particular cultural moment.

My own view is that the distinction between art and manufacture is as real as any distinction can get. Manufacture makes products with standards of excellence that are pregiven and articulable, ultimately, in terms of usefulness. Art directs itself to products whose standards of excellence, to the extent that there are any, are always open to consideration and reconsideration; it aims at investigation and transformation. It may be an accident of contemporary life that we appreciate this difference, that it matters to us. But this doesn't mean that the difference is our invention, or that it is arbitrary and without importance. Valid argument is one thing, and persuasive rhetoric is another, and that was so long before Aristotle set to work framing the means for elucidating the difference. So the difference between art and manufacture, like that between validity and persuasiveness, or truth and irony, can't be seriously questioned. This is so, by the way, even if, as is surely the case, works of art, in the past as well as the present, may in fact tend to participate simultaneously in *both* categories.

)•

I'm not an art historian and it goes beyond the scope of what I can undertake to offer a universal survey. I'd lay a bet, though, that the survey could be accomplished and that it could be shown that the strange-tools theory I am developing here in fact helps us makes sense of all art everywhere.

Part of what is at stake, it seems to me, is that art that is very old—or from a remote culture—sometimes no longer shows up for us as challenging and difficult. This may be because it falls under the category "important art" and is brought to our attention under glass in the art archives. Or it may be that the work is unfamiliar and we don't get what it is doing. In both cases, the works don't engage, challenge, or affect us, which is just to say they don't show up for us as art. Very often we find ourselves admiring old masters, for example, more or less solely for their decorative aspects, or because of their supposed historical significance or monetary value, or perhaps because they exhibit virtuosity in craftsmanship. And so of course it seems implausible that we admire works of this sort because of the way they subvert or undercut or abrogate the authority of what is normally taken for granted. After all, that's just not what these works do for us, at least most of the time. They have expired. Or stopped being artworks.

Until we learn to look again, that is. Until we learn to turn them on, or to let them show up in person, as it were, and not, so to speak, in poster-format reproduction. Once we do this, we begin to see that where there is art at work among the things we call works of art, it is always joined to the kind of transformation from not seeing to seeing to which I have been directing our attention.

Consider some examples from the Renaissance. They can give a feel of ways the view I am developing here can be applied to work that is in no sense contemporary.

To begin with: two paintings by Leonardo da Vinci, one a portrait of his Milanese patron Duke Ludovico's wife and the other of his patron's mistress. In one sense, these are just pictures of beautiful and beloved women, and Leonardo was presumably contracted to provide just that—exhibitions of these women that were at once celebrations of them. But in another sense, they are much more.

It is striking that in the portrait of Duke Ludovico's wife (*La Belle Ferronnière*), the subject stares straight out at us. She shows herself to us. We are given *her* by being given her eyes. It is also noteworthy that we cannot see her hands, which are concealed on her lap behind a low wall.

In Leonardo's portrait of the duke's teenage mistress Cecilia Gallerani (*The Lady with an Ermine*), by contrast, Cecilia looks away from us. But she is not concealed. We do not see her look, but we are able to see her hand. Her right hand, with which she holds the ermine, captures attention. It is enlarged, bony, powerful, masculine, and it juts forth. It is neither an accurate depiction of a young girl's hand nor an idealization of her beauty, or her person. It is almost caricaturelike.

These two portraits offer a fascinating contrast in composition. We see both women, but in the one it is the eyes, and in the other, the hand, that reveals the presence of the depicted person. To tie the eye and hand together in this way is to enable these portraits to become more than pictures of people. They become, for those who look with the right questions in mind, inquiries into the nature of portraiture itself—what is it to show someone in a picture? At the same time, Leonardo puts the lie to the conventional wisdom that only the eyes are the window to the soul. The soul, it turns out, shows up in the hands as well. And so, finally, we can suggest that the paintings accomplish the joining of seeing and knowing by the eyes with holding, making, and creating with the hands.

I know of only one painting of Leonardo in which the eyes of the person *and* the hands are open to our inspection. This is *Salvator*

Mundi, a portrait of Jesus Christ, the savior, but also the creator of the world. In this painting Jesus looks at us and makes the sign of the bless-ing. By putting hands and eyes in play as he does in his portraits of Duke Ludovico's girlfriend and wife, Leonardo puts Man and art and God into juxtaposition for our reflection. (Actually, there *is* another example where we see eyes *and* hands: the *Mona Lisa*. Perhaps this explains that painting's distinct quality and impact.)

Now, I don't claim that these remarks are more than a beginning. I have said nothing about materials, scale, color, etc. But what they do suffice to demonstrate is that these paintings put much more than these women on display, and, indeed, that *what* they put on display far outstrips whatever it was that Leonardo could possibly have been contracted to achieve. The paintings work with ideas.

A painting can be thus a fee-for-service rendering or documenta-tion of a person (that is, a piece of commercial art) and also at the same time an exploration of what it even means to participate in that sort of commercial, pictorial transaction. These works challenge and question and subvert, and it is here, in this, that they are works of art and not merely depictions. And I propose that wherever we find art, throughout our history or anywhere else, we find made objects and staged events that set up problems, and perhaps offer solutions, in just this kind of way.

Here is another example, also from the Renaissance. Andrea Riccio's diminutive statue of Moses originally sat in a church in Padua atop a fountain facing the altar. I suppose that most people visiting the church, then as now, would have paid the statue little heed. It was religious decor, one might be forgiven for thinking, nothing more.

But as the art historian Alexander Nagel has shown, closer in-spection reveals a surprising set of problems and puzzles; a certain kind of thoughtful engagement is required to bring these to the sur-face. Yet it is precisely these puzzles and problems that make the work interesting and important—and decidedly more than decor.

Consider: Moses is here shown, as he often is, with horns; it was the convention to interpret rays of light expressive of the holiness of the founder of monotheism as like horns rising from his head. But these horns are different; they are the horns of a ram. Perhaps the artist made a mistake. But this isn't very likely. A ram's horns, with their distinctive spiral, are decidedly not the sort of horns conventionally attached to Moses, but they are typical of the pagan Godhead Zeus Ammon. It's hard not to be struck, then, at least if you pay the right kind of attention, that this statue of the person who is in fact the founder of monotheism shows him looking, for all the world, like a pagan idol.

But that's not all. Moses is depicted holding a wand as he draws forth water from a rock. Moses had been commanded by God to *call* forth water from the rock, using words alone; but he uses pagan stagecraft instead.

What is depicted, then, is an episode of religious backsliding. Moses is pandering to the audience, a crowd that is made up, at least in part, of idol worshippers. Moses is represented here in the very act of disobeying God. Riccio's bronze—which lacks the lustrous patina typical of bronzework of the era and of which Riccio was himself an acknowledged master and appears, rather, to have been corroded through the passage of time as if dug up from a remote and ancient past—virtually trembles with theological ambiguity.

Again we see that there is art in this art, but it isn't where we think it is. It isn't in what we see, exactly, but in what we can't see, or in what the piece affords as a possibility for discovery.

This Moses is a strange Moses, one that, at the very least, must force its attentive contemplator to reflect on what is unsaid, or unmet, or unfulfilled. And it is here, in this staged interrogation, that the art work happens.

Let's consider another kind of example, again from the Renaissance. It is received wisdom that art in the Western tradition aims, in the words of Anne Hollander, at representing the visible world with conviction. Of course just what this entails is not so obvious. What is it to represent things, to show visible things in painting or sculpture, as they truly are?

There is a tendency, several hundred years old, itself perhaps a product of the Renaissance, to understand this representational project in psychological terms. The aim of the painter, it is often supposed, is to create illusion. So, for example, the art historian E. H. Gombrich writes of Masaccio's *Holy Trinity with the Virgin, St. John and donors* (1425–1428): "We can imagine how amazed the Florentines must have been when this wall-painting was unveiled and seemed to have made a hole in the wall through which they could look into a new burial chapel in Brunelleschi's modern style." It is in relation to these sorts of "illusions of depth" that the Renaissance invention and application of artificial perspective is typically understood. Perspective, it is supposed, gives the laws of sight; paintings made in accordance with these laws are able to fool the eye. They are good paintings because they are effective illusions.

But perspective, as the philosopher John Hyman has noticed, does not describe laws of *sight*. Its laws do not tell you what you *will* see when presented with a painted surface. Rather, they give rules for figuring out what will be visible, other things being equal, from a point of view. Artificial perspective provides a kind of instrument or calculus, a technical apparatus, for determining what would be visible and so it provides a useful tool for anyone concerned with painting how things look, that is, with showing what is there.

It may be natural for us to join Gombrich in describing Masaccio's picture as giving an illusion of depth. But notice that it is almost never the case that anyone is actually misled or confused, or genuinely amazed, by such an image. We are no more inclined to believe we are seeing through a hole in the church's wall when we inspect the altarpiece than we would be inclined to mistake an architect's balsa wood model for an actual house.

What is remarkable is that representational pictures—I don't mean art works, just pictures—purport to show us what is not present. And what is important to appreciate is that they carry this tension, this almost contradictory objective, right on their surface. So pictures afford us a sense of the presence, in the picture, of what is manifestly absent. It is crucial to remember, when we think about pictures and their power to depict, that our visual consciousness of pictures encompasses the fact that they are pictures; it includes their frame and their size, and their position on the wall, even as it also includes that which is depicted.

Pictures propose questions, at least potentially. Consider the whole issue of time in a representational picture. You may see in a painting actions being performed or events happening—a person running, a rider galloping, water flowing, clouds gathering (here I am thinking of Nicolas Poussin)—but the picture isn't moving; there is no time in the picture, or rather, time is stopped in a picture and movement is frozen. But how can you experience an event and see an action when time is at a standstill and motion has ceased?

Pictures offer questions of this sort. How do we see what is not there? But most of the time we leave the questions implicit. Indeed, it is this very fact—that we leave so much implicit—that enables pictures (like the images we see in the newspapers) to function, uncontroversially, as pictures. Most pictures come with a caption, either a literal one or one provided by context. How do you know that the bearded man on the cross is Jesus? Is it that you recognize his appearance? And how can we tell which portrait shows the duke's wife and which his mistress? Here context and communicative intention are everything. (I discuss all this later on in more detail.)

The thing about *art* pictures—that is, representational pictures that are doing the work of art, whether painted or photographed or sculpted or digitally constructed (note: not every picture is a work of art and not every work of art, not even every painting, is or aims at being a picture)—is that they activate the puzzles whose answers are normally taken for granted. Works of art illuminate the questions, as James Baldwin is said to have put it, that are occluded by the answers we already know.

And so, when it comes to works of art, we can't take for granted anything about regular context. But it is only because we can usually take context (or caption) for granted that pictures can be so unproblematically effective in depicting. And so, when we are dealing with art, we need to think about context itself, or about picturing, or picturing in a religious context. This is what art lets us do, this is what art requires us to do. And we see, at least if I am right, that Riccio's statue, and Leonardo's portraits, and Masaccio's altarpiece, each in its own way, does just this; they are artworks because they do the kind of work that it is art's special interest to perform, and this despite the fact that they also perform more straightforward pictorial (depictional, commercial, didactic, religious, decorative) functions.

•

I can remember, as a young teenager, visiting Jackson Pollock's paintings at the Met with friends. Sarah said: I don't get it. What the heck is this! Anyone could do this!

Hers was exactly the right response. At least it was the right *first* response.

Years later I was flying to California from New York and I was carrying with me a small metal sculpture by the artist Robert Goodnough. The piece was made of sharp steel bars bolted together and spattered here and there with paint. The guard at the security checkpoint—this was before 9/11—pulled me aside for interrogation. *What is this?* the young woman asked. It is a sculpture, a work of art, I replied. Ah, she said and smiled. And she looked again. She was calm and easy. She was in no hurry and she took a long look. Finally she announced: there's not a lot of art in this art! And she waved me through.

Exactly. The work presented itself to the guard as a puzzle, as something of dubious value. This is the right response to a strange tool.

Part of what stands in the way of our appreciating that these are appropriate, legitimate, and authentic responses to a work of art is the fact that we most frequently experience art by visiting, as it were, the art archives (museums). We are told that these are things of artistic value; that's why they're here in this museum, that's why they are on a pedestal. And so we go and look at them and try to understand what makes them so special. And we suppose it must have something to do with who made them, or with the skill and craft needed to make them, or with their beauty or their subject matter, or with their rareness, or with the fact that they (supposedly) are meant to give us pleasure. We look and we wait, hoping the magic will strike us. We take refuge in the words on the wall plaques, or we listen to the audio guide. What we don't do, because we can't, we don't feel safe doing so, is look and engage the work.

But this is to look for art in the wrong place. Let us return to the comparison with jokes. The value of a joke doesn't consist in the fact that it is difficult to invent, or hard to remember, or fun to hear. The value of the joke—what we might call its aesthetic value—consists in its affording us an opportunity to get it. You don't get a joke, however, just because someone tells you it's funny, by placing it, as it were, in the museum of jokes. Either you get jokes or you don't, and yet your getting them is something you achieve. It depends on what you know and what you expect and what you think you are doing with the teller of the joke. A joke functions always and only within a communicative setting. It takes almost as much wit to get a joke as it does to tell it. It is an achievement.

And exactly so with art. Art and joke telling are not in fact merely formally similar. The telling of jokes—or the use of irony in general—is, in a way, the quintessential art phenomenon. It is the subversion of what is expected or straight or unproblematic. We say something unexpected. We say what we do not mean. We startle our interlocutor and force him or her to think and make sense not just of what is said but also of what is not said, what is not sayable, of the whole situation and background presupposed by our conversation in the first place.

This viewpoint sheds light on the claim that art presupposes technology without being itself a technological practice. Art presupposes practices of doing and making without being manufacture, business as usual. Choreographers work with dancing because it so happens that we (Tony Manero, kids in Brooklyn, New Yorkers, human beings) are dancers. But choreographers are not dancers. They don't do what Tony does. They investigate dancing and so they investigate us! And sculptors like Goodnough aren't just making this or that, they are working with the impulses and materials and conventions that organize our familiar purposeful practices of making (and experiencing!). That's what the art is made out of. And that is what the art explores and exposes.

Another upshot of these ideas is that art is, really, a field of investigation. In this it is like philosophy. It is a research practice. This is yet another reason why it is mistaken to think that there could be a neuroscience of art. There can no more be a neuroscience of art than there can be a neuroscience of mathematics or philosophy. Or rather, anything that might call itself a neuroscience of mathematics or philosophy can have only the most peripheral connection to mathematics or philosophy. At best it can illuminate some of what is necessary for us to do mathematics or to undertake philosophy (namely, that we require brains!).

Finally, and this is a new point, these considerations also show why art requires criticism. Criticism is not a journalistic sideshow. Criticism is the oxygen of art. Art always gives us something to think and talk about. It happens, we might say, in the space of criticism.

This insight has two aspects. First, consider the case of jokes again.

We don't make a joke funny by explaining it. But, as we have already noticed, it is of the essence of a joke that there is something to get, and so, in this sense, there is something to explain. The same with art. It is never the end of the matter to say that you just like this or that artwork. That may be the best you can do. But if you value a work of art, it is always appropriate to ask *Why?* If, as logicians claim, a proposition is that for which the question of truth arises, a work of art is that for which the question *Why might it be valuable (or interesting)?*—or simply *What the heck is it?*—arises!

Gombrich wrote that there is no such thing as art. There are only artists. If there is any unity to the great variety of things we all are, then it is its story. Art, if it is anything, is one big history. Gombrich was responding to the fact that art eludes definition. It defies reduction to essential properties.

We are now in a position to see that this challenge that art poses—not only the challenge whether this or that work of art is any good but also whether this or that picture, or action, or object, or installation is even, in any sense, *art* at all—is one of art's basic preoccupations and questions. Art is a problem for itself. Art is always, whatever else it is about, an engagement with other art, with artists, and audiences, and teachers and students. Art is, really, *itself*, a critical practice.

9

Why Is Art So Boring?

Do you remember being bored as a kid?

I recall summer days during vacation that seem, as I think back on them now, to have been fantastically, impossibly long. Hot, endless, open, without organization. Irritating. The buzz of flies, fighting with my little brother, nothing to do. Parents remote.

By and large, there is no place for this sort of radical boredom in the life of an adult. As you get older, life gets organized around projects and plans and needs and goals, and the result of this congealing of activity is that time speeds up. Or we simply stop paying attention to the metronome and are captured by larger patterns of meaning and organization. Our days are over, one might almost say, before they have begun, for we have already defined the present moment in relation to what is yet to happen, in relation to the purpose, point, or plan. ("What did you do yesterday?" "I went to work.")

And this is all for the good, surely. It's a necessity. We *achieve* this. We do not live in the ticktock motion of sensations and buzzes and one thing after another. It is the mark of our development, of our integration—to use John Dewey's language. Our lives are not made up of a series of sensations; they are composed of experiences that demand to be named—*that dinner in Venice, going shopping, the softball game, my year in Berlin*—and these experiences integrate over time. Grown-ups don't get bored. Grown-ups *can't* get bored, for that distinct emotional state, vaguely painful, that sense of being trapped in the unending and meaningless, that state is available only in the absence of structure, plan, task, obligation. The preconditions for boredom are absent in adult life.

What does this have to do with art?

My conjecture is: everything.

The closest I have come as an adult to reliving the florid boredom of childhood is when in the presence of art. Don't get me wrong. I *love* art. I work with art. I study art. I was raised in a family of artists. Art matters to me.

And yet it is hard for me to think of anything more slit-your-wrists dull than some performances, or more excruciatingly sleep inducing than encountering—yet again!—a gallery space with pictures on the wall, each of which, to begin with at least, is closed, mute, indistinguishable, and off-putting.

It isn't just *bad* art that is liable in this way to induce that feeling of anxious capture by an endless and meaningless present. I have stood in galleries at the Met or the Frick or the Alte Nationalgalerie—places that are for me as close to sanctuaries as anything I have ever known—and found myself totally cold in the presence of work that I know and value. It is as if someone failed to press the ON button; the work stays off (or *I* do), and this time spent with art in the standby mode can be a torture.

I propose that the boringness of art is a clue to what art is and why it matters to us. Any adequate account of what art is and of its place in our lives must address the striking fact that art has the power to bore us. This is a power it maintains when everything else in our lives mitigates against boredom. Art affords us the opportunity to be bored to tears, when almost nothing else in our life does. And art's potential to be dull does not contradict the fact that art also moves and thrills and transforms and excites us. Indeed, it is the opposite side of the very same coin. Just as there is no encounter with love without the live risk of heartbreak, so there can be no confrontation with art that does not open up the possibility of getting lulled unconscious and bored to death. Art is valuable only in direct proportion to the degree to which it can, or might, bore us.

Why should this be?

We have the ingredients for an answer ready to hand.

Works of art are strange tools, after all. That is, they are tools we can't use, they are useless. They are texts with no practical content, or pictures that don't show us anything in particular. And so they require us to stop doing. To stop acting and to stop demanding application or even pertinence. Again the comparison with philosophy is apt. Philosophy doesn't yield positive nuggets of information that you can take away and put to work in this or that area of your life, the way physics, mathematics, or economics does. Art, like philosophy, is not practical in this sense. The pictures in the clothing catalog show you something you can buy; the architect's model lays out something you can build. But the choreography on the stage? The painting on the wall? These are cut off from dancing, or showing, or learning. They stop you dead in your tracks. That is, *if you let them*. If you suspend. If you interrupt. If you enter that special space and that altered state that art provides or allows. Art situations have this in common with religious spaces like churches. They are places where so much can happen but only because nothing really happens. They are spaces for self-transformation.

Works of art are cut off and they demand that you cut yourself off from your engaged living. This is obviously so in a practical sense. You can't talk and send email and carry on in the usual way when you are in the theater. And if you do so, then, to that extent, you are not present. You are not taking the bait or tuning in and turning on to what is there. Art settings, like philosophical ones, ask for a kind of suspension of the convictions and habits of engagement that take the winds out of the sails of boredom. To be confronted with art is to be like a child; it is to be made helpless. Art infantilizes and destroys.

This is an old theme in modern thinking about art. Tonio Kröger, Stephen Dedalus, these young art heroes, are enemies of the bourgeois society that gave them life. Art interrupts, makes strange, and so subverts.

This is one of the reasons why pornographic art is almost a contradiction in terms, as I mentioned before. Porn has a clear function; it is meant to turn you on. And to do that it needs to offer you images, ideas, fantasies, and opportunities to be what you are— sexually aroused, for example. Pornography leaves you and everything else as it finds you.

This is also one of the reasons why architecture—thought of in the Renaissance as the queen of the arts—is in many ways the most uncomfortable of all the arts. Always on the verge of collapsing into mere design, into the functional managing of human need and habit and practical life. It isn't surprising, when you think about it, that the buildings of great architects have leaky roofs and doors that don't quite close. Sound roofs and well-fitted doors are tools par excellence, tools whose excellence requires the perfect match to the prefigured need of the user. But artists are always concerned to abrogate just that, to disturb everything that is already, as a matter of habit and background, in place.

A true art of architecture would make uninhabitable spaces. And if there is a pornographic art, whatever else is true of it, it will not be good for masturbating.

Suppose you don't know baseball and you are brought along to a game. That can be a pretty boring experience. But the boredom is at best superficial. You are bored because you don't yet know what's going on. You haven't glommed on to the rules, to the story, to the point. You're confronted with someone else's language. Or someone else's job.

But when it comes to art—I don't care what kind of art—it isn't that you don't know the rules. There are no rules. There is no code for you to learn such that having learned it you can take the rest for granted and get on with the game. Art always puts the status of rules, the very idea that the game—the story, the depiction—has a point, on the block for reconsideration.

Art is boring *on purpose*. Or rather, it confronts you with a situation that makes boredom a natural, a spontaneous response.

Some artists make this explicit. The avant-garde composer John Cage is a famous example. He gave a series of lectures at Harvard toward the end of his life. The lectures were the close reading of several famous texts that had been scrambled together into a meaningless mix of words. By the third and final day, the audience of hundreds had dwindled to a handful of people. His admonishment to just listen, to find the music in the emptiness and the silences and the lack of intelligibility was too large a pill for most people—for most sensible right-thinking people, and even for the most sophisticated art audiences—to swallow.

But this is an extreme case of what is always at work wherever there is art. The lights dim. You are fixed to your seat. And now you must make something of what there is. If you can.

Most artists, but maybe not Cage, are motivated to work more directly with your desires and curiosities, with your natural tendencies to pay attention and then lose focus, to keep you entertained, at least to some degree. But the engagement with the work is always, necessarily, the most fragile thing imaginable.

Kids have boredom already; it comes for free with being young. They don't need art yet. It is almost impossible to get kids to play along with the art game.

But we, we who are creatures of habit, who are buckled in to a life whose mechanisms and rationales of organization are more complicated than any of us can really comprehend, we do need it. Or rather, we can be brought to need it. We can be educated in its importance. Works of art, whose first appearance is always opaque and disconnected, are in dialogue with what we already know, or think we know, and with what we expect, or think we expect, or what we care about, or think we care about.

The choreographer Jonathan Burrows has written that artists enter into an implicit contract with their audiences. The audience plays along. And the artist provides the clues, the materials, needed to complete the transformation. It's no good telling jokes the audience lacks the information to find funny. So there has to be dialogue or give-and-take.

This formulation is exactly right. But what can't be lost sight of is that just as we can't take for granted any code or rule or method for evaluating the artwork, for making sense of it or bringing it into focus, so likewise we can't take for granted criteria for artistic failure. Boredom is a pitfall, but it is a necessary pitfall, like the possibility of losing a race. Races don't fail because we aren't all winners. A critic may with justification condemn a work of art as dull. But that is at most the beginning of an explanation of why the work falls short.

•

Actually, there is another place in our culture where boredom is rife. Education. Students stuck in a lecture hall or classroom, made to follow, or to try to force themselves to follow along with a teacher's rhythms and tempo, may find themselves forced into a painful state of boredom.

I don't think it is an accident that teachers run this risk the same way that artists do. Teachers, after all, are performers, and if they take their task seriously, they are undertaking an artlike activity. Teachers do not merely report what is known. They are not transmitters. They are, rather, midwives whose project is to help deliver knowledge. They bring knowledge to the world and they do so by whatever means necessary.

Boredom is not desirable in the classroom. Who could challenge that? But it is very mistaken to think that boredom is the enemy of effective teaching. It is very mistaken to think that teachers are supposed to be entertainers (just as mistaken as the idea that artists are entertainers!). It is no measure of a teacher's effectiveness that the students enjoy the process. Students need to press the ON button. Students need to endure silences and awkward transitions so that they activate themselves and take on the work of achieving understanding.

It goes beyond my aims here to follow up this thread. Teachers are not artists even if they manifest, in this regard, an important kinship with artistic work. But I want to say enough about this topic to bring out that our culture's anxiety in the face of boredom, our expectation that learning, gaining understanding, growing, should be straightforward, is highly suspect. There are no rules for learning; there is no agreed-upon-in-advance metric for assessing a teacher's effectiveness. And, returning to art, there is no force at all to the idea that art has anything whatsoever to do with entertainment.

Artists are not entertainers, just as choreographers are not dancers and painters are not simply showing you something.

At first glance, this raises a big problem for popular art, pop music, and the movies. These are creatures of the marketplace, after all, and success and failure here do seem to be tied, as with pornography, to the degree to which they entertain or pander. It is unfashionable—it is terribly old-fashioned—to agree with Plato, and with arch modernists like Clement Greenberg or Theodor W. Adorno, that there is such a thing as pure art, that art is divorced from pleasure, and that an art that panders to accepted standards of taste is less than art.

I return to popular art—with emphasis on popular music—in a later chapter. I agree with the New York gallerist Jeffrey Deitch that fashion, rock and roll, graffiti, the art of the street are now vitally bound up with what art is for us. But it is a problem, for us, and for art, to understand how or why this can be. For a nonesoteric art, an art that doesn't cloak itself in invisibility, an art that seems to be free for the taking, an art that revolts against boredom and displeasure seems to be no art at all. For what can art give us if it just turns us on, makes us feel good, and leaves us as it finds us?

10

Art and the Limits of Neuroscience

What is art? Why does it matter to us? What does it tell us about ourselves? These are our questions. In chapter 8 I expressed skepticism about the neuroscientific turn, the program of using the methods and tools of neuroscience to illuminate problems of art. I return to this theme in this chapter. It is critical that I do so for two reasons. The first is that we can learn a lot about art and its importance to us by better understanding why the neuroart program fails. Second, despite obvious shortcomings and the absence of anything resembling interesting findings or results, the neural reductionist approach to art enjoys remarkable prestige and popularity. This fact itself reveals something disturbing about our culture and our values.

Part of the problem is that neuroscience is straitjacketed, not by the methods of science, to be sure, but by unacknowledged philosophical assumptions, not so much by a theory as by an ideology about what we are. Each of us is a brain in a vat of flesh and bone, or, to change the image, we are like submariners in a windowless craft (the body) afloat in a dark ocean of energy (the world). We know nothing of what there is around us except what shows up on our internal screens.

Crucially, this model—*you are your brain*, the body is the brain's vessel, the world, including other people, are unknowable stimuli, sources of irradiation of the nervous system—is not one of neuroscience's findings; it is rather a raft of assumptions that have been taken for granted by neuroscience from the start; it is Descartes's conception but given a materialist makeover.

Of course not every neuroscientist subscribes to the you-are-your-brain ideology. In fact, there are some thinkers, Francisco Varela and Antonio Damasio, for example, who have tried to shape a viable alternative. My own research in philosophical cognitive science, including joint work with Evan Thompson, Susan Hurley, and Kevin O'Regan, is meant to be not so much an attack on neuroscience as an effort to reform it from within by weening it away from its Cartesian default assumptions.

In fact, the problem of fitting the study of brain into a more comprehensive study of mind has been recognized to be a central challenge for cognitive science since the birth of the discipline in the last half of the twentieth century. David Marr's 1982 book *Vision* is a critical text here. David Hubel and Torsten Wiesel won the Nobel Prize for Physiology and Medicine the year Marr's book was published. They were awarded the prize for their work on the mammalian visual system, based on devising techniques for recording from individual cells. This research held out the promise that it might be possible to explain how we see from the bottom up, so to speak, cell by cell. What we see, they considered, is created by the activation of cells each of which is specialized, let's say, for shape, color, movement, orientation, and so on. Marr resisted this optimism. Trying to understand vision at the level of the individual cell, he warned, would be like trying to understand bird flight by studying individual feathers. The question ought not to be what the cells are doing individually. Instead we should ask what problem or problems the visual system itself is trying to solve. Or to put it in the terms Marr favored: What function is vision computing? Once you've figured that out, Marr reasoned, then you can ask the further question: How does a mechanism like the human brain—in contrast, for example, to a digital computer—implement the information-processing laws or algorithms that constitute vision?

It's tempting to view Marr as arguing that we needn't focus on hardware; to understand the mind, it is the brain's software that is primary. This would be half right. Marr's deeper point, I think, is not that we shouldn't be focused on the brain; the point is that insofar as we focus on the brain, we need to look to it not as a piece of meat, or an electrochemical system, but as, in effect, a computer.

No one has done more to sharpen this idea for cognitive science than Daniel Dennett. The brain, he argues, is a *synactic* engine (that is, an engine that makes use of purely formal, physical, meaningless properties of symbols). But it functions as a semantic engine (that is, as if it were sensitive to meaning and significance). The question is, *How?* How do the mere causal processes unfolding in the body's tissue come to have the world-referring, computation-crunching cognitive significance that they do have? Dennett urges that the way we get from mere neurophysiology to an understanding of the brain as subserving and enabling intelligent life is by framing questions about what the brain does in relation to the whole life of the animal. We shift back and forth from what the animal does and achieves to what happens in the brain, and so we tell a story about how what is going on in the brain belongs to and is a part of the story of the animal's life. Importantly, we don't reduce that life to the brain.

Dennett's account has a novel consequence. Suppose that a woman in France reads in the French papers about a murder committed by a Russian in Trafalgar Square in London. We read about the same event in our papers as do the Russians back home in theirs. All of us come to believe that a Russian committed murder in Trafalgar Square. But notice, there is no reason to think that this shared fact about our mental states is realized in the co-occurrence, in each of us, of one single brain state. We are different people with different brains and different histories in different places learning about what is going on by reading about it in different languages. The reason we all have the same belief about the same crime is not that our brains are, in any specific respects, in the same neurophysiological condition. That we share beliefs isn't a fact about our brains. And this is so even though, for Dennett, the brain is crucial for all our cognitive achievements. Beliefs, for Dennett, are something more like functional states of the whole person, states that supervene not on internal goings-on alone but depend on the person or animal's relation to its environment.

For Dennett, meaning isn't inside the head. So nothing inside the head—not the brain, not anything else—could be the source of meaning.

Despite the work of Dennett, Marr, and others on the conceptual foundations of cognitive neuroscience, it remains the case that most neuroscientists—although not those named above—even those not working on such grand issues as the nature of consciousness, art, and love—are committed to a single proposition that is in fact tantamount to the same Cartesian idea that they would be embarrassed to endorse outright. The momentous proposition is this: every thought, feeling, experience, impression, value, argument, emotion, attitude, inclination, belief, desire, ambition *is in your brain*. We may not know how the brain manages this feat, but, so it is said, we are beginning to understand. And this new knowledge of how the organization of bits of matter inside your head can *be* your personality, thoughts, understanding, wonderings, religious or material or sexual impulses is surely among the most exciting and important in all of science. Or so it is claimed.

The abiding idea here, then, is that our lived experience, our daily world, our everyday actions and reactions and feelings and concerns are events in the nervous system. The world itself is a domain of *we know not what* that acts on the nervous system and is screened off by its own effects. We find ourselves on *this* side of the wall of effects separating world and mind. We know things not as they are in themselves; we know only our brain's internal fabrications of them. Very few scientists openly assert such things—or if they do it is usually off the record or in popular books written away from the lab—but it follows ineluctably from the neural reductionism, the internalism, that is their starting point.

Some scientists try to escape this Cartesian vertigo by trying to have it both ways. They grant that we can't understand the value of money or the attachment between a parent and a child without taking up the standpoint of economics, and history, on the one hand, or the personal-level standpoint of love and caring, on the other. But this, it turns out, is simply a fact about us, about the kind of explanations we, owing to our cognitive limitations, find satisfactory. Love is a neural condition. The value we attach to money is a neurological fact about us and nothing more. Even if we find it hard to describe a mother's relation to her child without using the folk-psychological category of love, it would be possible to do so, at least in principle. If not to our satisfaction, then to the satisfaction of a better scientist than we ever manage to be.

I admit that the world acts on us, triggering events in the nervous system. Of course it does! But it is also true that we act right back. Every movement of the eye, head, and body changes the character of our sensory coupling to the world around us. Objects are not triggers for internal events in the nervous system; they are opportunities or affordances for our ongoing transaction with them. The world shows up, in experience, not like a picture in the head. It shows up, rather, as the playing field or arena for our activity. Not the brain's activity. *Our* activity. Not activity inside our head, but activity in the world around us. Our concern is with the active life of the whole, embodied, environmentally and socially situated animal.

The brain is necessary for human life and consciousness. But it can't be the whole story. Our lives do not unfold in our brains. Instead of thinking of the creator brain that builds up the virtual world in which we find ourselves in our heads, think of the brain's job as enabling us to achieve access to the places where we find ourselves and the stuff we share those places with.

It is widely admitted that, for the present at least, we can't explain consciousness in terms of patterns of neural activation alone. In truth, we are not much beyond Descartes when it comes to trying to make sense of why or how we are conscious, as I asserted in chapter 8. I've been arguing for some time now that this is because we've been looking for consciousness in the wrong place. Consciousness is not a neural event inside us, although it depends causally on such events. Objects are not triggers for events in the nervous system, although of course they produce many such effects. And experiences are not effects, events set off as a result of the bombardment of the nervous system from outside. Rather, experiences are temporally extended patterns of active engagement between whole living beings and their worlds (including, I might add, their social world). As Francisco Varela and Evan Thompson write: brain, body, and world make consciousness happen.

It may ultimately be an empirical question whether consciousness depends solely on neural processes or whether it depends also, constitutively, on the body and the world, including the social world, and their dynamic patterns of exchange. The possibility that maybe we need finally to get out of our heads to explain or make sense of human experience is not even considered as a live option. We just assume that the membrane dividing brain and environment is somehow the causally critical division between self and world. This is, I think, to borrow a phrase of Dennett's, "a dead giveaway of vestigial Cartesian materialism" that still holds neuroscience captive.

This is why I insisted, in chapter 8, that we can't take neuroscience for granted as an intellectual readymade and apply it to the problems of art that we care about. This is why I insist that neuroscience has yet to frame an adequate conception of our biological nature.

Indeed, if I am right, far from its being the case that we can explain art from the standpoint of neuroscience, it may be that the order of explanation goes in the other direction. That is, it may be that a better understanding of art will allow us to forge the resources to articulate a more plausible conception of ourselves, one suitable, finally, for laying the ground for a better neuroscience. Indeed, going a step farther, art—as I try to show in this book—is not a *phenomenon* at all, like digestion or eyesight, that stands in need of explanation. It is itself a mode of investigation, a style of research, into the crucial questions that interest us, e.g., our human nature.

The idea that art is itself a setting in which we study ourselves opens up the possibility for a very different kind of collaboration between art and neuroscience.

•

If you are at all sympathetic with the skepticism about neuroscience that I am advancing here, then you will perhaps find it plausible that so-called neuroaesthetics is just another instance of neuroscience's intellectual imperialism, just another chapter in neuroscience's attempt to come up with a brain-based theory of everything. But in fact neuroscience's recent preoccupation with art reveals something deeper and more fundamental about the neuroscientific project.

This comes out clearly when we turn to visual neuroscience and the primacy accorded there to "neural representations." Visual consciousness—what we really see, it is said—is given by a picture in the brain. Marr called this the 2½-D sketch. It is not quite a full-fledged model of the 3-D world; it is, really, its picture. Technically, it is the array of point-light intensities on the retina but transformed, in effect, into a line drawing, in which boundaries between objects are marked out. Vision may enable us to gain knowledge of a three-dimensional world, but it does so, it is widely stated in the vision literature, by giving us two-dimensional, or 2½-D, experiences.

Seeing a cube from this standpoint is having a picture of the cube—in effect a line drawing—in your brain (or in your mind). And this, in turn, explains why we experience a cube when we look at a picture of one. For the seeing brain, a line drawing is the cube's equivalent. This follows from the inexorable logic that the cube itself, in its three-dimensionality, is screened off by the optics of projection. The best we can have, in sight, is how things look from here, that is, the best we can have, in vision, is the cube's 2-D (or 2½-D) projection.

Neuroaesthetics—or at least the theory of pictures, pictoriality, depiction—is in play for visual neuroscience from the very beginning. So now consider the claim advanced by the Harvard vision scientist Patrick Cavanagh that artists, insofar as they are in the business of making effective pictures, "act as research neuroscientists"; their pictures are brain experiments. If I am right, the headline here that art is a kind of neuroscience or that artists act as neuroscientists is really a statement of first principles and marks no discovery. After all, it is axiomatic for visual neuroscience that the fact that we see a cube when presented with a line drawing of one shows that, for the visual brain, at least, a line drawing of a cube is the cube's equivalent. And so the fact that we don't immediately notice mistakes in a painter's rendering of shadows shows that the brain is not governed by a knowledge of physics in constructing its visual world. Cavanagh does not need to adduce evidence to support his claim that if we really saw the world in 3-D, then pictures would look jarring and inaccurate when we move. That pictures don't shock us in this way shows that we don't see the world in 3-D after all.

To repeat, the would-be discovery that artists are in effect carrying out neuroscientific experiments when they build pictures is not really a discovery at all. It follows from the familiar starting point idea that we are confined, in our experience, not to things themselves but to neural pictures of them. Cavanagh is reading his neuroaesthetics off his philosophical starting points.

One noteworthy upshot of the neural equivalence of representations with what they represent is that objects themselves, with all their specific, tangible substantiality, play almost no role in neuroscience. If you want to study object perception, it suffices to work with photographs of objects. The power or meaning of a picture of an object, according to the equivalency thesis, is exhausted by the power and meaning of what is depicted; and vice versa, there is nothing more to an object's significance (at least to vision) than is carried by a suitable pictorial rendition of it.

And so it should not be surprising that the psychologist and experimental neuroscientist Vilayanur S. Ramachandran offers an explanation of why we value an eleventh-century bronze statuette of the goddess Parvati by showing that, for neuroevolutionary-psychological reasons, "we" supposedly respond to full-figured women. And this notwithstanding the fact that, whatever else is true of the statuette, it is clear that it is not a full-figured woman. The treatment of the statue, the depiction, as if it were a transparency through which we encounter what it depicts, is justified by the equivalency thesis, or, in this case specifically, by the idea that the statuette is, neurologically speaking, the equivalent of a full-figured woman.

The equivalency of a picture and what it depicts, however, is deeply implausible. As I argue later on, it is one thing to see a thing and another to see its depiction. That is, whatever we say about why pictures have representational powers, it better not commit us to the idea that pictures give us the experiences we would have if we were encountering in the flesh whatever it is that they depict. When you see a picture of something, you have a sense of its presence despite the manifest and perceptually salient fact of its nonpresence. You may see a full-figured woman in the statuette. But you are manifestly not in the same state you would be in if you were actually in the presence of a full-figured woman.

A clever neuroscientist will object. If there is a difference between seeing a thing and seeing it in a picture, indeed, if the picture shows you something while at the time showing you that it isn't there, then this distinctive structure in the experience of pictures will itself be neurally realized. Neuroscience is not committed to ignoring this experientially important difference; it is committed only to the idea that there is no significant difference that is not, itself, ultimately, a neurological difference.

Well, we've already seen that the dogma that mental states of whatever kind—love, monetary value, conscious experience, etc.—are identical to brain events is not one that has yet been made good on. And anyway, the neural equivalency thesis—that seeing something and seeing its picture are states of the same kind—is implicated by Cavanagh's and Ramachandran and William Hirstein's analyses of representation in art. If you give it up, then we have to give up Cavanagh's claim that painters are neuroscientists, and Ramachandran and Hirstein's claim that the statuette is a super-stimulus, perfectly designed to titillate the brain just as a woman with large breasts and buttocks would.

In any case, there is a more pressing issue. Ramachandran and Hirstein's story leaves the *artwork*, with its distinctive values and qualities, out of the story. Everything we need to know about a work of art is clarified, for Ramachandran and Hirstein, once we do our real work, which is, they believe, explaining the sources of our titillation. And what titillates is not the picture but the world (or, in this case, women). Or rather, the picture (the statuette) titillates us only insofar as it is the world's equivalent. Ramachandran and Hirstein don't go so far as to offer an account of the specific work of art—with its distinctive look, patina, size, weight, religious significance, and so on. And this shouldn't be surprising. Just as the object falls out of consideration within the scope of neuroscience, so the *art object*, the work itself, plays no role, is never brought into focus, in the neuroscience of art (neuroaesthetics).

Indeed, it isn't clear how the artwork can ever make an appearance in neuroaesthetics. After all, for neuroscience, objects themselves are only triggers that are functionally equivalent to their neural representations. So the same is true of art objects. At best they are triggers for events in the nervous system; the object itself screens itself off thanks to its effect on the nervous system. And so it shouldn't be surprising that researchers looking at our aesthetic response to sculptural form conduct their studies in the absence of sculptures, confining themselves to pictures of sculptures, or that others identify aesthetic experiences as those triggered by the inspection, inside the magnetic resonance imaging machine, of digital photographs of paintings.

If the equivalency thesis is right—if a picture is the neurological equivalent of what it depicts—then the disappearance of the artwork itself from the study of art can be chalked up to good scientific method.

But if we grant, first, that it is one thing to see a picture of something and another to encounter it in the flesh, and second, that when it comes to art, we are interested, in part, in creations that capture our attention directly and in their own material person, so to speak, and not merely as transparencies through which to encounter whatever it is that they represent, then we've got a problem on our hands. Neuroaesthetics seems unable to bring its own subject matter, art, into focus as a subject of investigation.

At root this inability to bring the artwork into focus stems from the doctrine that the artwork's significance is its effect on our perceptual (or emotional) systems. The fact that experimentalists rely on pictures of artworks rather than artworks themselves means that they must ignore the more powerful response that would be triggered by actual artworks, a response that is sensitive not only to pictorial or representational content but also to such factors as scale and installation. But there is a deeper, less technical point, one that is prior to all that: artworks are not response triggers, and aesthetic experiences are nothing like events switched on in the brain. No stimulus could ever stand in for the artwork. Not even the artwork itself! For the artwork is not a stimulus.

Actually, as we noticed in chapter 8, this problem of bringing the artwork itself into focus in neuroaesthetics was already in evidence with the programmatic claim, advanced by Semir Zeki, that it is brains that see art and that the laws of the brain constrain art. To support this view, Zeki adduces such facts as that Mondrian's paintings exploit intricate details of human color perception and that no artist makes art from ultraviolet light, precisely because such radiation is, after all, invisible.

The problem here is that the brain constrains our experience of art. Not because of anything distinctive to do with art, or with the neural representation of art, or with the experience of art, but because the brain constrains our visual experience of anything we see. Insofar as works of art are to be looked at and visually examined, then it will be only insofar as we can see that we can engage with them. What we have here is not so much a false account of the neural underpinnings of artistic appreciation as one that leaves art and its distinctive neural underpinnings, if there are any, out of serious consideration. It never gets that far.

•

A more promising approach, perhaps, would be to turn attention to *aesthetic experience*—the intense delight we take in beholding the beautiful or the awe-inspiring (the sublime)—in order to investigate its neural correlates. This is the approach taken by Gabrielle Starr and her neuroscience colleagues Edward A. Vessel and Nava Rubin. But there are problems here as well.

Let us suppose that there are neural correlates of aesthetic experience. This doesn't mean that these correlates have any explanatory significance. Here's an example from a different domain. It has been claimed that there are differences in the brains of men and women; these differences are adduced as evidence that gender is hardwired. But the thing is, if there *are* differences between men and women, behavioral, cognitive, experiential—I am not assuming that there are, but *if* there are—then it stands to reason that these differences would make a neurological difference. How could they not? But that doesn't rule out the possibility that it is social, cultural, environmental factors that drive, cause, and so explain the differences. And so with aesthetic experience. If there are aesthetic experiences, then these experiences have neural correlates. Everything leaves a trace in the brain (as opposed to the brain's tracing everything!). That much is clear. There are neural correlates for everything. But it remains to be demonstrated that those correlates have anything to teach us about the experience that interests us. I am not aware of any evidence that they have done this.

Another problem has to do with the difficulty of laying out interesting or stable or necessary (let alone sufficient) hallmarks of aesthetic experience. Some aesthetic encounters are moving and some are not. Some are moving to me but not to you. Some are moving on one occasion but not on others. Most are not moving at all until we have, so to speak, learned to get moved. Can we pick out aesthetic experiences as those we rank as most moving, say, on a four-point scale? This is Starr's methodology. She and her colleagues ask subjects

ART AND THE LIMITS OF NEUROSCIENCE   131

to judge photos of canonical works of art as moving (or not) on a scale of 1 to 4. I doubt that we can operationalize aesthetic experience this way. And I suspect that this not an accident but rather itself a fundamental feature of aesthetic experience. I return to this below.

In any case, Starr and her colleagues treat the experiences of looking at digital reproductions of artworks in the fMRI scanner that are ranked 4 on the scale of degrees of movingness as "intense aesthetic experiences." And they argue that there are, in fact, striking neural correlates of such experiences, across different artistic domains (music, painting, and poetry).

Specifically, they argue that "intense aesthetic experiences," but not less intense ones produce activation in what has been called the "default mode network." This is said to be a network of associated brain areas that are believed to be suppressed, relative to a resting state, by task- or world-oriented activity but that regain baseline rates when attention is turned away from the world, during rest, daydreaming, imagination, thought, etc. It has been argued that the default mode network is a neural system for specifying the self. This claim resonates in an intuitive sort of way with the idea that this system is active when we are strongly moved aesthetically. It is as if being moved aesthetically transports us, turns us inward, removes us from mere seeing, mere object-oriented inspection to something more like contemplation.

This is a suggestive idea, but one that may not be well supported. For one thing, I would question whether the self can be specified, represented, or activated only by acts of withdrawal from the world. The self shows up not only as the *me* of self-reflection—as the research team of Kalina Christoff, Diego Cosmelli, Dorothée Legrand, and Evan Thompson remind us, drawing on ideas of William James—but also as the *I* of agency. There is also evidence, cited in the notes, that in fact the so-called default mode network is frequently activated during engaged involvement with tasks and the environment. It isn't clear, then, what default mode activation means, and so it is unclear what we should make of the putative correlation between such activation and what is getting labeled, for the purposes of these studies, aesthetic experience.

•

Now, I have already stated that I don't think you should think of perceptual experiences in general as events that take place in your head. So it isn't surprising that I also reject the idea that aesthetic experiences are a special species of event that happen in your head. But my worries here don't derive from my own "externalist" starting point.

A striking feature of aesthetic responses—I addressed this also in chapter 8—is that they are cognitive achievements, comparable, if not identical, to getting a joke. "Getting it" requires wit, insight, understanding. Crucially, the relevant scope of understanding concerns what is communicated and expected, and in particular what is expected about ways of communicating. Aesthetic responses are like this.

Here is another feature of aesthetic responses. We have them not only, as it were, in isolated encounters with works of art (as we do when we are in the brain scanner). We frequently *learn* to have them, and our responses are informed by what teachers, critics, friends, and family say and think about the work, by what works we have seen before, and also by what we do or are interested in doing in relation to the work. Aesthetic responses are not fixed data points, but are more like positions staked out in an ongoing conversation, ongoing in our day, in our lives, and also in the historical time in our culture. Aesthetic responses are cultivated and nourished and they are also challenged. Aesthetic responses are themselves the question art throws up for us, not something we can take for granted in making sense of art itself.

This brings me to a final feature (also mentioned in chapter 8). Aesthetic responses are judgments. We take stands on works of art. We don't just "like" them; we like them, as Kant said, in the "universal voice." That is, we expect others to like them, too, and if they don't, then we expect that there is a lot to be said about our disagreement. As the philosopher Alexander Nehamas suggests: aesthetic judgments are the beginning of conversations and not their conclusions. Art is experienced in the setting of argument, criticism, and persuasion. It was Kant's insight to realize that all this is compatible with the fact that it may be essential to the art encounter that there is no way of adjudicating disputes in this area, that there are no decision procedures, no rules, no way of proving who's right and wrong. But art nonetheless raises the question: *Who's right?*

Aesthetic responses, then, are not symptoms or reactions or stable quantities. They are actions. They are modes of participation. They are moments of conversation. There is nothing about which we can even ask: What are its neural correlates? And moreover, to look for neural correlates is already to have turned away from what deserves to be called aesthetic experience, to events or even feelings in our minds.

John Dewey made the paradoxical claim—quoted as this book's epigraph—that it is the very existence of art objects that stands in the way of our framing a plausible aesthetic theory. Exactly. It isn't about the objects. And it isn't about the effect the object triggers in us. Dewey said: art is experience. We can explain it like this: it's about what we do with the art objects. In that sense it is about the *work* of art.

To wrap this up, then: neuroscience is too individualistic, too internalistic, too representationalistic, too idealistic, and too antirealistic to be a suitable technique for studying art.

But there's a deeper point to be made. Neuroscience, as we have seen, treats art as a phenomenon and so it studies art the way it studies any phenomenon. Art objects are triggers distinguished by the distinctively "aesthetic" character of the experiences to which they give rise. I have argued that the trigger conception of art and aesthetic experience actually fails to bring either of these entities into the scope of investigation. Art isn't explained; it is explained away.

And now we get to the heart of the matter. Art isn't a phenomenon to be explained. It is, rather, a mode or activity of trying to explain. This idea is central to the argument of this book. I turn to it now in the next chapter, but it is only in later chapters that I'll be able to make good on the full significance of the claim. Art and philosophy are both species of a common genus: they are, as I put it, reorganizational practices. This statement turns out to have an important and surprising implication about the relation of both art and philosophy to biology, as we noticed in chapter 2. But it also helps us appreciate that the idea that we might reduce the aesthetic to the neurological is no less wrongheaded than the idea that we might reduce philosophy itself to events in the brain.

11

Art Is a Philosophical Practice and Philosophy an Aesthetic One

"Practice" is one of those words that get thrown around a lot by philosophers, anthropologists, and theorists of all stripes. Like any bit of jargon, it has its uses, but it also marks the spot where theoretical wheels may have a tendency to lose traction and spin freely.

My father was an architect. And he ran a bar in New York City. He used to say that he didn't think of himself as having given up architecture when he took over the bar. Running the bar was, for him, an architectural practice. I guess he meant something like the bar was a space for people, and architecture is the art of interior spaces.

My mother was a potter. Starting in the late 1950s, she made pottery in the vernacular of traditional American and English pottery. She was a production potter. She didn't make ceramic sculpture. She threw pots—pots for drinking out of and holding food and being put to work in the home. So in some sense she was a worker, a craftsperson, and yet hers, I maintain, was an artistic practice.

So running a bar can be an architectural practice, and making dishes and cups can be an artistic one.

In this chapter I want to call attention to deep affinities between art and philosophy, as practices and as fields.

A first striking feature common to both art and philosophy is that they are not limited in their subject matter. Yes, there are traditional topics that have captured the concern of philosophers—the mind-body problem, for example, or the nature of justice—and so too there have been artistic preoccupations, with regard to both media (painting, print making, water colors, etc.) and subject matter (still life, portraiture, etc.).

But surely these boundaries and groupings do not mark out genuine limits to art and philosophy as disciplines. Philosophers do philosophy, as a matter of fact, just about everywhere. Physics, neuroscience, chemistry, linguistics, and economics, but also talking, making decisions, loving, knowing, anxiety, and religion—these are all places where philosophy can and does happen.

And so with art. There is simply no way one can say "This isn't art" because this or that is not a suitable subject for art, or this isn't a possible domain in which to make art. Love, God, politics, humor, digestion, vision, food, you name it. Artists find their inspiration in the vicinity of all of these.

It is a striking feature of philosophy, then, and of art, that these practices have no subject matter that limits them in the way that history limits itself to historical facts and physics limits itself to the physical. If art and philosophy are unified, it is precisely as practices. There are shared traditions and a shared concern with methods and values and ways of carrying on. Think of art and philosophy as long conversations in which participants come and go, some joining in at the end, others at the beginning, others coming late but insisting on learning what was said earlier, while others intervene without a good sense of what is going on. Or compare art and philosophy to martial arts: the unity of the field is the unity of the teaching lineage. It is real human relationships—student to teacher to teacher's teacher to teacher's teacher's teacher, and so on.

What is philosophy, anyway? Every generation of philosophers confronts this question and does so with urgency. It has seemed impossible to take for granted that we know what we are doing or know what we are learning when we learn philosophy. This is why philosophers write histories of philosophy not merely as a way of reporting facts, of telling a story, but as a way of doing philosophy. And this is why philosophers, now and two thousand years ago, question philosophy and call its value into question. Philosophy is continuously renewing, revising, revolutionizing, and rethinking itself. Philosophy is a problem for itself.

Exactly the same is true of art. *What is art?* is one of art's central preoccupations. Is Duchamp's *Fountain* a work of art? Yes. But why? Or rather, how? He went to a hardware store in New York City and purchased a prefabricated urinal. Did the urinal become art because an artist bought it or perhaps because he signed it, or signed it with a made-up name? Or was it the act of putting it on display that made the bathroom fixture an artwork? Or maybe the bathroom fixture is *not* an artwork. The art is in the act of installing the urinal. Really, the work is a kind of performance. Duchamp's work poses these very questions. His work asks: What is art anyway and why does it matter? This is a striking and clear example, one distinctively characteristic of modernity. But all art, always, has been in exactly this sort of way preoccupied with other artists and with the nature of art itself.

And so, as with philosophy, art renews and revises and returns and remakes itself over historical time.

A further striking fact: we can speak of change and history and even evolution in philosophy and in art, but we cannot speak of progress. This has to do with the fact that there aren't breakthroughs or discoveries or results or findings in these fields, certainly not ones that invalidate or cancel out earlier ones or preclude future ones.

You don't read a philosophy paper or book for the bottom line. "Philosopher X thinks that p." "Descartes holds *cogito ergo sum*." "Kant believes that space and time are forms of intuition." First of all, these are not propositions established to the general satisfaction of a community of peers. They are, rather, moves in an important conversation; they don't bring the conversation to its close, however. Second, these sorts of philosophical theses have no self-standing content. You don't know what they mean unless you have followed along on the philosopher's journey. Simply put, there is no bottom line in philosophy. And there are no stand-alone nuggets of truth that can be put in the archives alongside findings of math, physics, and biology.

A philosophy text is more like a *score* than it is like a record of fact or finding. When an experimental scientist publishes a finding, he or she reports the work that was done beforehand. It is a trivial matter in such a case to write up an abstract. But a philosophical abstract is always dubious. A philosophical piece of writing *is* the philosophy, not a report of it. Like a score, a philosophy text is an instrument for undertaking philosophy in the style or in the locale of the text's author. To read a philosophy text is to participate in the performance of the ideas and feelings and puzzlements it traces out.

If aliens from outer space come down to earth and find a way of deciphering philosophical books, they will not be able to make sense of them. They won't share the puzzlements and curiosities, the predicaments and entanglements that are the presupposition of philosophy. Philosophical writings are of no use to someone who is untroubled by philosophical anxieties.

And all this is true, suitably reformulated, of art as well. Yes, some artists make objects and all artists make or do something. But these finished products are not self-sufficient accomplishments ready for storage in museum archives, even if, somewhat scandalously, this is how we as a culture tend to think of them. They are occasions for active engagement on the part of people who are disposed to do something with them. How else can we explain the fact that there is no physical unity to the work of art? What does a urinal have in common with a work on canvas, or a song, or a building, or an altarpiece? Artworks are dead in themselves, like mere noise or useless stuff. We bring them to life by putting them to work in thought, conversation, and appreciation. They have power in the way that jokes have power, as moves in a game of communication and reflection. Maker and public jointly undertake the work that makes art possible.

Art and philosophy, we may say, are practices. Their value is not in their result; method and result are one. And so, to repeat, while one can speak of history and evolution and meaningful growth and change—just as we can speak of these concepts in relation to a conversation, or a person's understanding, or a culture's practices—we can never speak of progress in a more definite sense. It's not as though artists make discoveries that are independent of the local curiosities and puzzlements and fascinations and hankerings that are their natural setting. Dewey was exactly right that, in a way, the museum is antithetical to art. As if you can see the art just by looking at it, or by taking note of what the audio program or docent tells you! As if art's values are delivered so easily! Works of art don't just sit there in the museums, shining for all the world to see. Audiences and makers engage with each other through the opportunities that artists manufacture. We enact art as much as we perceive it.

It is just these facts about art and philosophy that have made art and philosophy *problems* for culture. Artworks and artists are objects of suspicion. And so too philosophers. Sure, there is an art market, but it is insane and irrational and has no intelligible relation to what makes art important. And so it isn't surprising that governments and funding agencies struggle to justify why they should support art, or philosophy, in a world where there are so many urgent needs and high costs.

And how can philosophical research be a thing of value when it never yields settled agreement or certainty? And how can it be worthwhile to devote resources to making products that, by their very nature, refuse to be in the service of this or that function?

Plato's answer was that it isn't the conclusion to the argument that is the source of philosophy's value. Its value is the change in the way we understand how the different concepts and commitments and values that we hold at once all hang together. You are transformed in the course of a philosophical discussion. You start out thinking you know what justice is, or personal identity, and at the end, having faced up to the manifest and evident shortcomings of any view that you or your interlocutors can come up with, realize that you don't know. Yet your not knowing is infused with understanding. You may not learn anything new, but you see everything you already knew in a new light. Philosophy leaves everything as it finds it but reorganizes the way you think and reason. Philosophy changes us. Philosophy aims not at discovery but at understanding.

An aesthetic experience, understood now in a way that is true to the temporally drawn out, communicative, thoughtful, and argumentative character of our life with art, has exactly the structure of a philosophical dialogue in Socrates' or Plato's sense. We start out not seeing what is there. But by looking and interrogating and challenging, we come to see it. The work challenges us to reorganize our seeing, our expectations, and our thinking. The work of art, like that of philosophy, is the reorganization of ourselves. And this reorganization, this work, aims also at understanding.

I hear an objection. Art is not intellectual the way philosophy is; it is not a play of ideas. How can one compare reading a philosophy book to going to a dance performance, or dancing to writing a philosophy book?

As we have noticed already, one mistake implicit in this objection is that philosophy is wrongly described as cold. Philosophy is intellectual, yes, but that doesn't mean it is cold. Philosophy
is driven by the emotions of puzzlement, confusion, curiosity. It
is hot.

And at the same time, it completely sells the work of the dance
artist short if you think he or she is not solving problems or investigating structures or posing questions.

Critically, it is because the questions that underlie philosophical
and artistic projects are *important*—and as we have already seen,
these projects know no bounds—that our engagement with them can
be so significant to us.

•

From the standpoint of this approach to art as a philosophical practice (and vice versa), it is possible to explain three features of art for
which it is otherwise difficult to account (especially for neuropsycho-
logical theories).

First, as mentioned in the last chapter, it is a striking and abiding
feature of art that it makes us argue. It is a domain of dispute. We argue about whether this or that is any good, as art, and also whether
it *is* art in the first place. We argue about what art is, anyway. And
assuming that we think we know what it is, we debate whether it has
any real value.

If you care about art at all, then these issues really burn. Attitudes
on questions of art draw boundaries between people and show limitations to our ability to understand each other and get along. And
they also mark large-scale cultural and historical differences between
people.

My proposal is that aesthetic disagreement is a kind of philosophical disagreement (or that philosophy is, in effect, a domain of
aesthetic dispute). Unlike mathematics or physics, there are no proof
procedures in philosophy. But this is not because the problems aren't
real. It's that the problems don't turn on new facts or mere logical
consequence. Philosophical puzzlements concern getting clear about
where we find ourselves and what we think given what we already
know. Philosophical arguments are persuasive but also educational,

and they are practical. They pertain to the question of how we should carry on (in this intellectual or practical domain or that).

If art is a subspecies of philosophy, or if—as I would put it—each is a subspecies of a larger genus, then it shouldn't surprise us that art, like philosophy, is a field of disputation. Art and philosophy share a common aim: self-transformation and the achievement of understanding.

Second, artists make stuff. They tinker, they stage, they build, model, shape, mold, sketch, and construct. And yet as everyone knows, they are more than manufacturers. They don't make stuff merely in order to make better pictures or to be more entertaining. Artists who make pictures are, in my view—and I'll have a lot more to say about this as we go on—using picture-making technologies to put pictures and the role that pictures play in our lives on display in order to call them into question. This doesn't mean that it will not sometimes be important to the artist to make a realistic picture, or a pretty one. But that won't be the whole story.

And that's what the view under consideration helps us begin to understand. Artworks are *philosophical objects*, and if it is worthwhile doing philosophy with pictures, this is because, well, pictures are important to us. We do live with pictures and they do organize our lives; indeed, they do so in ways we have no real comprehension of or control over. We live with pictures and take them for granted. Painters—those in the business of making pictures, that is; importantly, not all are (e.g., Barnett Newman, Ad Reinhardt, Al Held)— do philosophy where the relevant forms of puzzlement and need arise: in the act of depicting.

Finally, as we have already considered at length, art can be very boring; it is always liable to bore us to tears. If works of art are strange tools, if art happens with the disruption of business as usual, always demanding that we look differently and try to see what we don't quite know how to see, then it isn't surprising that we run the risk of failing to see anything at all and just finding ourselves trapped and disengaged with the works around us and with our lives.

This modality of boredom, this distinctive pitfall, is a hallmark of philosophy, too. Philosophy doesn't yield up the results that help you carry on as you were carrying on before you did philosophy. It won't yield up the cure for deadly diseases or help you end global warming. And yet it helps you see differently, by enabling you to re-make yourself.

Not all art is boring. Ditto for philosophy. But the live possibility of boredom is always there for art and philosophy, and in exactly the same way.

PART III

The lived perspective, that which we actually perceive, is not a geometric or photographic one.

—Maurice Merleau-Ponty

12

Making Pictures

The scene: my son's first-grade classroom, music recital in progress. I look around at the other parents and to my surprise I see that none of them are looking at the young performers. Their gazes are fixed intently on the displays of their various video and photo devices. Some have brought tripods and expensive movie cameras; others content themselves with the their smartphones.

What I find remarkable about this situation is not the parental urge to substitute an image for the performance itself. Nor is this a special instance of the power of televisual images to capture our attention, even in the face of live performance. No, what's striking is that these parents *are* paying close attention to the performance, they are watching it, but they are doing it in a special way—by making pictures.

If you have ever tried to draw from life, then you know that it is staggeringly difficult. Where do you begin? How do you direct your attention? What matters? To draw effectively, you need to learn new ways of thinking about what you see—how the world is articulated and set forth and built. To draw something well, you need to study it *very* closely.

Nowadays, with digital photography, it's pretty easy, and pretty cheap, to make pictures. Making a digital snapshot can hardly be compared to drawing something painstakingly from life. But drawing and amateur photography do have this in common: making pictures— even digital video at the elementary school on one's handheld device—is a way of paying attention to what you are depicting. And so, it is a way of seeing. It is a special way of attending to what you see, just as dancing can be a special way of paying attention to the music you hear. Pictures are bound up with seeing, but not only with seeing; they are bound up also with thinking about what we see, and with the interest we take in what we see (and also in how we would like to be seen, and in how we would like to be seen *as seers*).

Notice also that the interest we take in our children when we film them at a recital is not an interest in their *visual appearance* in a purely optical sense (whatever that is exactly). We know what they look like. We are interested in who they are, what they are doing, and how they are performing. We want to show *them* off, not their appearances. Pictures, in at least one of their main varieties, are distinctively visual; they target the world as it shows up for us by way of sight. (More on *non*visual pictures later!) But pictures are not about looks. They are ways of displaying what we see, that is, things we care about (for whatever reason).

But the most important lesson we can glean from thinking about the scene in my boy's classroom is also the most obvious one. It is the simple, almost too-evident-to-state fact that we *make* pictures. We don't find them. They aren't natural occurrences in the way that reflections in the surface of a pond or on the chrome of my bicycle handle are natural occurrences, or the way a shadow on the wall is a natural occurrence. We don't stumble upon pictures. We *produce* them. They are artifacts. Bits of manufacture. Many of our picture-making devices—the digital or photographic camera—exploit phenomena of natural image making, reflection, and the like. It is a general fact about technologies that they harness nature and put to work our understanding of natural phenomena, as the Santa Fe Institute economist W. Brian Arthur has stressed. The point is that pictures are products of human handiwork, and picture making is a technological practice. A picture, in brief, is a tool.

•

We don't make pictures just for the fun it, at least not usually. Tools are devised for purposes and against the background of needs, expectations, problems. Why were all the parents concerned to make pictures? It's telling and important that that is not an easy question to answer. Not because of anything to do with pictoriality, as such, but because the motivations here are complicated, perhaps as complicated as our lives themselves. Why do we feel we need to document the lives of our children in pictures? What would we lose by not doing so? What are we accomplishing by doing this? It is not the job of a theory of pictures to answer these questions. But it is the job of a theory of pictures to notice that whenever we make pictures, we do so for reasons like these, reasons that are embedded in the complicated fabric of our lives. In this way, pictures are like words, or speech. Why do we speak? Let us count the ways! To close a deal, express an apology, find out how to get our bottle-deposit back, flatter the boss. Why do we make pictures? The answer to this question will be similarly varied and context specific.

The multiplicity of uses to which we put pictures doesn't mean we cannot usefully generalize. *Pictures are tools for showing things, for putting things on display.* This generalization captures the basic function of picture making without flattening out or ignoring the great diversity of background contexts that motivate and condition the practice of picture making. After all, why do we want to show something? We get all the diverse specificity we want when we try to answer this question.

But there is another value to this formula that pictures are a tool for showing. It puts pictures squarely where they belong, in the setting of our communicative exchanges with other people. To see a picture—and this is something we rarely acknowledge—you must appreciate what it shows you, and to do that, usually, you need to be sensitive to a very subtle background. This picture in the newspaper advertising supplement is showing me the chickens that are on sale at the market. For me to understand the picture, to perceive what it shows, I need to be sensitive to a vastly complicated background of commercial advertising and the like.

This fact is a general one about tools and technologies. Door handles (again!) are straightforward and easy to use. But not absent a natural (that is to say, a cultural) setting. Door handles presuppose that there are doors, that we live in buildings, that we need to pass from one room to another, that our bodies and in particular our hands are built a certain way and function as they do. Door handles may pose real obstacles to children, or the disabled, or visitors from remote cultures. But so long as the background *is* in place, so long as everything that we do take for granted can safely be taken for granted, door handles are so unambiguous, so simple seeming as, basically, to disappear from consciousness. We needn't look at them, think about them; we don't need to *try* to use them. They become like the ground itself that we stand on. We simply act in the world in concert with them.

And so, for the most part, with pictures. Outside the museum, pictures are only rarely things we inspect. That is, when I study the photograph of the jacket I'm thinking of ordering from an online retailer, it's not the picture I inspect; it's the jacket. And when I moon over the picture of my loved one, it is her beautiful face, and not the picture itself, that captivates me. When the setting is in place that lets us use pictures *as* pictures, to show or display something, the pictures themselves, like door handles, or the ground itself on which we stand, recede into the background.

•

Pictures are bits of manufacture. They are more like love letters than they are like fossils. We don't find them. We make them. I mentioned above that this is almost too obvious to require saying. What could be more obvious than that this photograph of a chicken, say, the one in my newspaper announcing the sale at the local market, is a move made in the complex social practice of advertising?

Plato disagreed, as we have already noticed (in chapter 5). It's easy to make a picture, he explained. You just hold up a mirror! A mirror image is a reflection, and that, for Plato, is what a picture is. Plato also thought that pictures were pretty useless. We're not interested in reflections, after all; we are interested in the world itself. Why think I can learn anything about the nature of the world around me by examining naturally occurring images like those on my belt buckle, or on the plastic of my eyeglasses, or on the surface of a puddle?

Plato's disdain for pictures is a disdain for the visual world. Seeing, for Plato, is itself just a way of reflecting things around us, and seeing, like mirrors, is confined to mere appearance. This idea that seeing is a transaction with mere images is, in fact, one of the organizing ideas of modern empirical thought about vision. It has its origins already in Plato but finds its mature treatment among the later scientific revolutionaries—Kepler, Leonardo, Descartes, Galileo, Newton—who laid the groundwork for the science of vision. Kepler was able to join a sophisticated understanding of the physical geometry of light rays with a correct description of the structure of the eye, and so of the way rays of light bend on entering the eye. Kepler was the first to be able to demonstrate that the eye is a kind of complicated image-making device, a sophisticated mirror or, better, a camera obscura.

Kepler and his contemporaries also noticed that the story of sight can't end with the retinal image. After all, we experience the world upright, and the retinal image is upside down. Something needs to be done with the retinal image before we experience what it shows us. It needs to be reinverted before the mind's eye. Late nineteenth- and twentieth-century scholars of vision carried this idea much farther. We don't see with the eye; we see with the brain. They appreciated that the retinal image is remarkably unlike the visual images of which we are conscious when we see. In addition to the fact that the images are upside down and there are two of them, the eyes are in nearly constant motion, yet we experience a stable visual world; there is a blind spot in each eye where there are no photoreceptors, yet we experience no gaps in the visual field; the resolving power of the retina is not uniform, yet we don't experience the world as blurry or unresolved at the periphery; toward the edges of the retina, color-sensitive receptors disappear, yet we experience the whole visual field as a colorful expanse; there are blood vessels and other materials crossing over in front of the retina, causing incident light to be blocked and bent, yet we don't experience these disruptions to clear vision; the retinal images are tiny, yet we experience the world around us at a human scale; finally, the retinal images are just that, images, in the mathematical sense; they are projections onto a two-dimensional surface (roughly, the surface of the retina is concave), and yet we experience the world around us as consisting of solid objects standing in fully three-dimensional spatial relations. We don't *see* our retinal images; they are at best the input to the image-making process that makes vision as we know it possible.

The vision science that comes down to us through this tradition— the vision science that rules supreme in universities today—shares Plato's basic idea that seeing is having images in the mind, that seeing is, rather like photography, a complicated process whereby what we see gets produced.

And of course this approach then shapes the way cognitive scientists try to explain our experience of actual pictures. So, for example, Steven Pinker writes, as if it is self-evident: "Whatever assumptions impel the brain to see the world as the world and not as smeared pigment will impel it to see the *painting* as the world and not as smeared pigment." The thought here is simple: we see the world when we look at a picture for the same reason that we see the world when we look at *the world*. And what reason is that? When you look at the world, what you really see, what you are really given, is a retinal (or neural) *picture*. All seeing is an encounter with pictures. So whatever impels your brain to see the world when you are confronted with the retinal picture will impel your brain to see the world when you are confronted with an external picture. How do pictures work? When you see a picture—a picture of your grandmother, say—according to this view, you encounter an object that produces in you just the effect—the image, the experience—that a direct encounter with your grandmother would have produced. You experience Grandma when you see the picture because the picture gives rise to an internal image of Grandma. A picture is like an externalized retinal image; it is the trigger for an experience. (I am reviewing points here already taken up in chapter 10.)

Now, this is a ludicrously inadequate explanation of our experience of pictures. If Pinker and his colleagues were right, then seeing a picture of Grandma would be an experience of the same kind as the visual experience of Grandma herself. But the whole point is that the phenomenon of seeing in pictures is not like seeing what is depicted. Any account of what we see when we see Grandma in a picture that appeals to the fact that the picture produces *the same* effect in us that would be produced by Grandma is, well, a nonstarter.

If the psychologists are right, we lose a grip on what is distinctive about seeing pictures, namely, that pictures present things visually as manifestly absent. We also lose a grip on what is distinctive about seeing. Crucially, the world we see does not show up in our experience like a simple projected image of surfaces. We visually experience much more than projects to the eyes. For example, I don't see only the projective properties of your body, shape, form, color. I see *you*. You show up for me, a person, a personality. I experience your personhood, your manhood or womanhood, and so much more. Or consider my visual experience of a tomato. I see its surface, to be sure, but I also have a sense of its hidden parts, a sense of its 3-D fullness. Or consider my experience of the meaning of the text of the letter you've written me. The meaning isn't there on the page in such a way as to be projected onto my retina and reconstructed in the production centers of my visual system. And yet I perceive it visually in looking at the letter. One last example: I don't experience the room I'm in as a uniform expanse of detail from the center out to the periphery, as it might be represented on a page. What I see has everything to do with what I'm looking at, what I'm thinking about. I may spend an hour talking with you and never notice, never "see," what you are wearing. Merely striking my eyes and giving rise to events in my brain is not enough for something to show up for me in my experience.

What is noteworthy about all these phenomena—as I've argued elsewhere—is that your nature as a person, or as a man, say, the hidden parts of the solid opaque objects I see, the meaning of the words, all show up for me thanks not to what projects into my eyes but to what I know and what I can do. I have access to the detail in the room, to the other side of the tomato, to your personhood, to the meanings of your words, and the ground of my access is my knowledge, my know-how, my ability (for example) to read, my mastery of pertinent concepts.

The very idea that vision is an *optical* process, one that consists, as Pinker suggests, in the receipt of an image, is itself a kind of ur-myth that we've been telling and retelling even though it barely makes sense. Seeing is no more about having images in mind than touching is. Seeing you is just another way of encountering you. Seeing isn't something that happens in us. It is something we do. And like everything else we do, it depends on where we are, whom we're with, what we know, what we want, and what there is.

So how do we use and understand pictures? How do we see with them?

13

Using Models

We don't get far trying to understand pictures by treating them as stimuli-generating images or pictures in the head. These proposals fail to explain the curious and subtle way things show up for us in pictures. So let's take seriously the significance of the idea that seeing is not a matter of entertaining mental pictures and that seeing *pictures* is not a transaction with mental pictures. Let us ask, instead: What do we *do* when we see, and, in particular, how do we use pictures to achieve access to what they depict?

My proposal is that pictures are a special kind of model. And that a model is something we use to stand in for something else. A model is a proxy. I am not using the word "model" in a technical sense. We are familiar with architect's models (in balsa wood, say), model airplanes (in plastic), fashion models, and model apartments, not to mention scientific models and animal models in the biosciences. What all these have in common is that they are things we put to work in order to think about or investigate something else. The property agent uses the model apartment to inform you of the nature of the unit you'd actually buy or rent. The scientist's model provides a structure whose investigation will reveal, say, the behavior of molecules under certain conditions. The fashion model shows you how the clothes look when they are worn at their best, and the animal model in biomedical science is an actual animal, whose reaction to a medicine (say) is supposed to carry information about how a closely related species (human beings) would react to the medicine.

We aren't tempted to think that the work of the model is somehow psychological. We aren't tempted to suppose that the model gives rise in us to a representation identical to one in a direct encounter with the thing we are modeling. The clothes look better on the model than they would on me. And the tiny balsa wood model of the house looks in so many respects nothing at all like the house.

No, when it comes to models, it is clear that their effectiveness, their power to show us something, has to do with the way we make them and, critically, with the way we *use* them. We look at them, study them, think about them. And because of the way we look at them and make use of them, they can inform us about something else, the thing that actually interests us: *How does this work?*

We use the model house as a substitute for the actual house. And so the question we really need to ask is, Why do we use it as a substitute? And also, What justifies, or what licenses us, to make this substitution?

It's worth noting two important things about models. First, nothing is a model by virtue of its intrinsic makeup alone. The balsa wood house models the house the architect plans. But he or she might have made the very same construction to serve, instead, as the record of a house built years ago. And indeed the very same structure could be used to function not as a model at all, but as, say, a toy, like a dollhouse.

Second, something is useful as a model only relative to our particular interests or purposes. Watson and Crick's model enabled scientists to *just see* how the structure of the DNA molecule enabled a certain pattern of information storage and exchange during biological growth. And the balsa wood house is very useful in showing, say, the scale of the house and its various proportions. But it conveys nothing about materials and very little about landscaping and the like. The crucial point is that models are ways of exploring the world or accomplishing certain goals. We use the model to pose and answer questions. A model is useful, successful, accurate just insofar as it achieves a purpose.

Models can be hastily put together for immediate needs. In order to show you where I'd like us to meet later, I can set up a little model of the city using a few forks and knives and the salt and pepper shakers.

"This is the Washington Square Arch," I might say. "And this here is the construction site at Fourteenth and Fifth Avenue." And then I can show you, using this provisional model, exactly where I propose we meet.

What justifies our selection of a model is the particular needs and interests that motivate us in the first place. Maps are models, and we select maps at different scales depending on what we're trying to do. All sorts of factors may influence our assemblages for purposes of modeling and investigating. I may find it more natural, for example, to use a penny as my stand-in for the construction site, the knife as my model for Fifth Avenue, and the salt shaker as my stand-in for the Empire State Building. This model may be preferred because, in some vague and finally unprincipled way, I think of the avenue as long and thin, the construction site as squat and flat, and the Empire State Building as tall. But there is no reason, in principle, why I couldn't switch these elements around. And remember, I choose one element rather than another to be mapped in the first place only because of accidents of our circumstances. Suppose I know that you know where the Empire State Building is. And I know you know how to get from there to the arch at Washington Square. In that case, I can show you what I want to show, I can guide you to a place you've never been before, by including those two landmarks in the map.

We can appreciate, then, that a critical feature of models, whether in science or in tabletop conversations, is that they achieve their work only against the background of shared context.

In one sense, then, we see, models are utterly arbitrary. In another sense, they are not arbitrary at all, for they reflect precisely what we might call our epistemic or communicative predicament. But there is a further, critical sense in which models are anything but arbitrary. Once we've stipulated where the Empire State Building and the Washington Square Arch are in the model, it follows with absolute determinacy where the building site is. We can choose this scale or that, but once we have, things follow. Now it is possible for us to acquire and communicate new knowledge from a model. Once we set up the projection of the model into the modeled domain—and crucially, it is we who set this up, in light of our needs and interests—then things are out of our hands. And so a good model really does capture relations among its elements. Not that we are compelled to accept the deductive consequences of our models. In natural science, if our model predicts something that does not in fact occur in the relevant circumstances, then we have reason for thinking the model is wrong in some way. But even here, where we are in the business of revising models in light of investigation, we are guided by the logical force of the model. Once we set up the isomorphism between model and the world, we let the model take care of itself and let it see to what we should do next.

To summarize: a model is a substitute for what we are modeling. Models are tokens we think with. We can use a good model as a substitute and therefore as something we can regard *as* the thing that interests us.

•

Now back to my proposal about pictures: a picture is a special kind of model, what might be called a *visual* model. It is a model that we make for the sole purpose of showing the visible features of a scene, the way things look. That a picture can actually serve to model how someone or something looks depends, as with the architectural model, on our interests, on our concerns. For example, most pictures are very small; they do a very bad job of informing us how somebody would look with respect to size if we were to encounter him or her in the flesh. Also, most of the pictures that clutter our lives are at a resolution that is much lower than that of vision itself. They leave a lot out. We don't usually make the mistake, though, of thinking that this aspect of the picture captures a feature of what is depicted. Just as we assume the architect isn't proposing to build a house in balsa wood, so we don't assume that Hillary Clinton is tiny and has perfect skin. And yet we need to remember that it is precisely because the picture has the properties it does have that we find it useful. We wouldn't be able to buy it for cheap in the newspaper if it were of too high a resolution. And the fact that the picture is small allows us to study it, if we want, to come in close, much closer than decorum or custom would ever allow in relation to an actual person.

My point with these remarks is that we need to resist the misguided idea that the picture depicts by affecting us exactly as we would be affected by that which it depicts. If it did, then every picture would be an occasion for whole-scale delusion about what we are seeing, and it isn't.

My argument does not entail that the resemblance of the picture to what it depicts is arbitrary. It is no more arbitrary than is the resemblance of the tabletop model to the bit of the city that it depicts. There is a difference. What the tabletop model reproduces, what it replicates, is the spatial relations among several specific landmarks in the city. But what the photograph replicates, what it reproduces, is how Hillary Clinton looks (for example).

It is tempting to say here that the model can show how something looks because it stands in a special kind of projective relation to what it depicts. And this would be right. But crucially, we *think* the projection, but we don't find it. It is not a natural projection. We set it up. Again, just as with the tabletop model, it is because there is a projective relation between the salt shaker and the Empire State Building and between the penny and the building site that the model shows what it does.

•

We need to turn to an objection that will have been brewing and that must now be met head on. The striking thing about pictures, it will be objected, is that we just see them, get them, understand them, and we can do so without any special training, without any need to participate in communicative activities let alone in activities of making and using models. You know what Mom looks like, so you are able to recognize Mom in a photo, at least if the photo is any good. Seeing Mom in the photo is, really, just an exercise of your ability to see Mom, an ability you could exercise if she were standing right in front of you. This explains the special status of photographs as evidence. President Obama famously refused to make public the photographs taken by a Navy SEAL of the assassinated Osama bin Laden. Why were the photographs taken in the first place? Presumably to confirm that the right man had been killed. Our concerns here are with the man and the deed, not with pictures or models or visual appearances.

The objection, then, runs like this: you can see something in a picture just because, well, you can see. Pictures are immediate in the way they deliver their content. The model/substitute theory, it would seem, given this, overintellectualizes pictures and makes them seem like constructs in a scientific theory, something that requires special sophistication to make sense of.

Another way to put the objection is like this: you need to know the language to understand what someone says. The language is the key. And knowing the language requires learning, training, a background, etc. But not so pictures. You don't need to learn to see pictures to get a picture. There is no implicit language that must be learned. And the proof of this claim, so the objector will continue, is that even children and some animals can recognize what is shown in pictures. Monkeys, pigeons, and other animals can be shown to be sensitive to elements presented in a picture. Indeed, according to some studies, male monkeys show sexual arousal when shown pictures of female monkeys in heat. And famously, even a human child who had not been exposed to pictures in the first years of his or her life was able spontaneously to recognize animals in pictures.

Are pictures natural, then? If pictures work for animals, does it follow that the optical approach to pictoriality and vision itself that I've rejected is right after all? For surely if all it takes to see something in a picture is to be presented with a picture, then what better explains this outcome than the fact that the picture produces in one the very effect (neurologically, psychologically, optically) that would have been produced by the actual state of affairs represented in the picture?

•

For the sake of argument, let's accept the empirical claim that babies and animals are able spontaneously to see what pictures show them. (In fact, as we'll see in a moment, there is room for debate here.) Notice, first, that this claim isn't enough to establish that babies and animals are sensitive to pictures in the distinctive way that is characteristic and, I would say, defining, of the way an adult human enjoys pictures. The critical thing about pictorial presence, as we've noticed, is that it is, to use the philosopher Richard Wollheim's idea, *double fold*.

To appreciate this insight, consider, as we have already remarked, that pictures do not ordinarily deceive us. It is only in the most unusual circumstances that, when looking at a picture, we take ourselves actually to be in the presence of that which is shown in it. The crucial point is that the fact that we know perfectly well what we see in the picture isn't really there does not get in the way of our having a sense, when we look at a picture, of the presence of what it depicts. The distinctive thing about pictorial seeing is that it is a way of enjoying a visual sense of the presence of something that is manifestly, visibly, *not* present. Making sense of pictures requires understanding them as giving you an access of a visual kind to something that is not present. To be fooled by a picture is to be doubly fooled, for it is to think you are seeing something you are not seeing (whatever is depicted) and for you not to know that you are seeing a depiction, even though you are.

No animals or babies see pictures in the rich sense in which we are normally able to see pictures, as when we admire Grandma's picture in the photo album, or Junior's graduation yearbook picture, unless they are sensitive to this distinctive presence-in-absence structure in pictures. And there is no evidence that animals or babies are sensitive to pictures, are able to make sense of them, in this way. Some babies may get fooled by pictures, but this just shows that they don't experience the picture pictorially.

To be sensitive to this double-folded content structure requires that we keep in mind that a picture (this made thing here before us) is something we use or display or put forward in order to exhibit features of something, right here in the picture, that is not (or at least need not be) right here before us. Compare it with sarcasm. To appreciate a person's sarcasm is not just to understand his or her words, what they mean. It is not just to understand, in this sense, what is said. It is to understand what a person is doing (suggesting, implying, implicating, expressing) in using those particular words. And so with pictures. To get a picture is to understand that one is shown something that is not present.

Some infants reach into pictures when they look at them, as if to pick up the ice cream, or touch the lamb's fleece. It is crucial to appreciate that this action, although it is loaded with understanding and cognitive sophistication, falls short of the kind of understanding that gets put to work in our familiar life with pictures. This is a prepictorial, indeed, an infantile, form of engagement with pictures. I submit that this is the sort of understanding that is known to be exhibited by infants and animals. We could epitomize this by saying that for babies and monkeys, arousal is the only possible response to a picture.

•

My objector will not be dismayed, however. Granted, the objector will continue, a sophisticated understanding of pictures requires, in just the way I have been describing, a participation in a cognitive practice of making use of pictures to stand in for what they depict. But we are entitled nevertheless to isolate a more primitive responsiveness to pictures as fundamental. And here the point is that seeing something in a picture is a matter of a pure optical encounter with a visual appearance, one that does not seem to be learned or practice dependent in the way I have been urging.

Not so fast. Yes, but. For simplicity, consider statues. Do we recognize the life-size wax models at Madame Tussauds because they produce in us the same effects that the originals on which they are based would produce? Maybe so, but what explains this conclusion is the prior and more fundamental fact that the models exhibit the same qualities as (they look like) their originals. And what makes this the case is not that they give rise to a sensory response in us, but the fact that they are shaped and painted, they are modeled, to be copies (in respect of perceptual qualities) of their originals. What enables us to recognize the dummy is the fact that we know the original.

And so with pictures of the familiar two-dimensional variety. Unlike mathematical modeling, pictorial modeling has been developed, over thousands of years, precisely to exploit *our* skills—visual, cognitive, and otherwise. Just as a computer's operating system can seem user-friendly even though it is the result of massive technological innovation, so pictures can seem immediate, even though they are an evolved instrument of modeling. Pictures are *user-friendly*. This, however, doesn't make them more natural than a good operating system.

And it is really not so surprising that if we find them user-friendly, other creatures with similar visual systems will, too. Pictures, like scarecrows, can produce effects across species without in any way undercutting the fact that they are bits of technology. The pictures were made for us, and for creatures like us.

Crucially, it is one thing to recognize what a picture shows, and it is another to have an experience of the distinctive presence of something in a picture. We can try to bring all this together by returning to our earlier formula: a picture is a tool for showing. To understand a picture, then, to see it with understanding, is to understand what it is being used to communicate. And once again we are forced back to the idea that *this* understanding is possible only for one who is alert to the communicative context.

The final test of my proposal is that, if I am right, it follows that a picture can be robbed of its content, can be blanked out and made unshowing, by obscuring its natural context. And this is indeed exactly what we find. Pictures have a rhetoric, that is to say, they have a story to tell, and if you are not savvy to the picture's rhetoric, you won't be able to see what the picture shows. The best example I know of comes from my own experience. My son—he must have been six at the time—was unable to recognize me in a picture, not because I was concealed or blurred, but precisely because he couldn't tell, roughly, what the picture was trying to do. It was a picture in which I was caught in a reflection. It was unclear to him what the situation was, why the picture was taken, what, if you like, the picture's caption might be. And this also explains the well-known fact that it is difficult to recognize faces in pictures when they are upside down, or in general when viewpoints are unexpected or nongeneric.

To sum up, the conception of pictures as models can explain why animals and infants might recognize what is depicted in a picture even as it also explains why a sensitivity to what pictures show—in contrast to a cruder sensitivity to what is pictorially but not really there—requires a sensitivity to rhetoric and background.

I think at least part of the reason that pictures have a rhetoric goes unnoticed is the simple fact that it is taken for granted (in much the way we take the background for granted against which the utility of a door handle presents itself to us). You are not puzzled by the array of pictures of family and friends on the wall of your friend's home as you might be, say, by the distinctive arrangement of imagery at a religious shrine. Roughly speaking, we understand *why* those pictures adorn the wall. They are expressions of pride and love, displays of filial connection and a desire to acknowledge and honor one's loved ones. And so for the images that crowd our newspapers and books and websites. For most pictures, most of the time, we ourselves could effortlessly write the caption. And of course so much of the time pictures come captioned and the caption provides the context that is needed to bring the image into focus.

•

There is a scene in Douglas Gordon and Philippe Parreno's film *Zidane* in which the soccer star's actions are impossible to make sense of in the game, not because they are blurry or out of focus, but because the filmmakers have managed to deprive the action on the soccer field of the narrative flow that ordinarily allows us to follow what's going on. Televised soccer usually contains carefully composed scenes from as many as twenty-five or thirty camera feeds. Gordon and Parreno, who are artists, not documentarians, took a different approach. They kept their seventeen cameras fixed on Zidane himself, from start to finish. As a result, although we see the man, we can never tell what he is doing. A glimpse of him in action but out of context in this way is the experiential equivalent of a blurred image. The film's subtitle is *A 21st Century Portrait*. The work this film does is precisely to investigate, question, and rethink what a portrait is, could be, or, for that matter, ever was. It achieves this end by removing the rhetorical setting and context that alone make conventional portraiture possible. This example provides our first hint as to what makes some pictures, in some settings, not really pictures (or portraits) at all, but rather, works of art.

14

Pictorial Strategies

Pictorial presence is not something that happens in the mind or brain. We achieve it, collectively, in our picture-making and picture-deploying practices. The idea that pictures are in this way technologies of presence has important implications.

If pictures are things we use, for different purposes, then we would expect there to be fundamentally different *kinds* of pictures, corresponding to the different sorts of uses to which we put them.

We have already seen that this is so. I've described pictures as a special kind of model. But I might just as well have said that models are a special kind of picture. In some languages the word for picture applies not only to 2-D pictures but sculptures as well. A 3-D model of a house by an architect need not be a visual model, in the way that a photograph of Hillary Clinton is. That may not be why we made it and that's not what we use it for. The architect's blueprints are also pictures (we call them diagrams); they model the building for purposes other than displaying its look. These are pictures, but not *visual* pictures.

A fascinating case is the medieval Christian icon. Byzantine Christians venerated icons but not necessarily because they believed that there was a magical connection between the icon and the saint depicted; nor are they likely to have believed that Jesus and Mary really looked the way they were presented in the icons. For one thing, the icons are not very lifelike. They are cartoonish in a way, for all that they are earnest. For another, different icons present one and the same saint, in certain respects, at least, very differently.

A Byzantine icon is not a picture in the sense that it is not a visual model, that is, it is not a construction that is meant to go proxy for something by displaying its visual appearance. An icon is not a likeness in the way that, say, a police artist's sketch aims at likeness. In another sense, however, we may say, and I gather seventh-century Christians would have said, icons do give a likeness. And we can be precise about what this likeness comes to: it is usually possible to tell, *by looking*, whom the icon presents. Figures are displayed in icons as conforming to a very precise set of visible criteria. We can use vision to identify them because we know the visual features that belong to their identity as defined in the tradition. In the same way, you can recognize a person as regal, even though there is no one look that all kings have, and in the same way you can tell, by looking, which piece is the knight in chess. A Byzantine icon is a depiction of a likeness in this sense. It is a picture in this sense. Not a visual model of a person, but rather an exemplification of essential properties of the concept of a person. It is, if you like, the visible articulation of the thought of the person.

This iconic conception of what a person is is not foreign to our modern sensibility, at least not entirely. For example: Don Giovanni and his manservant Leporello do not look alike. In Mozart's opera, however, merely switching clothing is enough to get Don Giovanni's enemies—his former lovers!—to chase Leporello. From a certain perspective, this is psychologically ridiculous. But we might say, instead, that within the narrative scheme of the opera, people are thought of not so much as people but as icons, as exemplifications of essential features, and this is marked in their uniforms or dress.

Back to Christian icons. An icon's significance is not exhausted by its exemplification in this way. For iconophiles, it was critical that the picture serve as a substitute for its original and, therefore, that it be licensed, by practice and tradition, to play this role. In *this* respect, then, icons are like what I have been calling visual pictures: they are a special kind of substitute. But where they differ is precisely in the relevant rules governing or legitimizing substitution. For *visual* pictures, what authorizes us to use the picture is the conviction that it models the physical appearance. For the icon worshippers there was, it seems, a twofold demand. First, it was required that the picture conform to a conventionalized way of exemplifying the qualities proper to Jesus or St. Jerome or whomever. Second, it was required that the icon be a copy of a legitimate existing icon and, in this way, one of a long line of copies, each of which has a role to play in religious worship. It seems also to have been required that this chain of copying originated in the act of painting the saint himself or herself. But what we need to remember is that the point of such an original act of painting would not have been to capture the visage in the way a mug shot tries to do, but rather to capture the essence in the way that a verbal description might attempt. Icons are revered because they participate, effectively, in a practice of standing in for one whom we revere. And they do this despite the fact that they may not "look like" that individual.

The Byzantine theory is a deep theory of the picture and one that comes much closer, in some ways, to exhibiting the essential nature of pictures—that they are substitutes we make for our own purposes and that they acquire their significance because of their place in a practice—than the modern idea of representation based on optics and perspective. It is superior to the modern view precisely because it is able to avoid our basic mistake: namely, psychologizing the picture, treating it merely as a stimulus for a reaction in the viewer's mind (or visual system or brain). For the Byzantine theory, what matters is not what pictures do to us, but what we do with pictures. (Or rather, the Byzantine theory gives us a whole new, clearer account of what it might mean to say that the pictures act on us.)

We can discern a similar distinction in basic styles of picture making in modern portraiture. For example, early modern portraits such as Lucas Cranach the Elder's famous renderings of Martin Luther are striking for their masklike wooden quality. In some sense they perfectly capture the visual appearance, the visage of the man, but they do so in a way that seems entirely external. They are like molds, or paintings of masks. The person is displayed, but not, so to speak, the inner man. Not the man himself. In one famous painting of Martin Luther, the religious thinker is shown holding a book open to the viewer, as if, by letting you see the words on the pages, you gain some insight into what he might have been thinking, as to what kind of man he might be. This was presumably a great innovation, a new kind of stagecraft! Is it that Cranach lacked the skill to show only the man, to exhibit his feelings and attitudes in the manner of his appearance?

Perhaps. But the view developed here gives us the resources to offer a very different sort of answer. Cranach wasn't making pictures of the man. Indeed, these are not portraits of the man at all, in this sense. Rather, they are exhibitions of the *person*, and the person is, according to a long tradition of thought, not the man. A person is a role that a man plays, much as an actor plays a role (much as Don Giovanni can be thought of as the one wearing the red cloak). Father, priest, theologian, founder of a new religion—these are roles a man can play. Cranach aimed at the person, in this sense, not at the man. And so it is as if he aimed at painting the knight, rather than this or that piece of wood carved this or that way standing on the chessboard. Later painters took a different interest: not so much in persons but in people, not in the roles we play but in the players of roles. However much greater Rembrandt may have been than Cranach, what marks his portraits as different is not a difference in degree of likeness but, fundamentally, in mission. Rembrandt and Cranach were not in the same business; they made different kinds of pictures.

•

We are now finally in a position to say something more general about pictures as art and also to address an important objection that will have arisen to my entire project.

There are different kinds of pictures. In this chapter I've discussed different kinds of portraits, and I've contrasted pictures as visual models with pictures as icons. There are also diagrams, sketches, cartoons, caricatures. The genus of all these species is *pictures as a technology for showing*. And it turns out that all these technologies function, in different ways, thanks to the principle of substitution. We use the picture as a representative of what it depicts—as a stand-in or proxy. And what explains the differences in the species of picture are the different rules, practices, conventions, interests that license or govern substitution. We substitute for different purposes and in different ways in different settings (and at different times and places). The criteria governing treating the icon of a saint *as* the saint are radically different from those governing the making use of a police artist's sketch to find out what an unknown perpetrator looks like. What licenses us to deploy a picture as a stand-in for its original depends on many factors that are as complex and multilayered as our lives and culture. This is

the stuff of anthropology. We are all agents in a picture-based economy, and to understand the pictures in our lives we need to undertake research into this economics.

Painting as an art (and drawing, etc.) aims at just this. Artists
don't make pictures (depictions) simply to take part in the preexisting
pictorial economy in which we are embedded. The catalog designer
aims at showing you the coat he or she hopes you will buy. The ico-
nographer participates in a ritual practice of copying in order to secure, for you, a legitimate object of veneration. The photographer
documents the events on the field of play. But the artist is never in
the business of doing any of those things. There's no art in that. The
work of art happens precisely when that economy, that function, that
rhetoric, that invisibly familiar practice, is disrupted. This can take
many different forms. Perhaps, as in the case of the contemporary
artist Robert Lazzarini, the objective is to put your perceptual and
emotional habits and values on display. Perhaps, as with Andy Warhol,
it is the very idea of what a portrait is, or what celebrity is, or what it is
to be original that is put on display. Maybe, as in the case of Johannes
Vermeer, it is the idea that it might be possible, in a painting, to exhibit
the interior life of a family or, perhaps, to conceal that life while recording it, that is where the action is. Or maybe, as with David Hockney, it is the artist's cascading manic impulse to sketch and doodle
and draw that itself is put on exhibition. When it comes to pictures
that are also works of art, only one thing is clear: you can't tell just by
looking. The work of art isn't visible to first inspection. It requires
interrogation. Returning to our slogan, the artwork says: *See me if you
can!* And it gives you the resources you need to try.

Contrast seeing a painting by an artist with looking at an adver-
tisement. The latter is successful when you don't need to ask what it
shows. The former is successful when you have to ask what it shows or
have to wonder even whether it is trying to show you anything at all.

Of course, these boundaries collapse, too. Clever ad people might
make a picture you can't understand in order to capture your interest
and get you to pay attention to a product it displays. As we have discussed in chapter 4, it is characteristic of art (a level-2 practice) that it
loops back and exerts an influence on the very activities (level 1) it
seeks to understand.

If it is true, then, that pictures organize our lives by shaping a communicative landscape in which we are wanderers, then pictorial artists provide us a way to bring this basic fact about our nature into focus. And this is the form of research that is proprietary to both philosophy and art.

A crucial caveat. Don't misunderstand me. I am interested in the work *the art itself* achieves. I'm not interested in the artist's self-understanding. Maybe all the great nineteenth-century German painter Adolph Menzel ever tried to do was make a good illustration of his subject. Maybe he took himself unreflectively to be in the picture-making business, like a good advertiser. And there can be no doubt that, whatever else he achieved, he did make pictures that served to display, for example, the activity on the factory floor, or on the battlefield. The point is that *if* his paintings are works of art, they are not just illustrations in the business of showing you this or that. And in fact it is the case that when it comes to many of his most interesting pictures, it is almost impossible to state clearly what they show you and this is because, really, before they show you anything, or in showing you something, they force you up against the limits of what is showable. As the art historian and theorist Michael Fried convincingly argues, Menzel, in his paintings of the 1840s, gives you artworks that appear to do one thing—show you a scene—but actually end up displaying something else—what it would be like to be present in the scene, alive, embodied, exploring. They give you not what would be seen, but what the seeing would be like. They are, in this sense, depictions of the visual field itself. These "pictures" are studies of embodied consciousness rather than documents of this or that. They are works of art.

15

Air Guitar Styles

"Pink Cadillac" is a lovely piece of writing about Hank Williams by the critic Dave Hickey. It takes the form of a letter from beyond the grave by the country music legend himself. Hickey gives us a vibrant sense of the artist and his art. It is striking that he manages to do this without any discussion of music. Melody, harmony, timbre, lyrics, innovation in the expression of musical ideas—all this goes unmentioned. The focus is the life of Hank Williams, or a kind of fantasy of that life. Drugs, sex, depression, life on the road.

It is an important fact about pop music—I'll use this term for a whole gamut of musical forms: rock, rhythm and blues, soul, hip-hop, top forty, reggae, but, importantly, not jazz, folk, or the music of the Broadway musical—that you can engage with it, in a serious way, without engaging with it *as music*. Indeed, to engage with pop music as music is, almost always, to fail to engage with it at all.

People don't crowd into packed arenas to *listen*, the way they do when they take their seats in the traditional concert hall. Ask fans of Bruce Springsteen, Tupac Shakur, Elvis Presley, Pearl Jam, the Rolling Stones, or Beyoncé what makes a concert experience memorable. They won't talk about music. They'll tell about the excitement, the thrill, the person or people on the stage, his or her sex appeal, how it felt to be there, in the presence of greatness, part of a crowd, a sense of connection to the star or to the audience. They'll recount how they danced and screamed. They might talk about the loudness and the light show. Maybe they got to touch her! Maybe they caught one of his guitar picks! They may mention which songs were played and how *they* felt. What matters is the event, and what makes the event special is not that it is an opportunity for careful listening. It is an opportunity of an altogether different kind.

It is tempting to denigrate rock and roll, or pop, for this reason. After all, it isn't "serious" music. The philosopher Roger Scruton, who has given a lot of thought to these issues, makes just this kind of move. He notices that fans idolize Kurt Cobain, but they don't, in a sense, listen to him. He might have added that there is as a matter of fact little in the music that would repay close listening. From Scruton's standpoint, Nirvana is a cult of personality and a Nirvana concert simply an excuse for excess and abandon. In place of rhythm there is only pulse, and in place of voicings there is only Cobain's cry and the dull pounding of "power" chords. Scruton sees in Nirvana, and the rise of rock and roll more widely, a breakdown not only in musical but also in the broader culture. In place of a community of music makers and listeners skillfully bending their ears and their minds to articulate musical gesture, there is only an unrestrained giving in to immediate gratification and primitive, untutored impulse.

Scruton gets it wrong, I would say, but maybe not because he underestimates the *musical* significance of Nirvana. He is almost right. He is right that, with Nirvana, it's not about the music; it's about Cobain, or the character Cobain manifests through song. And he would be right to think that Nirvana's music, in a sense at least, does not invite, and maybe does not even repay, close listening. You don't need to pay attention to *music* to get it. The sources of its significance are elsewhere.

But what Scruton doesn't consider is the possibility that that's the point. To criticize Nirvana or any pop act for this failure is like criticizing the Impressionists for failing to offer sharper, more delineated renderings of their subjects. That wasn't what these painters were interested in. And so with Nirvana—or Lou Reed, or David Bowie, or David Byrne, or Jay Z, or the Rolling Stones, or Chuck Berry. These artists aren't in the close-listening business.

It is a commonplace that you don't need a "good voice," technical virtuosity, or formal training to make a mark in the world of pop. But it is a mistake to conclude that this is because pop music is easy to play or undemanding. If this were so, then you'd expect musicians

with "serious" training and "good voices" to do it better. But that's
precisely not the case. Almost every singer in the world has a better
voice than Bob Dylan. But who sings better than Bob Dylan? Your
average studio musician may play better than the star member of a rock
band, but we're not interested in the studio musician. And when classically trained musicians turn their attention to pop music—you know,
opera singers doing Simon and Garfunkel or the Beatles, pianists
doing Neil Young—the results are, at best, no longer pop music—that
is, they lose their pop zing and relevance. When you distill the music
out of the pop you lose the value. At worst, these forays into the
world of pop are cringingly embarrassing. These talented musicians,
like Scruton—who is a classically trained musician and composer as
well as a philosopher—don't get it. It isn't about the music. It's about
something else.

What is it about?

•

Pythagoras is said to have lectured behind a screen so his followers,
known as the *akousmatikoi*, were made to attend not to *him* but to his
words. This "acousmatic ideal" (hearing without seeing) has shaped
attitudes to music in recent centuries. Music, according to this principle, offers a soundscape that is detached from its makers. Musicians
are implicated only as remote causes of the sound product that is the
real concern, namely, music and its forms and meanings. This is why
the orchestra sits out of view, sunk in its pit.

Recording technology adds fuel to this acousmatic fire. In an age
where most people know music not by way of an encounter with live
performance but by downloading, live-streaming, or turning on the
radio, or putting on a CD, the idea that to listen to music is to pay
attention to a performer seems quaint and untrue. Recorded music, it
is thought, reveals music for what it is, something that peels away from
the instruments needed to realize it. This idea finds expression in the
image of the audiophile perched in a chair at the acoustic optimum
in his or her living room, manipulating sound equipment to produce
the ultimate sonic situation. The music happens with eyes closed, in
your own head.

From this standpoint, electronic music—music coded on a laptop rather than plucked, thrummed, pounded, strummed, blown, hollered out, or sung—is the truest expression of what music is. Music is acoustic, or acousmatic; that is to say, as I am using the term here, it is *music*. And musical creativity consists in the creation of structures in a field of sound; musical understanding is knowing your way around these impersonal structures.

But there is a different musical ideal that is, as a matter of fact, no less influential in our culture. It is lively and important, although it is never really made explicit; it bears no name. According to this different ideal, the artist is not a vehicle for music; instead, the music is a vehicle for the artist. Music, accordingly, is a mechanism for the artist's display of himself or herself.

And *that* is the essence of pop music. You don't need virtuosity to be a pop musician. What you need is personality. And when we love pop music, what we love, really, truly, is not so much the music; rather, we love the one, the star, there in the spotlight. Lou Reed, Bob Dylan, David Bowie, John Lennon—*they* are the object of your fancy when you love their music. For their music, their art, is *them*, or some idea of themselves, put on display. Pop music is exhibition. It is demonstration. It is music, sure, but really it is *spectacle*, something for you to take in with your eyes. You don't so much listen to pop music as you witness it. You don't participate in the performance; you are, rather, its accomplice. You are part of the club, the *fan* club.

We have already noticed that from the standpoint of the acousmatic ideal, pop music can seem, well, *bad*; musically speaking it may be simple-minded and unsophisticated, clichéd and predigested. Take Bob Dylan: his songs are conventional, they embody folky, bluesy clichés; his voice is scratchy. Or the Rolling Stones: even when they are at their best, they are sloppy and chaotic, as if vaguely out of tune and out of sync.

And yet: Bob Dylan and the Rolling Stones are artists; their work shines. Captivating, enthralling, distinctive, and inimitable. But musically—harmonically, rhythmically, melodically, structurally— the work is simple. How can this be?

Music doesn't do the heavy lifting here because this is not, in the relevant sense, a musical art.

A comparison with recent art history can help sharpen the idea.

From the standpoint of visual art that is rooted in a craft practice—think Cézanne, Matisse, Picasso—the work of many contemporary artists—think Sol LeWitt, Bruce Nauman, Jenny Holzer, Barbara Kruger, Chris Burden—can seem, well, *devoid* of art. Not merely devoid of skillfulness, or virtuosity, but devoid of anything lyrical or articulate or beautiful. If these *are* artists—I take it for granted that they are—then they are working with different means. They look like *visual* artists in the way that Gustav Courbet and Rembrandt are visual artists, but they are not.

And so with pop music. It looks like music, but it isn't.

When it comes to art, the question we need to ask is: In what does the *work* of art consist? Or better: Where is the work happening? When it comes to artists like LeWitt, the art is not in the specific gesture, or the hand, or the look, or the individual object; it is, finally, in something like the conception. When it comes to pop artists like Mick Jagger and Keith Richards, Jay Z, or David Bryne, the work is not in the music; it is located somewhere else.

Pop music isn't directed to music. The artist himself stands large and demands that you pay attention to *him*. The music is, at most, a way of directing your attention to him; *he* captures your attention and your fascination. His music is like his words. You look through the music to the person, or to an artistic model of the person. It's not the *what* of sound but the *what* of action and personality that interests us when we are engaged with pop music. Or, to give a different image: when it comes to pop music, the artist stands between us and anything musical. And he does this *on purpose*.

This basic fact—that pop music is about the man or woman, the group, not the music—sheds light. From this standpoint we can appreciate that it is no accident that pop music is the music of fandom and the cult of personality, or that it is now unthinkable that there could be pop music without the music video. It is in the attention to style and attitude and posture and politics that the art of pop happens. Pop stars are sex symbols, and when we love them, we want in some sense to be like them, or at least to be with them, to have them, to belong to their tribe. Pop music is always tribal. And that's why it is also always generational. Pop music is directly concerned with identification and with why we want to identify with something new or different, or with something old that is new again, or something new that is really old.

Air guitar is the truest expression of pop musical appreciation. When we play air guitar, we don't ape the music, we ape the player. We identify with the player, and with the playing—with the display rather than the production. Pop music is always about the player.

We can also appreciate why pop music is time-bound and an occasion for nostalgia in a way that music (in the other, acousmatic sense) never is. Hearing a pop tune can take you back to a summer, or an evening, or an emotional state. Hearing a Beethoven piano sonata doesn't have that kind of effect, or if it does, that is incidental to the music's significance. This is because a pop song, but not a work of music, is precisely a positioning in a space of stylistic possibilities that is temporally and culturally local. To get the song is to get its position in that space, and to identify with it or imaginatively take it up. Pop music, even the best and most enduring, dates itself, not just in the sense that you can read off its date, but in the sense that pop music directly engages sounds, looks, attitudes that are specific to a time and place.

And it does this in fantastically subtle ways. When Robert Zimmerman, a Jew from Minnesota, changes his name to Bob Dylan and adopts the musical quality of traditional American folk music, he's giving more than a few nudges, winks, and nods about himself, music, the culture, his culture, and probably much more. By treating traditional forms as a vehicle for storytelling of a personal, contemporary, and untraditional sort, Dylan drives your attention away from mere music and forces you to think about what it is that he is doing anyway. This is a quintessential art moment. But it is one in which music takes a backseat to attitude, posture, identity, and public image.

The Rolling Stones engaged in a very similar kind of culture and personal play in their wholesale adoption of sounds and styles of the blues and also soul and rhythm and blues and later disco and other forms of music that were invented by African Americans. The Rolling Stones are not inauthentic, no more than Bob Dylan. The very term "authenticity" doesn't even apply. The whole question of what it would be to be authentic is their subject matter, in matters musical, but also sexual and in other domains such as drink and drugs.

But this isn't new. This sort of identity play, with its layers of re-sistance, contrast, lust, and rejection, is already at work in the black artists who inspired the Stones. Robert Johnson, the famed King of the Delta Blues, was dead at the age of twenty-seven. He was any-thing but the King of the Delta Blues, even though he was from the Mississippi Delta. If you listen to Robert Johnson's surviving record-ings you hear a man flawlessly playing blues in a whole range of different styles. The minor-keyed moaning of Bentonia, Mississippi, on one track ("Devil Got My Woman"), while other tracks are straight Clarks-dale, Mississippi, or in the blues styles of Florida, Texas, or the Virgin-ias, as well as more urban-sounding music. Johnson came up in the jukebox era, so he was not confined in his musical experience to a single vernacular style. He played with style itself, mastering it in all its varieties and putting them all on display. And more than anything else, putting himself, or an idea of himself—*made a deal with the devil down at the crossroads, sold his soul to find his genius*—at the center. To listen to Robert Johnson's music is to listen to *him*, just as was the case with Jimi Hendrix and Kurt Cobain, to name two other artists who also died at the age of twenty-seven.

Professional musicians may express contempt for the idea that you need to be black to play the blues or, even more absurdly, that there is something to the crossroads myth about Robert Johnson. It's hard not to be sensitive to the proximity of something like racist thinking in the vicinity.

But the scruples of these musicians wanting to preserve Johnson's honor, and to do so on *musical* grounds, sort of miss the point. Not to deny that he did make distinctively musical contributions. Johnson managed to make it sound like there was more than one guitar play-ing. But even this celebration of his virtuosity starts to sound like the celebration of *him* rather than the music itself. "He's so amazing! The King of the Delta Blues!" The point is that Johnson was a virtuoso inventor of himself and brilliant manipulator of *preexisting* folk styles. Johnson was a *pop* musician. You can't play his music. Or rather, you can, but there's no more than historical interest in playing it the way he played it. *That's* not something you could say of Beethoven. A good Beethoven show is of more than historical interest. Robert Johnson's performances are distinct, dateable, specific, individual stylistic com-mentaries and interventions.

This quality helps us better understand the distinct pop world phenomenon that is *the cover*. Orchestras don't *cover* Beethoven when they perform his music. It's about the music, always, and never about the man. The same is true of blues and folk music. When Jack Owens plays Skip James, he's playing their shared music; he's carrying on in their lineage. The music is in charge, not the personalities. And this is why when the Rolling Stones play "Mannish Boy," they aren't covering Muddy Waters (even if they gave him songwriting credit).

But when Patti Smith plays Bob Dylan ("Changing of the Guards"), or Heart performs "Stairway to Heaven," or David Bowie sings the Pixies ("Cactus"), these are comments on Dylan, Led Zeppelin, and the Pixies respectively, they are elucidations or assertions of where Patti Smith, Heart, and David Bowie stand in relation to these other *stars*, to these other shared cultural landmarks. Again, this is decidedly not what's going on when the jazz pianist Brad Mehldau plays Radiohead. Mehldau is oriented to the music. Radiohead is transparent. Indeed, it is a striking fact about Radiohead that they occupy a sort of in-between place, a position in the world of pop while at the same time consistently concealing themselves behind their music, creating music that commands attention and fascination *as* music. And there are other cases in between. When Sinéad O'Connor sings "Nothing Compares 2 U," it is possible to forget that she is covering Prince; the same is true when Generation X sings John Lennon. But these are covers, that is, these are samplings not of the original songs but of the attitude, understanding, outrageousness, and punk spirit of the original artists.

•

I've been advancing the idea that pop music isn't primarily music. It's an art of display. In particular, as we have begun to appreciate, pop music is the art of personal *style*.

Let me explain.

Everything a person does is marked by his or her distinctive style. You can tell an artist by his makings and identify a person by her signature. As for individuals, so for communities and even epochs. A person who knows can look at a picture and tell when it was painted, and where, even when he or she can't say for sure, or has no direct or specific knowledge about, who made it.

Style makes imitation possible—it gives you something to imitate—but it also makes forgery possible. For just as everything we make is inflected by our ways of making, ways that we learn just as we learn to dress and to walk and to speak, so the way we *see* things is informed by our sensitivity to style. Almost anything goes in the realm of dress and fashion. Despite that, it is easy to spot someone wearing the clothes of a different era. But just as style is directly perceptible, just as we can see it, so it also constrains us and limits what we can see. It is difficult to tell a forgery, not because there is no difference between the forgery and the original but because the forgery is made to match our current time-bound preconception of the original. Forgeries, it turns out, have a short life span. As the art critic Peter Schjeldahl remarks, they are best served up hot. They are made for *us, now*. Twenty years or so after a forgery is made, it is usually obvious that it is a forgery. Why? Because we no longer take for granted what we and the forger had both taken for granted, and so the distinctive stylistic hallmarks of the forger's own time now jump out for us. Take a look at *Butch Cassidy and the Sundance Kid*. At the time of its release, in 1969, this was a period Western. You can't look at it today without noticing the 1960s cut of clothes, hair, and even language. Interestingly, this is not true when we watch John Ford's great Westerns of the 1930s and '40s (for example *Stagecoach*). And this is not because these are better. I suspect what explains this difference is the fact that Ford's Westerns are *our* original when it comes to thinking about the Wild West. For us they smack of the real, or the authentic, as if we were traveling back in time. Go back farther to Buster Keaton's equally great films and you are once again struck that the hairdos are wrong. For a different sort of example, revisit Ridley Scott's masterpiece *Blade Runner*. The story is set in an indeterminate distant future. The movie is striking for its manifest futurism, and yet when we see it now we can't help noticing all the 1970s haircuts and jacket geometries that were imperceptible when the movie was made (and that would have stood out like a sore thumb, calling attention to themselves, had they not been like that!).

There is no seeing outside of style; style enables and disables our seeing. This effect operates at many levels. Since everything we do is inflected with style, and since style is always contrasted with other

styles, there is a sense in which our lives are comparative and historical through and through. I don't mean only that styles change so that
the ways we live have histories. I mean, further, that our histories are
noteworthy and questionable for us. Every new style is noticeably an
amendment to, a sampling of, or a quotation of a past style. To be
interested in the latest styles in clothing is, at the same time, to be
sensitive to the ways they differ from what was in the mode last sea-
son. At some point, though, our fluency with this progression of styles
breaks down. Maybe you can recognize 1980s style, or '70s, or '60s, and
even the '50s. But at some point, unless you are an expert, everything
blurs into "old-fashioned." For a child there is no way of telling apart
Shakespearean dress from that of the eighteenth century. They both
just look *old*. But our sensitivities also break down when we are very
near at hand. Can any of us say how the style of the first decade of the
twenty-first century differs from that of the '90s? Or indeed from our
own decade?

My reason for this digression into style is that I want, first, to note
that art is always preoccupied with style. Painters (for example) borrow,
copy, sample, and innovate off of each other, and so, in this sense,
style—the *way* a line is made, understood against the background of
all the ways we know it has been made before—is the very subject
matter of the artist's investigation.

But I also want to propose that pop music is an *art of style* in a
more direct way. Painters investigate style *as it finds expression in the
language of picture making*, we might say. And musicians—acousmatic
musicians—are students of style in the domain of song and melody
and the like. Pop musicians, in contrast, are interested not in a distinctively musical style, but in fashion, in style as a personal and so
also as a collective and a generational marker. Pop music, we might
say, is the art of fashion. And if fashion—I mean clothing design,
etc.—is itself an art, then I suppose we could say that pop music is a
form of fashion art.

This is why if you want to understand the music of Hank Williams, if you want to celebrate it, you turn your attention not to the
music but to the man himself and to the personality he offered the
world through his music. Pop music is the art of pure personal style.

Now, of course every art form has to deal with style. Painting, sculpture, installation art, performance—all position themselves in a space of style; they respond to what others have done and what is expected, or what is taken for granted as tasteful. Art plays with style.

But pop music is concerned with personal style in a more direct way. This is why, when it comes to pop music, music is political. We sort tribes by their music. The hippies, the punks, the jocks, the mods, the rockers, etc. Black music, white music. These differences matter.

●

It will be helpful to frame the present point in relation to the idea of the two levels that are at the heart my argument. Pop music takes as its level-1 materials the ways our lives are organized habitually, in ways that can be marked out as stylistic. How you wear your hair, how you walk, the slang you use, the music you dance to, the stuff you find cool (or dope or whatever).

Because style is an abiding and defining facet of our perceptual and cognitive lives, pop music's concern with style should not be construed as superficial or trite. Indeed, we can bring this distinction out by noticing that there is, to my way of thinking, a tight connection between the very concept of a person and the concept of style. In its original, etymological meaning, a person is a mask; from there this word ("person") acquired the meaning of a role, as in, the role played in a drama by an actor who wears a mask (as in "dramatis personae"). The face of a person is a mask, and the person, in truth, is a role, not the one who plays the role. This idea connects to other crucial ideas.

First, John Locke argued that person is a "forensic" concept. By this he meant that a person is, in its basic conception, the bearer of responsibility, the actor, the one deserving of praise or blame. For Locke the point was that a person is not the biological animal—the man or woman—but rather the agent. Again, as with the idea of person as role rather than player, we have the idea that personhood is something social, something performed, something undertaken. Something defined, crucially, in relation to praise, blame, and evaluation. So persons are citizens, they are fathers and mothers, they are employers and employees, they are baseball players and philosophers.

They *are* these things. That is, these are the roles we play, better or worse, successfully or unsuccessfully, in our social lives. We are persons insofar as we are subject, always and implicitly, to the standards of our community.

Personhood is performed, I said above. This brings me to the second linked idea: that of performance. In one sense, "to perform" is simply the most general verb of action. We perform actions in the course of our lives. But it is also possible to distinguish between things we simply do and the actions that, in doing, we perform. It is a difficult exercise to figure out just what principle marks that line, but it has something to do with the fact that when we perform, as distinct merely from acting, we act in view of the evaluation or standards or rules and norms of others. We speak of sexual performance, performance on the job, athletic performance, performance at school, and, of course, performance on the stage. Whether you are actually subject to the evaluation of another—maybe you are practicing handstands in your room or making drawings for your eyes only—you are still performing, for what you do is open to the possible, if not the actual, assessment of others. And crucially, that's how we experience it, too. The fact that you are alone rarely ever means you are truly alone, for almost everything we do is framed by the roles we are playing and the standards to which we are subject. Can you think of exceptions?

Turning to art, we can now appreciate why it is that performance is, as in some sense it is, the most fundamental of all the arts. The performing artist makes these facts about our lives raw material for his or her own practice. We are fundamentally performers. Not as a matter of choice, and not as a matter of biology, but as an inescapable condition of being a person. A performing artist is one who places himself or herself on the stage and says, "Watch me do what I do," all the while knowing that you are watching him or her do it.

Pop music is a species of performance art, if I am right. And its central preoccupation, as I have already said, is with distinctively personal style. This explains the endurance of pop music despite its seeming preoccupation with the trivial and also the relative absence of inventive or skillful engagement with musical ideas.

•

Now, the view I am defending here—that pop music is an art of personal style, that with pop, the music is a vehicle for work done in a different medium, the medium of style—faces a serious, even daunting objection.

Surely, whatever we say about pop music and style or fashion or personality or display, the fact of the matter is that pop music is, plainly, a kind of music. It is preposterous to say that the musical qualities of Bowie's "Space Oddity," George Harrison's "While My Guitar Gently Weeps," and Otis Redding's "Try a Little Tenderness" are not a crucial part of what we love when we love these songs!

This is a worthy objection.

I respond in two ways.

First, I do not want to deny that pop music is a species of music any more than I would want to deny that Barnett Newman, Al Held, Ad Reinhardt, and Andy Warhol are visual artists. But if we think of traditional visual art, namely, painting, as concerned fundamentally with depiction—not a very controversial claim, but anyway just a stand-in for whatever we think is the preoccupation of painting from the 1400s through to the end of the nineteenth century—then it's clear that these later painters are doing something radically different from their predecessors. Pop music is sort of like this: it uses musical language and ideas, just as Newman, no less than Rembrandt, used oils on canvass, but, as in the case of Newman, to a radically different kind of effect. Newman's paintings are not pictures, or rather, they are pictures only in a very attenuated sense. The songs of the Beatles, the great ones, are fine songs, but their greatness lies elsewhere, in, as I can say now, their social meaning.

Second, we noticed earlier that pop music investigates, in my sense, first-order material including not only style in general but also style as it finds expression in song and dance. This puts us squarely in the vicinity of the sort of robust looping that is central to grasping art's place in our lives. Pop musicians put the ways we are, in my sense, organized by song and dance—style—at the first order. We sing to celebrate, or communicate, or rock our child to sleep. Pop musicians put that on display. The existence of such representations of our song-and-dance practices alters the way we sing and dance and thus provides new material for artistic play. This generative process doesn't stop. The result, over time, is a highly sophisticated, intelligent musical practice. But crucially, I insist, it is not by virtue of exploration of, as I am calling them, distinctively musical ideas or problems, that pop music rises, or can sometimes rise, to the level of art. It is thanks to the ways, as I have been urging, that pop music puts ourselves as stylized on display.

16

The Sound of Music

In the last chapter I argued that when we listen to the music of artists such as Maurice Ravel, Sergei Prokofiev, Johann Sebastian Bach, Charlie Parker, Bill Evans, or Charles Mingus, our interest is not personal. We don't care about *them*, about what they think or feel or want, any more than we care about the personality of a mathematician or physicist when we read his or her work. The focus of attention is what these folks are doing or making, not on them. The performance is a vehicle for musical work. You gain no insight into Bach by investigating his sex life or whether he took drugs.

As we have learned, things are the other way around when it comes to pop music. Now the music, properly understood, really is just a vehicle for something else. The music is a presentation of, or the fabrication of, a character. This is why rock stars have fans and this is why the fans don't only admire the artistic powers of the musicians, but they want to be like them, want to party with them, even want to have sex with them. Bob Dylan, the Rolling Stones, the Beatles, Neil Young, the Sex Pistols, Jay Z, David Bowie, Tupac Shakur, and Kanye West, and also Aretha Franklin, Madonna, and Beyoncé, and on and on. Our interest in these artists is an interest in them, and the music is their direct manner of acting out for us. Whereas the classical musician displays the music in his or her performance, the pop musician displays himself or herself.

If that's all there were to the acousmatic conception of music—that when it comes to "serious" music, it's about the music, not the artists—

then we could happily leave matters there. But, as we have already noticed, the acousmatic idea is much stronger than this. It is the idea that what matters in music are structures in a domain of sound that have at most a causal dependence on the human activity that produces them. Music, as Scruton puts it, is the art of pure sound.

Indeed, what the philosopher Peter Kivy has called *the* main problem in the philosophy of music is that of understanding how *mere* sound—in contrast with, say, the meaningful sounds of speech—can be enthralling and captivating and important to people. This is the question expressed by the neurologist Oliver Sacks, when he remarks, "What an odd thing it is to see an entire species—billions of people—playing with, listening to meaningless tonal patterns, occupied and preoccupied for much of their time with what they call 'music.'"

For many, the idea that music is sound devoid of meaning is all the justification needed for thinking of music, essentially, as a "construction" of the mind. "We humans," writes Sacks, ". . . perceive tones, timbre, pitch intervals, melodic contours, harmony, and (perhaps most elementally) rhythm. We integrate all of these and 'construct' music in our minds using many different parts of the brain."

Music in this view is subjective, interior, neurological, for the simple reason that sound is all these things. This is the received wisdom. The neuroscientist Daniel Levitin, for example, offers no supporting argument when he instructs us that

> The word pitch refers to the mental representation an organism has of the fundamental frequency of a sound. That is, pitch is a purely psychological phenomenon related to the frequency of vibrating air molecules. By "psychological," I mean that it is entirely in our heads, not in the world-out-there; it is the end product of a chain of mental events that gives rise to an entirely subjective, internal mental representation of quality. Sound waves—molecules of air vibrating at various frequencies—do not themselves have pitch. Their motion and oscillations can be measured, but it takes a human (or animal) brain to map them to that internal quality we call pitch.

But should we think of sound as subjective and interior in this way? And anyway, what *does* music have to do with sound?

You might say the answer is obvious. Music *is* sound. Or rather, it is organized sound, or sound put together so that it is worth listening to. Musicians are sound artists. Sound is the basic material with which musicians work.

In this setting, we naturally compare music with speech. Speech is also sound organized for listening. To speak is to make noises and, in doing that, to communicate thoughts, feelings, ideas, intentions. Just as with music.

But with a difference. Aliens from outer space would quickly conclude that speech encodes messages, and with time and luck they'd break the code. But music, they would be forced to conclude, is governed by no such code. It may be organized sound, but it is not organized in the same way and toward the same ends as speech. Whereas speech is put to intelligent work, the aliens might come to believe that music seems to be devoid of content; it is mere noise.

Even so, it's hard to accept the conclusion that music is mere noise. Music may not encode questions and descriptions, but its phrases and gestures seem, well, they seem precisely like phrases and gestures, they have structure and import and coherence. A melody is something we encounter, and its fixity, its firmness, its givenness are palpable and, in our experience at least, undeniable.

And yet it is hard to challenge the premise that music is sound and that since it doesn't encode messages, since its elements don't refer to the world itself, that music is, well, *only* sound. And so we are thrown back on the question: What is this strange kind of sound we humans call music?

Enter neuroscience. According to some neuroscientists, as we have already noticed, the qualities we find salient in music—pitch, melody, harmony, rhythm, dissonance—are not physically real. They are subjective. They are *in the head*. They do not correspond to anything determinate in the physical stimulus. To understand these qualities, it is thought, you need to look at the way physical stimuli bring about effects on the nervous system and produce these qualities in our mind. Music, from this point of view, is internal and psychological; it is neurological and biological.

It's no surprise that we experience a unity or coherence in the musical sound. That's how we're built. And there's no surprise in the fact that alien anthropologists would be, literally, deaf to the meaning, organization, and structure in what we are doing when we make music. To get music the way we do, you need to be put together the way we are.

But let us pause here. Let's consider an alternative to the idea that music is distinctively or particularly tied to sound.

Obviously, we *listen* to music. And when we compose or make music, we do so with an ear to how it sounds. And even when we don't like a piece of music, and so make no effort to listen to it, it may very well be that we can't help but hear it when it plays. Music can engulf us as sound.

But the fact that we hear and listen to music doesn't mean that music is just sound.

Consider: we study paintings with our eyes. Paintings, by their very nature, it would seem, are concerned with the visual. But it is a mistake to say of a painting that it *is*, as it were, mere visibilia. Visual arts are not just *sights*, so to speak.

You might object that this difference is precisely the important one between music and painting. Painters make objects. And we take an interest in them—we look at them, we hang them, we even buy and sell them. And when we think about how they look, we are always interested in their distinctive, substantial, constructedness out of real stuff. Paintings are material and their materiality counts. Not so music.

But in fact exactly analogous points go for music. When we listen to music, we listen to the actions of performers, not only making noise but playing instruments, playing instruments together, in a real-world setting; or we enjoy a recording that was produced by real people, artists and engineers. The idea that a piece of music is just a patch of sound is no more plausible than the idea that paintings are just visual impressions.

With music, no less than with painting, we pay attention not only to sounds or looks. We also look and listen and pay attention to the work. The work is not just colors or shapes, nor is it ever just a sound.

It should not surprise us that there is pressure to reduce music to sound and sound to the subjective. Neuroscience, as we discussed earlier (in chapters 8 and 10), tends to hold to a trigger conception of experience, and neural approaches to art frequently treat works of art as precise triggers for certain kinds of experiences. Whatever a painting is, the aesthetic experiences paintings deliver are decidedly and, indeed, essentially visual. And so for music and sound. Music lives in our heads, whatever its causes, for sounds are inside us, not in the world around us. Or if they are in the world around us—if we mean by sound the disturbances in the medium—then it is surely not that which interests us. We care about the singing in our heads, not the waveforms in the air.

The nature of sounds and colors and other qualities, such as the sensation of heat, which philosophers call "secondary qualities," is one of the most controversial, and interesting, questions in the philosophy of perception. Although thinkers since Galileo have been inclined to make pronouncements to the effect that the colors you see are in your head, not really there where you think you see them, there is ample reason to doubt this. My own view is that colors and sounds are ecological properties. They depend in complex ways on the nature of objects and events and their interplay with environmental conditions. Human sensitivity to this interplay depends on the way we are built, on our nervous system, to be sure. But to grant that we couldn't detect these dynamic properties if we were built differently is not to imply that these properties are in any way unreal, let alone that they are internal.

But for our purposes there is a more pressing point. When I am startled by the siren of the passing fire engine, it is the fire engine, that big noisy red machine, to which I direct my attention. And what I succeed in hearing, when I listen to it, is the vehicle itself racing by.

We can bring this point out by turning back to language. It is sometimes said that language, like music, is just sound. The difference is that language is semantically significant sound. And thus the question is: How can semantically insignificant sound enthrall us as it does?

When I listen to you speak, I do not listen to the sounds you make. I listen to you. It is you, and what you say, that is, your meaning, your action, to which I pay attention. If I get caught up in the sounds of your voice, I am likely to fail to understand what you say. It is true that I perceive your speech by listening to what you say, and that depends on the qualities, as noise, of what you are doing. But the idea that what you are doing is just emitting noise, or that it is just noise that I perceive, *really*, is a bit of ideology. And it wildly distorts our experience.

Linguists sometimes say that the task a child faces when learning a language is finding the mapping of sound to meaning. But that's nuts. It seems nuts not only because we have inherited habits of intellectual reflection according to which, for example, we find it plausible to think that what you see, really, when you see a tomato, is a locus of qualities, qualities that could be present in your consciousness even if there were no tomato there. But in fact, your impression of the tomato is an episode of your engagement with and interaction with a tomato. I don't mean that it isn't possible for us to be mistaken—even totally deluded. Perhaps we are the victims of a *Matrix*-like scenario in which we are undergoing manipulations by evil overlords. But even then, even if that were true, what it is that we are experiencing, falsely, is a tomato, not mere sense impressions. You can't get the tomato out of the story.

That's exactly what the traditional philosophical view holds: if you were to describe what you see, faithfully, refusing to import any assumptions about what there is outside the fragile scope of your consciousness, then you would confine your description to only those features of consciousness that certify their presence immediately. The idea of a world beyond consciousness, such as it is, is one that we construct or build up out of the data of sense. The world is a confabulation constructed out of the data of sense. This is how Cartesian philosophers and modern-day neuroscientists tend to describe our predicament.

To repeat, however, there is no accurate, no faithful description of how things seem—of our conscious experience itself—that is not (for example) already the description of such things as tomatoes, resting atop other tomatoes, being illuminated by the lights of the grocery, there for purchase. If we want to confine our attention to what we really know, then what we really know is that *that* is how things seem to be. As the philosopher P. F. Strawson famously argued: we don't step forward from sense data to build up a conception of the world.

We step back from the world, in thought, to contrive the idea of sense data.

Back to language. Words, meaningful utterances, are like tomatoes and all the rest. It is a fantasy of what our lives are like to suppose that as children we are confronted by empty noise and that we foist meaning onto it, or figure meaning out. I no more figure out that some noises are words than I figure out, as James Joyce's Stephen Dedalus observed, that the wet bedsheets are cold and that Mommy smells better than Daddy. We live among language the way we live among people, and bedsheets, and the beer on Daddy's breath and the smoke from his pipe.

Back to music. Music is the stuff of human activity. In this it is like speech. And our sensitivity to music is, finally, a curiosity in relation to the ways we act and about the things we make. In particular, it is an attention to the way we sing, or play instruments other than our voices; and this playing is, just that, *playing*. We do it for the dancer or the audience, and we do so by banging, plucking, hitting, blowing, and hollering out. There is sound, to be sure; just as there is when we talk. And there is rhythm, to be sure, just as there is when we talk and walk and do anything. This is the stuff of music.

Music, as an art, puts these structures of tone and timing and intention and melody themselves on display. The idea that music is just sound, detached from making activity, detached from performance, is no less a fantasy than the sense-datum philosopher's fantasy about human consciousness.

Why is music meaningful? Why does it enthrall? Because we are rhythmically and melodically and tonally organized; this is a fundamental feature of our embodied living. Music investigates these ways. And it does so, in part, by inventing new ways of entraining ourselves, new ways that build on, refer back to, and play with the old ways (both musical and nonmusical). And because every musician responds to the ways of the musicians before him or her, music refers to a vast body of collective understanding, collective intelligence, collective humor and insight, about all that.

In a remarkable study, ordinary listeners were presented with recordings of the finalists in a classical music competition. Their task: to decide, by inspecting the recordings, who won the competition.

When they were given an audio recording alone—with no video— it turns out they were very poor at deciding whose performance was best and who was likely therefore to have won. They were at chance in guessing the winner (that is, they were right no more than 50 percent of the time). Their score improved somewhat when they were given a video to accompany the sound track. But they performed like experts when they were given the video track alone, without sound. The conclusion: it is easy for listeners, as a group, to decide which musical performance is best, but only when they see it without the distraction of hearing it, too!

Of course if you ask the judges what matters to them when they evaluate a musical performance, they will insist that all that matters is the sound.

How to make sense of this bizarre result?

You might suppose that it just goes to show how poor our ordinary powers of auditory musical discrimination are. Precisely what makes a musical expert a worthy judge is that the expert knows how to *listen* without getting distracted by mere visual noise.

It turns out, according to the University College London psychologist Chia-Jung Tsay, that experts perform no better than novice listeners. A group of experts are unable to agree on which snippet of audio recording is a winning performance, but unanimity is swift and secure when they ignore the music and pay attention to the soundless video track alone.

Now, you might chalk up this surprising result to "visual capture," a phenomenon well known to psychologists. The sound appears to come from the ventriloquist's dummy's mouth and not from its actual source. That's visual capture. We seem to hear what we think we see.

I suspect, too, that there may be a temptation to think that these findings somehow debunk or undercut our love of music. As one musician friend of mine put it, this is every musician's worst nightmare. It's not the music that moves people, it's what they see!

But these worries are misplaced. What is challenged by these empirical results is not the value of music, or the legitimacy of the results of musical competition. Music is human performance, just as recorded music is a trace made of such performance. Music is as people do, and what people do—how they express themselves, articulate, emphasize, intone, and sing—is manifest not only in the sounds they make but also in their visible display.

It should not surprise us that what we see makes a difference when it comes to making sense of and evaluating what we hear. We are interested in ourselves, after all. Not noise.

Yet there are still some surprises here. Granted, it's easier to tell who won from the video recording than the audio, but most of us would have expected that video + audio would be the best of all. After all, it gives you the most information about what happened on the stage.

This finding remains puzzling. Perhaps the explanation lies in the curious nature of the task. What we are asked to judge, in this experiment, is not the music—its qualities—but merely the question of who won. It is plausible that the simplest access to this information—who carries on as a winner does—would be on the basis of what we see. It doesn't imply that listening isn't critical for a genuine assessment of the music.

•

My criticism of the acousmatic conception of music, of the idea, that is, that music is a phenomenon of pure sound, divorced from production and setting—leaves intact a humbler and more reasonable version of the view. Namely, that with music—as distinct from pop music—it is precisely the music that concerns us and not the particular character of the performers. Crucially, however, music, thought of this way, is not meaningless sound. Even serious orchestral music is people playing with ideas and gestures whose familiarity, and importance, are things they take for granted.

PART IV

To be an artist is not a matter of making paintings or objects at all. What we are really dealing with is our state of consciousness and the shape of our perception.
                                                    —Robert Irwin

17

A Very Abbreviated and Highly Opinionated History of Aesthetics

According to Plato, art is a bad thing. He believed that there was no place for art in a just society; artists should be banned.

You don't need to have any particular knowledge of war, or sports, or love to make up enthralling stories about soldiers, athletes, and lovers. And while artists captivate and titillate with the tales they tell, they teach nothing, for they have nothing to teach. Art imparts no knowledge. Really, it is worse even than that. For although it delivers no knowledge, art passes itself off as if it does. It seems to show or display or inform. Art corrupts us because it leads us away from reality to make-believe, and it does so in a way that conceals this very fact from us.

For Plato, art, in its essence, is a kind of pornography. It titillates. It does so always in a way that bypasses truth, information, reality, and value. Art misinforms.

The idea that all art is the equivalent of pornography will strike many today as prudish and outrageous. And the proposal that we should reject art and banish artists from our midst is not one that many of us will find appealing.

But Plato's idea is not so remote from contemporary ways of thinking as we might think at first blush. It is generally accepted that children should be shielded from some works of art. Not because kids won't like them. We fear that the exposure would be harmful. Images of violence or sexual behavior, it is widely felt, can damage. It isn't easy to unpack our attitudes. But I'd wager that what motivates us here is less the desire to protect kids from unpleasant realities than our appreciation, or suspicion, that art is not a reliable guide to the fraught and complex matters it sometimes deals with. Would you want your child to frame his or her conception of what sex is, or what sexual desire and pleasure are or can be, on the basis of access only to pornography?

We can separate two claims in this line of thought. First, pornography is dangerous—it imparts a distorted account and harms our sense of what is real. Second, all art is pornography. The first claim is more believable than the second.

But even the second carries more weight than we might be inclined to grant at first.

One domain I know a fair bit about is life on a university campus. It never fails to surprise me, when I watch films or TV, how inaccurately, and how downright awkwardly, college life is represented. The college campus, when it shows up as a backdrop for a police investigation, or a love story, or whatever, is invariably shown according to a small number of well-established clichés and stereotypes. What is especially interesting to me is the fact that most, if not all, people writing movies or publishing stories have been to college. They draw, in their tellings, not on what they know but on images that are invariably simple-minded and unlikely.

Maybe here we should bring to mind the comparison with pornography once again. Just as the sex-movie maker does not (could not possibly, dear me!) draw on his or her real-life sexual experiences to come up with "material," but offers a *fantasy* of what sex is or could be like, so what explains the proliferation of ivy-covered buildings, handsome young professors in horn-rimmed glasses and tweed standing forth heroically before classrooms full of rapt admirers, is that this presentation gives vent to fantasy.

And surely there is something at least potentially dangerous about taking fantasy for reality, about letting one's experience of reality be too shaped by a package that has been delivered, as it were, from on high.

An example from my childhood: there used to be a TV show called *Welcome Back, Kotter*. It described life in a Brooklyn high school classroom. It was macho display, charming and charismatic acting up, and chaos from start to finish. It truly served for me, when I was in third grade, as a picture or model of what it would be like to be in high school. Sure, I knew it was comedy and fiction. It was play. But something stuck. The sitcom provided a direction, a model to understand my own options for life in the classroom.

Welcome Back, Kotter may have been harmless. But its mechanisms are at least potentially dangerous. This is why people are rightly worried about portrayals of race, gender, and ethnicity in the media—they can and do perpetuate stereotypes.

From Plato's point of view, what else can the arts possibly do but perpetuate stereotypes? Artists aren't scientists, or theorists. They are image workers, and every image is a falsehood. Neither the directors, nor the actors, nor the viewers have the first bit of knowledge of what they are dealing with. Entertainment requires not knowledge but the appearance of knowledge. Art is rank imitation.

I thought of Plato's argument not long ago when there was public outcry over a movie about the hunt for Osama bin Laden. The movie contained scenes of torture and seemed to make the case that torture played an important role in the U.S. effort to gain information about bin Laden's whereabouts. Some critics argued that the movie got the facts wrong—torture is, as a matter of fact, an ineffective means of gathering information. Others argued that even if torture is effective, it is morally unacceptable, so the movie is to be condemned for portraying that practice in a positive light.

Isn't there something ridiculous about this hue and cry? Not that the issues themselves are not of grave concern. Of course they are. But what silliness to think that this movie has any relation to what matters. After all, it is a bit of storytelling, made for money, by people with little knowledge of or responsibility to the truth and sold to people who are just as detached and uninformed. What vanity to think that we, as a culture, are coming to grips with the great issues of the day when we go to the movies!

For Plato the issue is simple. Artists make pictures, tell stories, or stage dramas. Their material is image. They work with appearances, projections, and make-believe. But appearances—let alone appearances chosen because they titillate—are no guide to the true nature of things. If you are interested in warfare, you don't speak to a storyteller but to a soldier, or maybe a politician. If you are interested in the solar system, you don't turn to the creators of *Star Trek* but to scientists. The work of art, for Plato, is twice removed from the things themselves. Artists make representations of what are, at best, the appearances of things, events, mere phenomena. Art trains us to look away from reality to a doubly falsified realm of imagery.

The idea that art is inherently dangerous and worthy of suspicion is a serious one. Even if we find Plato's censorious attitude hard to endorse, I at least admire Plato's earnest commitment to the importance of the question: How can art be valuable if it does not rest on knowledge, if it does not impart knowledge, if it is confined to appearance? How can art be valuable if it is imitation?

And yet there is a beautiful irony in the fact that Plato's own work, at least from the vantage point I have urged us to take up in this book, doubly undercuts his attack on art.

For one thing, Plato, in his writing, tells stories and enacts dramas. He works with his material exactly as an artist would. He offers us not what was said, or shown, or proved, but fictional displays of what might possibly be said or thought or admitted by imagined interlocutors.

But also, Plato is a philosopher, and philosophy, as I have been arguing, is by its very nature an artistic project. For philosophy, like art, is in the business of bringing out our organization and reorganizing us.

Plato is exactly right that art threatens to disorganize the soul. But where he goes astray, we are now in a position to appreciate, is in thinking this disorganizing and reorganizing is always harmful. Where he is right is in his appreciating that it belongs to the very nature of art (and philosophy) to be harmful *potentially*. Art and philosophy are serious business.

The fact is that Plato's own creative example should lead us to recognize that art can be a source of learning. Plato's work gives us the resources to make sense of the idea that a tragic drama, or an epic poem, for example, could in fact constitute a form of investigation and enable a distinct kind of knowledge. Not knowledge about warfare, to be sure, or sex, or the true look and feel of life on a college campus, or the movements of the stars. But knowledge—a kind of self-knowledge—pertaining to our appreciation of the way our own ideas, values, commitments hang together, or, as the case may be, fail to hang together.

From this point of view, the fact that *Zero Dark Thirty* gets facts wrong, or that its author is mistaken or misguided, is no obstacle to the movie's providing us with an opportunity for learning and reorganization. What is activated in such a film are our responses and our thoughts not about actual events but about possible ones, or perhaps our responses to our responses to *possible* events, to ways things might have been or might be or might unfold. There is room for error here, too, of course. But not factual error. Ignorance of the facts is no obstacle to productive investigation of the meaning, for us, of war, torture, etc.

Aristotle appreciated this point exactly. Art is more profound than history for Aristotle, precisely because it is concerned with more than just what happened, with what is true. It is concerned with what is possible, with what could possibly happen, and so, with a more fundamental reality; it lets us think about the real natures of things that constrain and determine what can happen. Art looks at things not under the aspect of their being true, or real, or having actually happened. It looks at things in the light of all the different sorts of significance they could possibly have. Every play, every poem, every painting, for Aristotle, is a *thought experiment*, and its value, as such, is, at root, philosophical.

It is in Aristotle that we find, for the first time, an explicit appreciation of the idea that literature and art can be philosophical, indeed must be, if they are to succeed even as entertainment, or depiction, or titillation, an engagement with ideas and meaning; art must rest on something like an investigation of reality. A story must be intelligible. It can't be too long or too short. It must have a beginning, a middle, and an end. It must represent not only events happening in any old order but also a meaningful arrangement of events structured around a very special kind of event, namely, human action.

Aristotle allows that Plato is right that art is in the business of imitation. But he insists that our interest in imitation—in imagery, in make-believe, in appearance—is productive, a good thing. For it is an interest in nature in the deepest and most encompassing sense. It is an interest in our world, organized as it is by values, concerns, biographies, introductions, and conclusions, rather than in random events happening in succession.

Aristotle argues that literature is research of a distinctively philosophical variety and, therefore, that criticism—the evaluation of art with regard to such questions as whether it works *as* art, that is, as drama, or poetry, or whatever—is a legitimate philosophical project.

And this view in turn explains something that might be puzzling if we thought that art was merely in the titillation or entertainment business. How is it that we take pleasure in seeing the same play again and again? Why can we enjoy an epic poem not only once, but many times over? And why is it that we can get as much out of a play by reading it as when we see it performed on the stage? This shows, if anything does, that it isn't just spectacle—stagecraft, suspense, or surprise—that is at work in the work of art. And this shows, as clearly as anything can, that the feelings and emotions we enjoy when we participate in art—fear, pity, sorrow, empathy, anger—are not merely *reactions* produced in us, triggered, as it were, by unreal events. Our engagement, and our feeling, are engagements with *problems of life* themselves. A bad end befalling a bad person may be just as affecting as a bad end befalling a good person. But what engages us, aesthetically, Aristotle believed, is the special circumstance of a bad end befalling a good person who acted from some flawed but comprehensible and natural, even good, impulse. We find tragic drama moving and significant, in the distinctive ways that we do, because the drama is putting ourselves, and our frailties, and the very meaning of what it is to be an agent whose life can be thought of as having a bad end or a good one on display. We don't tire from repeated viewing of the same play because engagement with a play's problems does not yield, all at once, the understanding or the reorganization that we seek. And we benefit from the reading of a play because the play, really, is a work of philosophy, an opportunity for engaged thinking.

Again we are struck by the similarity with philosophy. Philosophers do not ever definitely settle the questions they work on. Philosophy doesn't come to an end. What would bring it to an end would be the absence of puzzlement or confusion about ourselves and our lives. But it is the nature of our lives not only to be complicated but also to be organized in ways that we cannot, from the inside, as it were, comprehend. Human being is always a problem to itself. And so philosophy never gets old. And neither does literature.

Plato may be right that in an ideal world there would be no need for art, or philosophy, just as, in an ideal world, there would be no need for medicine. If we accepted things as they are, at face value, and acted out of good and natural impulses, well tempered by good judgment, we would have no need for art or philosophy. But what we are thus imagining is a distinctively nonhuman, perhaps, indeed, an animal existence. It is a form of existence not available to us.

It is the hallmark of our existence, as Heidegger said, that we are a problem to ourselves. Heidegger was clear, as few other thinkers have been, that the work art does is philosophical. Its job is bringing into the open, and putting on display, and at the same time instituting and so setting up, the structures and values that, as I would put it, organize us. It reveals organization and it also reorganizes.

Heidegger starts from the idea that the world shows up for us in many different kinds of ways. Sometimes we look around and contemplate what we see, or touch, or smell. But this kind of deliberate and knowing access to what there is around us presupposes that we are, as Heidegger would say, already embedded in and at home in a world. So much of what is there for us is there not as an object of contemplation but rather as the ground itself on which we stand, or the gear and equipment with which we engage what matters. We can study shoes and think about them, but insofar as we simply *wear* shoes in order to carry on our work and move about, we don't think about shoes, or experience them; we abide with shoes, we rely on them, we use them. Shoes can be objects of contemplation, but this presupposes that they are also "ready to hand" as gear for living, and being ready to hand is not a matter of contemplation. Insofar as shoes are just used, they are taken for granted, and this distinct way of being there for us, being there as taken for granted, requires, precisely, that we don't look at and think about them. The shoes, to be there for us in this way, need to have receded from the foreground.

But this raises a puzzle. If for the shoes to be there for us as equipment for living presupposes that they have receded into the background, how can we put that very fact—as Heidegger puts it: the equipmentality of equipment—itself on display? The minute you turn your attention to the shoes and think about the role they play in your life, you have changed the situation, broken the magic. You are faced no longer with the equipment you sought but with an object. How can we bring the shoes themselves, as we live with them, into view, into the open, if it is precisely the characteristic feature of the way shoes show up for us, when we take them for granted, that we do not notice them?

According to Heidegger, this is a job for art, and it is a philosophical job. It is the distinctive *work* of philosophy. A painting of shoes, for example, one of Van Gogh's famous paintings, can have the power to make perspicuous the way the shoes are coordinate to a whole way of living, what Wittgenstein might have called a form of life. To understand the shoes is to understand what it is to be one who depends on shoes to get through the day. This is the sort of thing a painting can exhibit. A painting can let us catch ourselves in the act of unthinking engagement with the world.

But Heidegger makes a stronger claim to the effect that shoes can be this way for us, can be equipment, only if there is art. It isn't just that art shows forth the structure of our world, it is that it sets up that world. *Without art there would be no world.*

Here is one way to understand this puzzling idea. Heidegger is getting at what I have called the need for art and philosophy as ways of finding ourselves when we are lost. We human beings are a problem to ourselves. It would be nice if we spent our lives happily caught up in the flow, engaged in the manner dictated by the first-order modalities of our organization. But such an automatic life is not human. Perhaps it is animal. But the striking thing about our engagements, our participation in organized activities, is that these always become a problem for us. We are lost in schemes of organization of which we are not the author and about which we command no clear understanding. It is the same with writing and language. Writing presents itself to us as a way of modeling our language for ourselves. But it turns out, as we have seen, there could in fact be no language if we did not confront the need to model it and adjudicate it and try to understand it better. It is precisely our engagement with what we take for granted that allows us, then, to carry on taking it for granted. You can't eliminate philosophy and art because philosophy and art are the ways we create precisely the worlds which, at some moments, thanks to this normative work, we can then let recede from view and reside comfortably in the background.

The work of art is to set up our worlds just as the work of writing is to make language possible.

Heidegger takes up the challenge that Plato raised and that Aristotle tried to answer: understanding how art can be a thing of value when it is not science, when it is not governed by our learning how things are. But Heidegger's treatment is very abstract and removed from our actual thought and talk and experience of art. Two other thinkers in the history of thought on this subject provide a more nuanced filling-in of the details.

The first is Kant. Kant appreciated, as I will put it, that art happens in *the space of criticism*. Let me explain.

Kant drew attention to two striking and undeniable but apparently incompatible features of our responses to art. The first is that aesthetic response is, as he put it, a matter of feeling. Some works of art move us. We find that we like them. We are touched. We care. And crucially, our responses are immune to argument. There are no rules that dictate how one ought to respond. You can't convince me to find an artwork beautiful, or stirring, or important—or, conversely, not. As Kant put it, we are not in the realm of concepts or rules here. We are in the realm of pure feeling.

But, and this is the second point, it is also the case that we take our responses to a work of art to be achievements or insights. When I judge a work of art to be important, or worthwhile, or beautiful, I don't ever mean merely that *I* like it or that it is worthwhile *to me*. I mean *it is a thing of value*. And I expect or trust that others will or at least should agree with me.

One way to make this idea clear is to appreciate that it makes sense, when we are dealing with aesthetic response to works of art, to speak of genuine disagreement. If I like a wine's taste, and you do not, we don't really disagree. After all, I'm right about what it is like for me, and you're right about what it is like for you. It tastes good to me but not to you. But when we talk about beauty, or other forms of aesthetic value, we never mean merely that something is beautiful *to me*. For Kant that doesn't even make sense. If I find something beautiful, that is because it really is beautiful.

And so we have an apparent conflict. Aesthetic judgments are subjective; they are matters of feeling and response. And at the same time, they seem, by their very nature, to carry, as we might put it, *inter-subjective* significance.

Kant argued that aesthetic judgments are made in "the universal voice." They may be subjective. But they aren't reflective of my arbitrary, accidental, subjective tastes or attitudes. When I judge a work of art, I do it as a person, from my point of view. But I take myself, in doing so, to be speaking not for me alone.

Kant's solution is to insist that disagreement about the value of a work of art is always the *beginning* of a conversation and never its end. It is never enough for one to say: I like the German artist Adolph Menzel. You need to be able to deliver on this pronouncement. You need to be able to say why you like Menzel or what you like *in* Menzel. Judgments about art thus initiate discussion, conversation or, more generally, criticism. And criticism is, by its very nature, a communicative activity, one that unfurls between people and requires that people be respectful and open to each other.

And the remarkable thing about critical discourse of this sort is that, in fact, it *can* change minds, it can transform how and what we can appreciate. Good critics do not merely describe a work, they also bring to our attention qualities we had missed, or persuade us to give weight to features that we had ignored or failed to consider. Criticism doesn't proceed by logical argument; there is nothing like knockdown argument in this vicinity. Criticism proceeds by persuasion. Critics are educators. They teach you to see. Insofar as we are art lovers, we are all critics.

Of course it sometimes happens that criticism breaks down. It may be that you just can't take seriously what I respond to in the work. That is, ultimately it may be that you cannot take *me* seriously. And that is what is at stake in aesthetic criticism: our ability to understand and, I might even say, *love* one another.

Kant famously said that aesthetic evaluation must be disinterested. This should be obvious. I am surely likely to take pleasure in my son's musical performance. And that's well and good. But if I like it because it is the work of my child, then I don't like it for aesthetically significant reasons. The fact that my son makes the music is not a reason for someone not partial to my son to take an interest in it.

For an aesthetic evaluation to be genuinely aesthetic, it must be an impartial response, one that is indifferent to who owns the work, or who made it, etc.

And yet, crucially for Kant, as we have noticed, there can be no objective test of whether a thing is deserving of our aesthetic praise. Aesthetic value is not a feature of a thing, like its weight or color, that we can detect or perceive or discover.

But this means that aesthetic disagreement is never really about the art thing itself; it is about our response to the thing. That is why Kant describes aesthetic response as a "free play of the imagination." The thing doesn't dictate how we experience it the way that the fact that a thing is a car dictates that we come to learn it is a car when we inspect it.

What is at stake, finally, in aesthetic evaluation, is what kind of person you are. That is why aesthetic disagreement, when it is un-resolvable, can spell the breakdown of a relationship. And it is also why art requires of us that we commit ourselves to the importance of conversation and criticism.

And this brings us back to philosophy. Philosophical disagree-ment is, in exactly this way, aesthetic. You can't prove a philosophical position any more than you can prove that a painting is or is not a worthwhile work of art. For what's at stake, finally, is you, and your commitments, and what you need to see your way clear of the puzzle-ments and confusions that hold you captive.

The fact that philosophy is not a science, that it does not admit of experimental methods or other forms of decision procedures that settle the facts, once and for all, does not mean that philosophical disagreements are not real. They are real. They are objective. But what's at stake is not the facts. What is at stake is how we assimilate, make sense of and, finally, evaluate the facts.

Art has value, then, exactly as philosophy has value. Not because it produces knowledge in the way that science does. But precisely because it is the domain in which we grapple with what we already know (or think we know). It is the domain in which we try to get clear about the ways we think and respond and assign value.

Just as choreography isn't dancing, so philosophical investiga-tion and aesthetic criticism are not domains in which we gather more facts. They are domains in which we try to put ourselves as information gatherers, as perceivers and, indeed, as perceivers whose evaluations may very well tend to be interested and biased, on display before ourselves.

The last author I want to mention, as I bring this brief and opinionated history of aesthetics, and this book, to a close, is John Dewey. It is in Dewey that we find, I think, the synthesis of the ideas that take form in the readings I have offered of Plato, Aristotle, Kant, and Heidegger. Dewey, more than any other single thinker, brings the nature of art, as I understand that nature, into focus. In Dewey, as in Plato, Aristotle, Kant, and Heidegger, we can frame a conception of art that shows how it is necessary, inevitable, natural, and philosophical.

Like Heidegger, Dewey is not interested in aesthetic experience. He is interested in the work art does, or in its meaning and significance. But for Dewey, this has everything to do with the nature of experience.

Experience, as Aristotle appreciated, but as later philosophers (such as David Hume and John Locke) tended to forget, is more than a sequence of sensations. Sure, there is a sense in which, at any given moment in time, we are confronted by brute sensation, by what William James called a blooming, buzzing confusion. But experience proper, John Dewey argued, does not refer to that. We don't reside in a meaningless series of sensations, in haphazard sequences of feeling and imagery. The experiences that make up our lives, the experiences we know and enjoy, are more structured than that. They are, as Dewey says, *integral*. They are nameable. The experience of dining together in Venice. The experience of studying at university. The experience of buying a house. The experience of trying to fall asleep last night. The experience of having a child.

The thing about experiences that are, in this way, thematically structured and integral is that they are achievements. We make them. We don't just have them. We manage them. If you think of living as a stream of doing, and undergoing, then the achievement of meaning and integration that is characteristic of our actual lived experiences is a thing of value.

Every experience, insofar as it is *an* experience, is integral. It has form and meaning. And it is made. It is achieved. In other words, for Dewey, it is *aesthetic*. Life itself is a meaning-making activity. All experience, insofar as it *is* experience, happens in an aesthetic space. For to be integral, to be integrated, to be organized, is to *be* aesthetic.

Perceiving itself, thinking, wondering, no less than dancing and singing, are aesthetic. For Dewey, to fail to be aesthetic is not to fail to be art; it is to fail to be experience at all.

So in a way it is Dewey's view that we are all artists. For we are all engaged in the making of experiences, in comprehending the form and meaning in the cycles of doing and feeling, of acting and undergoing the consequences of our actions, that organize our lives at the most basic biological level. Life itself is an activity of making experience.

And that is exactly what art is. Art is experience, for Dewey. Artists don't make things. They make experiences.

But now we confront a circle: art is experience. Artists make experiences. But we all make experiences. So we are all artists. But Dewey doesn't leave us trapped in this circle.

True artists don't only make experiences. They make objects (paintings, performances, whatever) that afford precisely the opportunity for integral experiences whose integration is, as it were, made manifest. The painter scores the canvas with an eye to how it looks, and then makes further changes based on his perception of the results of his own actions. In making the painting, he recapitulates the very circular processes of experience making and life itself. And when you view the painting, you encounter something that was made for you to encounter; you encounter it precisely as an opportunity to encounter what it is for an experience to be made. And you yourself must now make your own experience of the artwork. You don't do that by seeing it. You need to activate it by activating yourself. Artworks give you an opportunity to enact the ways in which our lives unfold. In which experience happens. In which we achieve our active lives. The art stands forth for you—as Heidegger might say, it shines—as exemplary. It *is* an experience. It affords you an experience.

The work of art puts our fundamental nature as makers, that is to say, as experiencers, on display. The work of art exhibits our manner of organization to ourselves and it does so in a comprehensible and recognizable way.

I opened this book with a quote from Dewey. He expresses this idea: it is the existence of art *objects* themselves that gets in the way of understanding the nature of art. We look to the things themselves. But art is experience. It isn't the things that matter. It is the experience of those things. But those experiences don't come for free. We need to make them. Art is an opportunity to make experience, to make ourselves, and so to live.

And so, in a way, it turns out that we are artists one and all. We all live, and life is a process of making experience, of creatively responding to what we do in the face of what is already happening.

But art is more than that. Art is philosophy, after all. It is putting all that about our condition and nature on display.

But we *are* all artists to the extent that, as Dewey holds, and as I have been arguing, the need for art, the need for philosophy, the need for understanding are all present wherever *we* are present, wherever there are human beings.

This doesn't mean that the making of art is universal. Art is no more universal than is writing. There are cultures that don't write their language.

What I have aimed to show is that these considerations bring out the ways art *is* universal, and for exactly the same reason that the writerly attitude to language flourishes even in cultures that do not write their language.

Art is not manufacture. Art is not performance. Art is not entertainment. Art is not beauty. Art is not pleasure. Art is not participation in the art world. And art is definitely not commerce.

Art is philosophy. Art is putting our true nature on display before ourselves. Because we need to. Art is writing ourselves.

Acknowledgments

I grew up in a household of artists. I was surrounded by art and by people for whom the value of art was paramount; indeed, art was the standard against which all other values were measured, or so it seemed to me. The ability to understand art, to see it and discriminate, to get it, was prized very highly, but not quite so highly as the power to make art. Is it a dark power, as my father's friend the artist Tony Smith suggested in a conversation with him? I imagine that the humble and admiring tones my father reserved for discussing the greatness of artists is comparable to the way, in other homes, one might have talked about the saints and their troubled and inspiring lives.

But it wasn't just my house; it was the Greenwich Village I grew up in. It was a weave of crisscrossing lives and styles, and art was the common thread. My friends and I used to get on the nerves of the painters next door. I can remember Leon Golub's angry frustration with us as we ran up and down the hallway outside the loft he shared with Nancy Spero. Another friend's dad made movies—sex movies. (I visited his loft with anticipation and trepidation.) The potters came and went day and night downstairs in my mom's pottery; our back neighbors worked at the Electric Circus and later took off to do lights for the Rolling Stones; Mick Jagger once stopped by to eat strawberry pie. Dove Bradshaw asked my eight-year-old brother to lead a sculpture workshop. I performed as a ten- and eleven-year-old in productions of Kikuo Saito at La MaMa Experimental Annex over on East Fourth Street. (I also played Curley in an elementary school production of

Oklahoma! and I played Buffalo Bill in Brian Kahn's production of Arthur Kopit's *Indians*, a work we performed for a very short run off-off-Broadway.)

According to one online guide to Greenwich Village, Bob Dylan, Graham Nash, and David Crosby all lived in the small redbrick tenement I grew up in. My parents owned it from the early 1960s on and had lived there as tenants before, so I'm in a position to know that Dylan and Co. in fact never did live there. The painter Robert DeNiro, Sr., did, however, and his young son Robert, the actor, was a not infrequent visitor (so my parents have told me). And Dylan did stop by, at least once, to see about pottery lessons in my mom's shop. Although I was too young to have known Barnett Newman, Tony Smith, Jackson Pollock, or Mark Rothko, these men, especially Newman and Smith, had been close friends of my father's in the years before my birth.

I tell all this not to drop names but because, looking back on it now, I want to acknowledge how remarkable it is to have grown up in this art community.

I also put down these personal memories because they help me to state my motivation to undertake the research of this book. For me, art isn't just another phenomenon to which I can apply my theory. It is personal. The question of art, the question of why it matters, what it is, how it figures in our lives, is in some ways my very first problem in philosophy.

The artist in the anecdote mentioned in the preface, the one who challenged me to rethink the very nature of seeing, was my father, Hans Noë.

I admit that this book's central claim—that art is a philosophical practice and philosophy an artistic one—serves me rather well. It can be understood, finally, as my defense of philosophy and its value, a defense of my work, in the setting of my family's engagement with art. If art is the most important thing, and philosophy is art, then it turns out I'm an artist after all. Look, Dad!

But there are seeming accidents as well that bring me to write this book. My first book, *Action in Perception*, which was published in 2004, has been widely read in the contemporary dance community and, to a lesser extent, in the world of visual arts. This was never my intention. I wrote that book for an audience of philosophers and cognitive scientists—it grew out of my collaborations with the philosopher Evan Thompson (and also his mentor and friend Francisco Varela) and also the experimental and theoretical psychologist Kevin O'Regan—and did not expect this. Rebecca Todd, the dancer, choreographer, and now cognitive scientist, who also happens to be Evan Thompson's wife, organized a workshop with me and Lisa Nelson (and a number of other dancers, including Karen Nelson, Susanna Hood, Margit Galanter, Heike Langsdorf, Alexander Baervoets, and members of the Paul Deschanel collective in Belgium, as well as the dramaturge Jeroen Peeters). This was my first encounter with the idea, so beautifully exemplified in Lisa Nelson's practice, that dance, or rather choreography, was or could be a research practice, a modality for investigating communication, perception, and consciousness. A few years later I was contacted by William Forsythe and his collaborators, Freya Vass-Rhee, Liz Waterhouse, Rebecca Groves, Norah Zuniga Shaw—and still later I came into contact with Nicole Peisl, Fabrice Mazliah, David Stern, and Roberta Mosca, as well as other members of the Forsythe Company including the dance scholar Scott deLahunta. I jumped into this world and began to learn to see dance, to think about what we see when we see dance, and to start the process of learning about what choreography can be. Scott deLahunta and I spent hours talking about what a dance-philosophy-science mutual engagement could be (in part in the setting of what came to be known as Motion Bank). Nicole Peisl and I have now choreographed and performed together, as well as jointly taught workshops. She is a source of inspiration. Our collaboration is ongoing (and not only professional: we live together and have a child). And Forsythe and I, over the last five years, have undertaken a passionate and ongoing conversation about the philosophy in choreography and the choreography in philosophy. This book has been formed by these conversations and is, in some ways, a record of them. I have recently begun a new collaboration—the development of a joint performative-lecture event—with the choreographer Deborah Hay.

However accidental it may be that I came to be invited into the dance world in this way, it all felt like a return to beginnings. My dad's girlfriend, and my sister Adi's mother, had been a dancer; back in the 1980s, when I was a boy, she used to take us along to Dance Theater Workshop. And, as I have already indicated, my father figures in my story and this project from the very beginning.

There are a number of other stations on the way to writing this book that I would like to mention. In 1997 I was invited by Larry Rinder and Marina MacDougall to give a lecture on perceptual consciousness at the California College of the Arts. The purpose of the meeting was to brainstorm on art and consciousness, a topic on which I had not yet begun to think seriously. This meeting was a turning point for me. It got me started on the topic, for one thing. Also, it was at this meeting that I met, for the first and only time, the distinguished philosopher of art Richard Wollheim; I now teach "his" aesthetics class at UC Berkeley. And I think it must have been a consequence of my participation at this event, and in a follow-up symposium with Vilayanur S. Ramachandran, Bill Viola, and others, that I was invited by Michael S. Roth to be part of a workshop on art and neuroscience at the Getty Research Institute in Santa Monica in 1999. The cast of characters at this meeting was impressive—Elaine Scarry, David Freedberg, Barbara Maria Stafford, Pietro Perona, Claude Imbert, Tom Crow, John Mazziotta, Patricia Churchland, among others. As I recall, Crow didn't like what I had to say about art; Freedberg and Churchland didn't like what I had to say about neuroscience. Scarry spoke up in my defense, but I had the impression that she was motivated less by genuine agreement and more by the spirit of charity. I was a bit bruised, but I came away with the conviction that there was work to be done in this area that was not being done and that I wanted to undertake it.

Fast-forward almost a decade: I spent the 2007–2008 academic year with my then wife the artist Miriam Dym and our two sons at the Wissenschaftskolleg zu Berlin. I wrote *Out of Our Heads* there, and it was during this year that I began to think in earnest about problems of art. I took inspiration from Horst Bredekamp and Luca Giuliani, who are both permanent members of the Kolleg, and also from Michael Fried and Alexander Nagel, who were fellow fellows. Our conversations about art took place against the background of Berlin and its art treasures. I also owe a special debt to the Humboldt University philosopher John Michael Krois, whose work on embodied approaches to art and experience also served as a source of inspiration. Miriam Dym, I should add, had always been my teacher about art, and her influence, or that of her practice, is all over this book. She had a show that year in Berlin that is never far from my consideration when thinking about strange tools.

It has been a challenge to write *Strange Tools*, in part because I had so many different people and audiences in mind while writing it. I wrote this book for the people I have already mentioned, but also for others I have come to know, either in person or through their writing, either very well or not very well at all. This book is for them, too: Whitney Davis, Hubert Dreyfus, Moriah Evans, Liza Fior, Michael Fried, P.M.S. Hacker, Edward Harcourt, Deborah Hay, Christopher M. Hutton, John Hyman, Robert Lazzarini, Sina Najafi, Warren Neidich, Jonathan T. D. Neil, Richard Sacks, Leo Treitler, Christopher Wood, and Alexi Worth. I owe a special debt to my friends Blake Gopnik and Lawrence Weschler, who have been inspired, spirited, and insightful companions and teachers about all things art.

I would also like to acknowledge the members of the Bildakt Symbolic Articulation group at Humboldt University: Horst Bredekamp, Mark-Oliver Casper, Maria Luisa Catoni, Katharina Lee Chichester, Franz Engel, Hanna Fiegenbaum, Joerg Fingerhut, Sascha Freyberg, Yannis Hadjinicolaou, Einav Katan, Marion Lauschke, Sabine Marienberg, Anja Pawel, Philipp Ruch, Johanna Schiffler, Pablo Schneider, Jürgen Trabant, Jörg Trempler, Stefan Trinks, Patrizia Unger, Tullio Viola, and Frederik Wellmann. Their careful reading and generous criticism of a working draft of *Strange Tools*, at a workshop in Berlin in September 2014, moved me to make big changes to the book's organization. I am enormously grateful to them. And also to my graduate students Caitlin Dolan and Charles Oliver O'Donnell, who traveled to Berlin to participate in the workshop and who offered generous and insightful criticism. I am especially grateful to Caitlin, who has also been my research assistant on this project.

I would like to thank my agent, Russell Weinberger, of Brockman, Inc., and my editor, Joe Wisnovsky, of Farrar, Straus and Giroux, as well as Wright Bryan and the *13.7: Cosmos & Culture* team at National Public Radio. Thanks also to my colleagues at the University of California, Berkeley, for their support, and also to former colleagues at the Graduate

Center of the City University of New York. I am grateful to the John Simon Guggenheim Memorial Foundation for giving me a fellowship to support my research on this project in 2012.

But there are two people I'd like to mention in more detail.

The first is Dominic Kahn. I've known him since I was eleven or twelve. He is very dear to me. He lives in Berlin and has made cameo appearances in my writings over the years. He is one of my critics, sometimes harsh, always faithful. But the thing about Dominic is that when it comes to art, I would say, he is the arch-skeptic. He likes what he likes but refuses to be taken in, as I imagine he would say, by the sham that is so much art. What meaning, let alone what magic, could there possibly be for him in a plain Barnett Newman canvas or a John Cage musical composition? And what does a painting of a crucifix, whether by Rubens or Titian, have to say to him?

I read some time ago of a janitor in a London gallery who was fired for sweeping up the cigarette butts and beer cans left on the floor after a late-night opening. He had no way of knowing that what he had swept away was the art itself! I myself, some months ago, called over one of the guards at the Städel Museum in Frankfurt to let him know that there seemed to be a leak—there was water all over the floor near a freestanding sculpture—only to have him explain that this was actually part of the piece! For Dominic, as I imagine his viewpoint, this would be grist for his mill. If the boundary between what is art and what is not art can't be clearly articulated, can't even be seen, then surely what we call art is just a matter of what "we," the members of an "in crowd," say. Which is to say that we are all in the position of the boy who looks around in puzzlement and has the courage to say, The emperor wears no clothes!

A very similar attitude is sometimes expressed about philosophy itself. Is there progress in philosophy? Are there philosophical results? Scientists, in particular, sometimes pose these questions mockingly. In one sense, clearly, their answer must be negative, at least when compared to the results of investigations in physics, or mathematics, or even history. It isn't just that findings are in dispute; it's that it can seem as if philosophy is nothing more than a field of disputation. Plato himself, the greatest philosopher, understood this. The Socratic dialogues don't end with an established conclusion or anything like a discovery. They end in confusion, with no positive finding. But can confusion be a thing of value? Socrates was put to death, remember, for corrupting the minds of youth, for confusing them, for shaking their confidence in their conventional ideas. So this isn't an idle worry. But Plato saw that this question deserves a positive answer. And he was right. It's worth noticing that Plato chose to investigate this very question of philosophy's value by exemplifying the philosophical method in the form of a conversation between Socrates and a slave child. The conversation proceeds, in part, by enabling the boy to make a drawing, or rather, by showing how a drawing can afford a method for thinking things through.

It is no accident that philosophy and art stand together; to make sense of one is, I believe, to make sense of the other. This is a theme to which I returned again and again in this book.

In any case, I write this book for Dominic. I don't know whether he can be won over. But I think his challenge, or at least the challenge I think of him as posing, is a real one and I want to address it.

My friend the art historian Alexander Nagel is the other person I would like to mention. We lived on the same floor of a dormitory at Harvard in 1989 and 1990. And since then he has been my constant interlocutor about art, its history and its meaning. Together we have walked the streets and visited the art galleries of New York, Washington, D.C., Paris, Berlin, Dresden, Venice, Syracuse, and Toronto. We were fellows together at the Wissenschaftskolleg in Berlin. In the fall semester of 2011, we jointly gave a seminar in New York, cross-listed at CUNY's Graduate Center (my home institution at the time) and NYU's Institute of Fine Arts (his), on style and its critical importance not only for art, and fashion, but also for human being in general. Without his collaboration and friendship, and without the model of his own writing, I doubt I would have written this book.

Finally, I would like to express my heartfelt gratitude to my children, August, Ulysses, and Ana Rosa, and also to my partner, Nicole Peisl.

Notes

These notes supplement the main text of this book. I provide chapter summaries, additional discussion of topics raised in the text, and references. It is my hope that these notes will enhance the book in something like the way that talking about a baseball game with a friend as you watch it can enhance your experience of the game.

PREFACE

> We have only to open our eyes, and spread out before us lies a banquet of colours and shapes, shadows and textures: a pageant of rewarding and threatening objects, miraculously captured by sight. All this, from two tiny distorted upside-down patterns of light in the eyes.

These words of Richard L. Gregory in *Eye and Brain* (p. 1) give nice expression to the orthodox idea that the problem of vision is that of understanding how we see so much on the basis of so little, how we get from "in here"—from images in the eye or brain—to what is "out there," in the world. I criticize this idea in more detail in *Out of Our Heads: Why You Are Not Your Brain, and Other Lessons from the Biology of Consciousness*, chapter 6, and the limitations of such a viewpoint is a running theme, and basic commitment, of my first book, *Action in Perception*.

In *Action in Perception*, I presented what I called "the enactive approach" to perception. This view was for all intents and purposes the same as the "sensorimotor approach to vision and visual consciousness" presented by the French-American psychologist J. Kevin O'Regan and me in our paper in *Behavioral and Brain Sciences*. I chose to relabel our sensorimotor approach "enactive," first, because the basic idea of the view is that experience is something we enact or perform; it's not something that happens in us or to us. But also because I wanted to honor the work of the neurobiologist Francisco Varela, who had died in May 2001, and whose use of the word "enactive" seemed to me important and closely allied. "Enactivism" now refers to a cluster of views roughly united in holding that the human mind is active, that its workings can be understood only in relation to the living body, and that the exercise of distinctively intellectual skills such as calculation or representation is not its fundamental mode.

•

I. GETTING ORGANIZED

In this chapter I introduce the concept of an organized activity and I argue that it is a pervasive phenomenon of human life. We are by nature organized. Any account of human biology needs to be able to accommodate this fact.

•

For more on breast-feeding and its critical place in our lives and development, see Kaye, *The Mental and Social Life of Babies: How Parents Create Persons*. Nothing in what I say here about breast-feeding turns, so far as I know, on *breast*-feeding as distinct from bottle-feeding. And although I refer to "mother" or "Mama" in the text, this is not meant to exclude caregivers who are neither female nor the mother.

In the text I refer to humans as the linguistic species. It is of course very controversial whether human language is unique or whether animal communication is a kind of language. I didn't mean to take a stand on that here. It is enough, for my purposes, to notice that the distinct place of language in our human lives may have something to do, as I indicate, with breast-feeding.

•

The idea that conversation is, in my sense, an organized activity has been appreciated for a long time now and has been the subject of exciting research.

When people talk:

- There is convergence in dialect, that is, they tend to talk, in relevant respects—vocabulary, slang, pronunciation, etc.—the *same* way. (See, e.g., Giles, "Accent Mobility.")
- There is a tendency for them to speak at the same general rate. (See Street, "Speech Convergence and Speech Evaluation in Fact-Finding Interviews.")
- They tend to adopt the same vocal intensity or loudness. (See Natale, "Convergence of Mean Vocal Intensity in Dyadic Communications as a Function of Social Desirability.")
- They pause with the same frequency. (See Cappella and Planalp, "Talk and Silence Sequences in Informal Conversations III: Interspeaker Influence.")

Moreover, speakers tend to:

- mirror postures and gestures (Condon and Ogston, "Sound Film Analysis of Normal and Pathological Behavior Patterns"; Kendon, "Movement Coordination in Social Interaction: Some Examples Described"; LaFrance, "Posture Mirroring and Rapport"; Shockley, Santana, and Fowler, "Mutual Interpersonal Postural Constraints Are Involved in Cooperative Conversation.")
- coordinate rhythms of speech and movement (Condon, "An Analysis of Behavioral Organization.")
- synchronize their patterns of movement ("postural sway") (Shockley, Santana, and Fowler, "Mutual Interpersonal Postural Constraints.")

For a general discussion of this broad range of phenomena, see Shockley, Richardson, and Dale, "Conversation and Coordinative Structures," where the citations above, and many others, are given.

According to one promising line of investigation, what explains this convergence and coordination when people talk is that the speakers, together with their environment, in the setting of whatever task it is that they are performing, come to form one single "dynamical system," one amenable to (nonlinear) mathematical modeling and analysis. A crucial fact about this sort of dynamical systems model is that it rules out the idea that, as it were, the speakers themselves are in charge. Which does not mean that we can't speak of intelligence here. But it's the intelligence of *letting things happen*, of *letting the situation organize you*, rather than the intelligence of deliberation and rational agency. See Kelso, *Dynamic Patterns: The Self-Organization of Brain and Behavior*, for a groundbreaking contribution to this topic.

•

There is a large literature on distracted driving and the use of cell phones. One remarkable study, carried out by Brian Scholl and his team at Rutgers, showed that cell phone use brings about a marked impairment in *visual awareness* during driving or any attention-demanding task. (Brian J. Scholl, Nicholaus S. Noles, Vanya Pasheva, and Rachel Sussman, "Talking on a Cellular Telephone Dramatically Increases 'Sustained Inattentional Blindness.'") It is also well known that the distraction of phone conversation is considerably greater than any produced by talking with someone sitting with you in the car. (See, for example, S. G. Charlton, "Driving While Conversing: Cell Phones That Distract and Passengers Who React.") In the text I offer an explanation of why this should be so; talking on the phone while driving creates a conflict between two organized activities. The result is disorganization and so blindness.

•

The idea that it is our nature to acquire *second* natures is an Aristotelian one, developed in his *Nicomachean Ethics*. For example, he explains (1103a) that virtues are acquired "not by a process of nature, but by habituation. . . . Thus the virtues arise in us neither by nature nor against nature, but we are by nature able to acquire them, and reach our complete perfection through habit." It is also an important theme in the work of the University of Pittsburgh philosopher John McDowell, in particular his *Mind and World*.

•

In *Out of Our Heads*, chapter 5, I discuss the topic of habit. We have already noticed that Aristotle was one major thinker who did not neglect this topic. Another is William James, who writes in a chapter devoted to habit in the first volume of *The Principles of Psychology* (vol. 1, p. 104): "When we look at living creatures from an outward point of view, one of the first things that strike us is that they are bundles of habits."

An interesting thing about habits is that they open us up even as they close us off. Just try to violate the task-dependent imperatives that both enable you to talk and walk and communicate and eat and prevent you from, as it were, acting with perfect freedom. Insofar as you are a skillful driver, you drive along without guiding or directing your own actions at the embodiment level of your organization. And this enables you to travel the world's roads, see new things, accomplish new goals, but also to pay attention to the landscape around you or to listen to the radio. The idea that habits (or skills) disable as well as enable was pointed out to me by the Humboldt University art historian Horst Bredekamp.

•

In the text I introduce the notion of the "embodiment level." The crucial thing about the embodiment level is that it is neither entirely *personal* (conscious, controlled, governed by thought and planning), nor is it properly *sub*personal (automatic, reflexive, independent of thought and understanding). Subpersonal-level activity unfolds on time scales of milliseconds. Personal-level action, in contrast, takes place at much larger time scales of minutes, hours, days, weeks, and lifetimes. The embodiment level, as Dana Ballard, who first introduced this idea, understood, unfolds at an intermediate level, on the scale of seconds. This is the time scale at which we coordinate our looks and reaches, at which we communicate with a glance or a nod. The developmental psychologist Linda Smith has shown that children and their caretakers participate in organized communication, teaching, and learning at precisely this level of looks, reaches, handlings, nods, and pointings. For more on the embodiment level itself, see Dana H. Ballard, Mary M. Hayahoe, Polly K. Pook, and Rajesh P. Rao, "Deictic Codes for the Embodiment of Cognition."

•

The distinction between the personal and the subpersonal was introduced into philosophy by Daniel C. Dennett in *Content and Consciousness* (pp. 93–94):

> When we have said that a person has a sensation of pain, locates it and is prompted to react in a certain way, we have said all there is to say within the scope of this vocabulary. We *can* demand further explanation of how a person happens to withdraw his hand from the hot stove, but we cannot demand further explanations in terms of 'mental processes.' Since the introduction of unanalysable mental qualities leads to a premature end to explanation, we may decide that such introduction is wrong, and look for alternative modes of explanation. If we do this we must abandon the explanatory level of people and their sensations and activities and turn to the *sub-personal* level of brains and events in the nervous system. But when we abandon the personal level in a very real sense we abandon the subject matter of pains as well.

Later, in *The Intentional Stance*, Dennett insists that it is the job of empirical psychology, *cognitive psychology*, to explain how the personal level arises out of and depends on the subpersonal level. Crucially, he insists, any genuinely *scientific* cognitive psychology will be a psychology of the subpersonal level. Thereupon hangs many a tale and thickets of controversy. And for just the reason that Dennett originally recognized: when we turn to the subpersonal, we abandon the subject matter of the person's active thought, life, and experience, for these have no reality at the level of cells and their causal networks.

2. REORGANIZING OURSELVES

The basic claim of this chapter is that art is a reorganizational practice; art takes as its raw materials the different ways we find ourselves organized (naturally, biologically, but also culturally). Choreography, which I take as my example, isn't in the business of dancing; it's in the business of putting dancing, or, really, the fact that we are dancers (as it were by nature), on display. As with choreography, so with the other arts. Painting as an art, for example, investigates picture-making and picture-using activity (technology) in something like the way choreography investigates dancing activity.

•

People dance on purpose but they don't decide how to dance. This is a delicate issue that I will come back to later. The point here is that dancing, like conversation, is an activity with its own dynamics; doing it well requires that one let oneself be caught up in the activity, that one let the demands of the tasks at hand make decisions for you. Note, though, that I don't mean to suggest that it isn't possible to be a thoughtful or self-aware dancer. Just as we can engage in free-flowing spontaneous conversation and nevertheless notice our own slips of the tongue, or other kinds of linguistic infelicity, just as we can talk and think about what we are saying as we talk, so we can participate in the organized activity of dancing with both self-awareness and self-control. Note also that my comment here is not meant to apply to professional dancers. Professional dancers are certainly capable of thoughtfully monitoring their own action as they dance. Of course professional dancers are not really dancers in my sense. They work with dancing.

The whole issue of expertise and self-monitoring, and the connection of these themes to that of organized activities, is one I hope to take up elsewhere. For related discussion, see Barbara Gail Montero, "The Myth of 'Just Do It.'"

•

The idea that choreography is not dancing but that it is directly engaged with dance invites an important criticism. A fair bit of art dance over the last fifty years has taken its start not from dancing at all but from other sources entirely. One important preoccupation of some choreography is movement, or the body, or somatic experience itself. Another source is *performance*—dance performance, but other kinds of performance, too.

I don't mean to rule any of this out! My crucial point is that choreography is related to the organized activities that are its antecedents in something like the way philosophy is related to natural science. Philosophy, however closely tied to science in the framing of its concerns, is not just "more science." It does something else. Something more or something less. Crucially, something different. (Wittgenstein, in the *Tractatus*, wrote (§4.111): "the word 'philosophy' must mean something which stands above or below, but not beside the natural sciences.")

•

Choreography and organization: my claim in the text is that choreography, insofar as it is an art, does not aim at better dancing or better realization of the dancerly way of being organized; it aims at displaying ourselves to ourselves as dancers. It is worth contrasting this idea with another related one according to which choreographic problems are, precisely, organizational problems, where this is understood in a technical or perhaps an engineering sense. In this sense, one might say that choreography, like music, is concerned with managing structures in space and time. Thought of this way, it is possible to see choreographic principles and problems at work and at play not only in arts like music and architecture, but also in business, in urban planning, and in setting the table and eating dinner. This in turn opens up the idea that choreography—which you might have thought was a branch of show business, relegated to putting dance on the stage as entertainment—is in fact a legitimate and authentic place for research into a broad range of ideas, principles, and strategies all of which have application outside show business and some of which might be closely related to problems or phenomena of interest to engineers, mathematicians, and physicists. This is a striking position, and one with which I am in broad agreement. It is worth stressing, though, that my conception of choreography as a *reorganizational practice* is different. Choreography's interest in organization is not that of the engineer or the technologist; the aim is not to be the master of one's activities, or to bring out the physical, psychological, or dynamic principles that govern organizations of one kind or another. Choreography's concerns are before all that, or after all that. They are philosophical and aim at bringing ourselves into view for ourselves.

•

Humberto Maturana and Francisco Varela present the theory of autopoiesis in *Autopoiesis and Cognition: The Realization of the Living*.

Evan Thompson's *Mind in Life* offers a detailed discussion of the importance of autopoiesis not only for biology but also for the study of mind. Thompson stresses a point that informs my comments in the text: that Darwinian natural selection offers a framework for explaining changes in frequency of traits across populations of organisms; the theory doesn't explain, it doesn't *try* to explain, the origin of organisms, of life, in the first place. Immanuel Kant, writing in *Critique of Judgment*, presumably had the outstanding need for such a fundamental explanation of life itself, of the organism, in mind (¶400):

> It is . . . quite certain that we can never get a sufficient knowledge of organized beings and their inner possibility, much less get an explanation of them, by looking merely to mechanical principles of nature. Indeed, so certain is it, that we may confidently assert that it is absurd for men even to entertain any thought of so doing or to hope that maybe another Newton may some day arise, to make intelligible to us even the genesis of but a blade of grass from natural laws that no design has ordered. Such insight we must absolutely deny to mankind.

•

Ludwig Wittgenstein, in *Philosophical Investigations*, states (§124): "A philosophical problem has the form: 'I don't know my way about.'"

3. DESIGNERS BY NATURE

In this chapter I argue that technologies are basic for human beings. They are hubs of organization. And this explains art's abiding concern with manufacture and technology, with making and doing and building and displaying, even though art's significance is never exhausted by, or even, really, approximated by, any pregiven measures of how well we do this. Art works with technology because technology—in the guise of pictures, language itself, dress, building—organizes us and holds us captive. Art is not technology. But art presupposes technology as irony presupposes straight talk.

•

On art as a making activity, John Dewey writes in *Art as Experience* (p. 48):

> Art denotes a process of doing or making. This is as true of fine as of
> technological art. Art involves molding of clay, chipping of marble, cast-
> ing of bronze, laying on of pigments, constructing of buildings, singing of
> songs, playing of instruments, enacting rôles on the stage, going through
> rhythmic movements in the dance. Every art does something with some
> physical material, the body or something outside the body, with or with-
> out the use of intervening tools, and with a view to production of some-
> thing visible, audible, or tangible.

"As true of fine as of technological art," says Dewey. Of course this raises a question
and a puzzle: we know why *technology* is a process of doing or making. Technology—
engineering, manufacture—is in the business of problem solving. It serves utility.
But why should art itself be so bound up with making? Or why should it be
concerned with production in the way Dewey names? These are the questions I
have set myself in this book. Dewey goes on to offer a clue (p. 50): "Man whittles,
carves, sings, dances, gestures, molds, draws and paints. The doing or making is
artistic when the perceived result is of such a nature that *its* qualities *as perceived*
have controlled the question of production."

•

I assert in the text that pictures are technologies and that picture use is an organized activity. A lot more needs to be done to flesh out this proposal. Picture use is
variegated, after all. There's making pictures. And then there's the way we handle
them, for example, when we flip through the pages of a catalog, or click on links on
a website. Of the six criteria of organized activities enumerated in chapter 1, all but
two apply straightforwardly to the case of pictures—pictures are cognitively sophisticated, our uses of them are spontaneous and unauthored, pictures serve useful,
function-oriented transactions, and pictures and our use of them can be a source of
pleasure. But what of the first and third criteria? According to the first, organized
activities, as I put it, are basic, primitive, natural. Can it be seriously maintained
that picture-using activities are basic in this sense? Actually, I think it can. It is a
striking fact about our engagement with pictures—I take this up in chapters 12
and 13—that pictures *feel* immediate and independent of knowledge and learning.
With pictures, it is as if we actually see what they show. We don't need to interpret
pictures to get at what they display, at least not in the usual case. Now, in fact, this
appearance of immediacy is something that needs to be explained and, finally, explained away. It takes knowledge and an awareness of context to understand pictures and see what they try to show us. But the point of the criterion—our main
concern here—is not so much that picture use, any more than language use, is
unlearned or primitive or natural in that sense, but that it presents itself to us as

immediately intelligible; we don't need to secure its intelligibility by argument or reasoning. Picture use, picture seeing, we might say, is profoundly habitual. In this connection it's worth remembering, as I note a few times in the text, that the history of our use of pictures is *at least* thirty thousand years old, and is one that we share, it now seems, with closely related species such as the Neanderthal (according to recent findings; see Joaquín Rodríguez-Vidal, et al., "A Rock Engraving Made by Neanderthals in Gibraltar").

As for the third criterion—that organized activities have distinctive modes of spatial and temporal organization—it is, strictly speaking, an open question whether our use of pictures (as manufacturers and as consumers) has this kind of organization. I bet that it does. Picture making and picture using—like all tool use—involves entrainment in activities with their own distinctive rhythms and patterns of movement in space. The further investigation of this is a challenge for future research.

Some anecdotal evidence for the claim that picture making is organized in my sense: I have twice sat for artists, and during the sittings I had the opportunity to watch the artists carefully as they rendered me. In both cases I was struck by the activity and dynamism of the portrait-making process. There was nothing detached and contemplative about it. The artists hungrily kept me in view even as they turned to their work surface. Far from being *contemplated*, it was as if I was sampled, tasted, handled, in the ceaseless and energetic back-and-forth of making looking, looking making. There really was something dancelike, something rhythmic and physical in this picture-making activity. It was physical and active, but also strikingly thoughtful and intelligent. Dewey gets at this (p. 47):

> Because perception of relationship between what is done and what is undergone constitutes the work of intelligence, and because the artist is controlled in the process of his work by his grasp of the connection between what he has already done and what he is to do next, the idea that the artist does not think as intently and penetratingly as a scientific inquirer is absurd. A painter must consciously undergo the effect of his every brush stroke or he will not be aware of what he is doing and where his work is going. Moreover, he has to see each particular connection of doing and undergoing in relation to the whole that he desires to produce. To apprehend such relations is to think, and is one of the most exacting modes of thought.

•

There is a lot written on technology and human evolution. Some books I found particularly helpful, and on which I rely in this chapter, are Haim Ofek's *Second Nature: Economic Origins of Human Evolution* and Matt Ridley's *The Rational Optimist: How Prosperity Evolves*. I learned a lot about this topic from the University College London geneticist Mark G. Thomas; he and I were fellows together at the Wissenschaftskolleg zu Berlin in 2007–2008. He introduced me to the idea that there are alternatives to the idea of that we became psychologically modern thanks to a change in our brains (a "brainy mutation").

•

On the prehistoric origins of clothing, see Ralf Kittler, Manfred Kayser, and Mark Stoneking, "Molecular Evolution of *Pediculus humanus* and the Origin of Clothing." This is discussed with great care and insight by Nicholas Wade in *Before the Dawn: Recovering the Lost History of Our Ancestors.* See also his "What a Story Lice Can Tell."

•

An excellent book on technology and its distinctive mode of evolution is W. Brian Arthur's *The Nature of Technology: What It Is and How It Evolves.*

•

Thanks to my friend Dean Moses, who is a Salesforce software engineer, for information about the Salesforce product Chatter and its workings.

•

About the importance of notations for thinking: notice that because we sometimes think in notational schemes, it is possible to investigate our thinking by looking into the workings of our notational systems. In the branch of logic and mathematics known as proof theory, it is possible to establish, for example, that a written language (a "formal system") is *complete* (that is, capable of being used to establish all the truths in a particular domain), or that it is *sound* (that is, that all the theorems are in fact true). These are investigations of the mathematics of the structures of our notations themselves.

•

That tools can extend our minds as well as our bodies has been a theme in the work of Andy Clark. See his *Supersizing the Mind: Embodiment, Action, and Cognitive Extension,* and also, especially, his paper with the New York University philosopher David J. Chalmers, "The Extended Mind."

But the idea of the extended mind is probably much older than their discussion. Maurice Merleau-Ponty, for example, writes in *Phenomenology of Perception* (p. 144):

> Without any explicit calculation, a woman maintains a safe distance between the feather in her hat and objects that might damage it; she senses where the feather is, just as we sense where our hand is. If I possess the habit of driving a car, then I enter into a lane and see that "I can pass" without comparing the width of the lane to that of the fender, just as I go through a door without comparing the width of the door to that of my body. The hat and the automobile have ceased to be objects whose size and volume would be determined through a comparison with other objects . . . The blind man's cane has ceased to be an object for him, it is no

longer perceived for itself; rather, the cane's furthest point is transformed into a sensitive zone, it increases the scope and radius of the act of touching and has become analogous to a gaze. In the exploration of objects, the length of the cane does not explicitly intervene nor act as a middle term: the blind man knows its length by the position of the objects, rather than the position of the objects through the cane's length.

Here, very clearly, Merleau-Ponty treats the cane, or the car, or the feather, as, effectively, part of an extended body and so, insofar as the extended body is a knowing, feeling, sensing, and also problem-solving body, as belonging to an extended mind.

Merleau-Ponty is influenced by Heidegger's treatment of tools in *Being and Time*. For Heidegger, the crucial thing about tools is that they don't show up for us as objects that we inspect, think about, evaluate, and apply. In a sense, they don't really *show up for us* at all. We take them for granted. We rely on them, much as we rely on the ground itself. They recede into the background, at least when we know them, when we understand them and are their masters. Tools are not really things, they are bits of equipment. Heidegger does not argue that tools extend the mind by extending what we can do; he argues, rather, that they make up our world in a way that can't be made sense of on the model of subject and object.

For Heidegger, as for Merleau-Ponty, and Clark and Chalmers, the boundary between person and environment or self and world is not defined by the limits of the skull. (This is also the theme of my own *Out of Our Heads*.)

A closely related family of concerns is expressed by Ludwig Wittgenstein in *Philosophical Investigations* when he writes (§626):

> When I touch this object with a stick I have the sensation of touching in the tip of the stick, not in the hand that holds it. When someone says "The pain isn't here in my hand, but in my wrist," this has the consequence that the doctor examines the wrist. But what difference does it make if I say that I feel the hardness of the object in the tip of the stick or in my hand? Does what I say mean "It is as if I had nerve-endings in the tip of the stick"? *In what sense* is it like that?—Well, I am at any rate inclined to say "I feel the hardness etc. in the tip of the stick." What goes with this is that when I touch the object I look not at my hand but at the tip of the stick; that I describe what I feel by saying "I feel something hard and round there"—not "I feel a pressure against the tips of my thumb, middle finger, and index finger . . ." If, for example, someone asks me "What are you now feeling in the fingers that hold the probe?" I might reply: "I don't know—I feel something hard and rough *over there*."

We can read Wittgenstein as bringing out what Merleau-Ponty has in mind when he says that we don't treat the cane as a middle term to draw inferences about the position of objects. Merleau-Ponty's focus is on the phenomenon: to suppose that we infer the location of things from the experience we have of the stick would greatly distort the way things show up to the cane user; as Merleau-Ponty says, we know where the cane is from the position of the objects rather than the other way around. Wittgenstein's focus, as always, and in contrast with Merleau-Ponty, is on *what it makes sense to say* about, for example, *where* one feels the hardness and roundness.

Wittgenstein also takes up this theme in an earlier work, *The Blue and Brown Books* (p. 16):

> It is correct to say that thinking is an activity of our writing hand, of our larynx, of our head, and of our mind, so long as we understand the grammar of these statements. And it is, furthermore, extremely important to realize how, by misunderstanding the grammar of our expressions, we are led to think of one in particular of these statements as giving the *real* seat of the activity of thinking.

Wittgenstein does not want to deny that we are correct when we say that thinking is an activity of our head, but he wants to remind us that this doesn't mean that our head alone *really* does the thinking, any more than it would be right to say that the hand alone really does the thinking.

4. ART LOOPS AND THE GARDEN OF EDEN

This chapter forms the heart of *Strange Tools*. The arts (and philosophy!) do not merely investigate, model, and display the ways we find ourselves organized. They change the ways we are organized; they loop down and reorganize us. And they do this essentially because they give us new resources for thinking about what we are doing, and so they give us resources for doing things differently.

•

I draw here on the Canadian philosopher of science Ian Hacking's beautiful idea of looping concepts and looping effects in his book *The Social Construction of What?* Categories like *heterosexual, professor, cheerleader, black, white, woman, man,* for example, exhibit what Hacking calls "looping effects." They don't just *apply* to people, grouping them on the basis of features that they may share. The categories supply people a way of thinking about themselves. Being straight, for example, isn't just a matter of acting in certain ways or being so disposed to act. It's also a matter of thinking of yourself in a certain way. And with this way of thinking about yourself comes a whole complex of associated qualities, limitations, and also expectations, stereotypes, etc., that loop back down and influence how we act or are disposed to act. Insofar as straight people act straight, gay people act gay, boys act like boys, and girls like girls, and so on—insofar as we even know what it means to speak this way—this is so in good measure because people identify with themselves as falling under a certain category and they make choices, both consciously and unconsciously, to conform to what the category says they are. We carry ourselves the way we think we are supposed to carry ourselves and dress the way we think we are supposed to dress. In my terms, we enact, or create ourselves, by fulfilling the demands of a label or a category. As Hacking puts it (p. 34): "Looping effects are everywhere. Think what the category of genius did to those Romantics who saw themselves as geniuses, and what their behavior in turn did to the category of genius itself. Think about the transformations effected by the notions of fat, overweight, anorexic."

It is sometimes noted that anorexia, for example, is a newfangled disease, one that exists only in the Western world. It is, as it is said, a social construction. Maybe so, but this doesn't mean it is unreal. We can make real the categories in terms of which we understand ourselves. Take race. The fact—I take it to be a fact—that "black" and "white" have no meaningful biological foundation—doesn't mean that the distinction has no reality. If how I am labeled affects how people treat me, and what options I have, who I am likely to mate with, where I am likely to live, and so finally what I take to be likely or plausible or probable about myself, then, in no time at all, we have manufactured (or evolved, or constructed) a *real* difference where there was none before.

What these sorts of examples show is that you can't segregate first-order and second-order facts about identity. What category we belong to shapes how we experience things because among the things we experience is the fact (such as it is) of our belonging or being treated as belonging to one category or another.

This isn't just a delicate philosophical point of academic interest but one that can make a big difference in our lives.

Consider one study, discussed by the psychologist Cordelia Fine, in which students at a private college were asked to perform a spatial-reasoning task. Before the test one group of students filled out a form on which they were asked to report their gender. The other group was not asked this question but was instead asked to name their university. In this way, one group was "primed" to consider themselves in the light of gender identity, whereas the other was primed to think of themselves under the category "private college student." Men primed to think of their gender performed markedly better than men who were primed to think of themselves as students at a college. The opposite was observed in women. Those primed to consider their status as students at a college significantly outperformed women who'd been primed to think of themselves as women. The mere questions—male? female? student?—by reminding the students what kind of person they are, determined how well they performed on the test.

If biology is the measure of all things, then many of the categories we use to group ourselves into kinds of person—man, woman, gay, straight, black, white, professor, cheerleader—are, in fact, ungrounded. You don't find them in nature as it is apart from our attitudes and beliefs about that nature. At the same time, what could be more real than the way we experience ourselves as being? This shows that biology is not the measure of all things.

See Cordelia Fine's *Delusions of Gender* for a smart discussion of the psychological literature on implicit bias and stereotype. My discussion of this here draws on my "Gender Is Dead! Long Live Gender."

•

Motion Bank is the name of a research project organized by the Forsythe Company, under the direction of William Forsythe and Scott deLahunta, to develop online digital scores of choreographic works and also to encourage the investigation of choreography. I was involved with the project from the beginning and I recommend the website: www.motionbank.org. Forsythe came up with the term "motion bank." We all have a stock of remembered images of what painting looks like, say, or what sculpture is. But we lack a similar "bank" of images of what dance is or what it looks like. The project aimed to take a step in the direction of (starting a conversation to begin) supplying that needed motion bank.

•

The idea that writing shapes our thought and experience of language is a central preoccupation, and original insight, of the linguist Roy Harris. I took classes from Harris in Oxford in the late 1980s. His books have made a strong impression on me. See, for example, *The Language-Makers* and *The Language Myth*. Of special importance for the topic of this chapter is Harris's *The Origin of Writing*.

•

The long quotation from a linguistics textbook that I give in the text is from the chapter on linguistic structure at the start of Andrew Radford's *Transformational Syntax: A Student's Guide to Chomsky's Extended Standard Theory*. This book was assigned to me in one of my undergraduate linguistics classes back at Columbia University in the late 1980s.

•

This idea that writing distorts and regulates language, and that it privileges some forms of speech over others, is a familiar one. It is tied to the well-known distinction between prescriptive and descriptive grammar. Prescriptive grammars tell you how you *ought* to speak, whereas descriptive grammars, so we are told, simply examine how people actually talk. It also informs the famous quip, attributed to the Yiddish expert Max Weinreich, that "a language is a dialect with an army and navy." This is usually taken to suggest that all ways of speaking, in all communities, are on a par as far as language is concerned. This is all well and good. No doubt High German is just another German dialect, not in any intrinsic way different from (let alone superior to) dialects spoken in small villages. But it is important to be alert to the ways the supposedly extrinsic factors—writing, dictionaries, universities, television and radio—in fact give speakers of a language resources that enable them, in effect, to think differently about their lives with language. As is always the case with looping effects, we're in the domain of self-fulfilling prophecy. There's a local point and a more general point to be made about this. The local point is just that the linguistic-cultural apparatus of writing, spelling, style, and all that provides speakers a model of their own practice that they can leverage as language users. Your awareness of writing changes the linguistic environment. The more general point is that, for us, now, the contrast between language, as it is shaped by the social, political, and ideological trappings of the nation-state, the university, writing and schools, the publishing industry, dictionaries, and all the rest, and language as it really truly is at some simple linguistic core, is no longer a meaningful one. This is one of the main points of this chapter: our lived experience of language is thoroughly shaped by writing and all the rest. We can't strip away the extrinsics. We can't return to Eden.

•

The philosopher David J. Chalmers uses the idea of Eden in a way that is related to my use here in the chapter. Chalmers uses the notion to capture some of our primitive commitments on the nature of our own conscious experience. In Eden, he tells us, before we ate from the Tree of Science, there was no gap between appearance and reality. Things really were the way they seemed. Science challenges this primitive Edenic phenomenology; we come to learn, for example, that the redness we see is not in the tomato itself but is an effect in us of the tomato's action, by way of light, on the nervous system. I deploy the idea of Eden to a different end in the chapter. You'd have to go back to Eden, I suggest, to find a mode of linguistic engagement that was uninfluenced by shared norms of how we are supposed to talk. Which is really just to say that there is not and never has been speech unaffected by a language ideology. See David J. Chalmers, "Perception and the Fall from Eden."

•

Plato's attack on poetry is centered around book X of the *Republic*.

•

For more on orality versus literacy, see Walter J. Ong's *Orality and Literacy: The Technologizing of the Word*. For more on Plato on poetry, see Eric A. Havelock's *Preface to Plato*.

•

We don't invent writing to represent speech; we apply the already existing instrument of writing *to* speech. This is a central claim of Harris's book on writing.

•

My thinking about language, writing, and the themes of this chapter has benefited from conversation with Christopher M. Hutton, the University of Hong Kong linguist.

•

Thanks to the musicologist Leo Treitler, whom I got to know at meetings of the New York Humanities Institute, for conversation on Beethoven and musical scores.

5. ART, EVOLUTION, AND THE PUZZLE OF PUZZLES

In this chapter I argue that pictures change the way we see. What we call "the aesthetic sense," I suggest, is something that would be impossible without pictures, or at least without the pictorial attitude. As a species, or as a culture, we've been making pictures for tens of thousands of years. Against this background I discuss attempts to understand art and aesthetic experience within broadly evolutionary frameworks. Evolutionary approaches to art as such, I insist, are unsuccessful. The prospects for an evolutionary conception of the aesthetic sense, however, are more promising.

•

Plato discusses pictures and mirrors in book X of the *Republic*. Here's the crucial passage. Socrates speaks first.

> But now consider what name you would give to this craftsman.
>
> What one?
>
> Him who makes all the things that all handicraftsmen severally produce.
>
> A truly clever and wondrous man you tell of.
>
> Ah, but wait, and you will say so indeed, for this same handicraftsman is not only able to make all implements, but he produces all plants and animals, including himself, and thereto earth and heaven and the gods and all things in heaven and in Hades under the earth.
>
> A most marvelous Sophist, he said.
>
> Are you incredulous? said I. Tell me, do you deny altogether the possibility of such a craftsman, or do you admit that in a sense there could be such a creator of all these things, and in another sense not? Or do you not perceive that you yourself would be able to make all these things in a way?
>
> And in what way, I ask you, he said.
>
> There is no difficulty, said I, but it is something that the craftsman can make everywhere and quickly. You could do it most quickly if you should choose to take a mirror and carry it about everywhere. You will speedily produce the sun and all the things in the sky, and speedily the earth and yourself and the other animals and implements and plants and all the objects of which we just now spoke.
>
> Yes, he said, the appearance of them, but not the reality and the truth.
>
> Excellent, said I, and you come to the aid of the argument opportunely. For I take it that the painter too belongs to this class of producers, does he not?

Of course.

But you will say, I suppose, that his creations are not real and true.

And yet, after a fashion, the painter too makes a couch, does he not?

Yes, he said, the appearance of one, he too.

•

Anne Hollander's *Seeing Through Clothes* is an exciting work and I take inspiration from it in this chapter. It is a history of the treatment of clothing, and the clothed body, in Western art. In chapter 6, which is devoted to mirrors, she writes: "The mirror gazer participates (not always consciously) in the imaginative act of making art out of facts: the aim is to mold the reflection into an acceptable picture, instantaneously and repeatedly, with no other means than the eyes themselves." Some of my remarks on Hollander's ideas are adapted from a short "appreciation" of her that I published after her death: "The World Looked Better Through Anne Hollander's Eyes."

•

As cited in the notes to chapter 3, evidence that Neanderthal participated in picture-making practices is presented in Joaquín Rodríguez-Vidal et al., "A Rock Engraving Made by Neanderthals in Gibraltar."

•

The idea that vision itself is cultural is a central theme in the research of the UC Berkeley art historian Whitney Davis. Heinrich Wölfflin, one of the foundational figures of art history, had said that "vision itself has a history." Davis extends this idea: vision, he says, has an *art* history (p. 10). For Wölfflin, in Davis's words, "styles of depiction—culturally located and historically particular ways of making pictorial representations—have materially affected human visual perception. They constitute what might literally be called *ways of seeing*" (p. 6). As a result of processes of this sort, vision, in Davis's terms, "succeeds to visuality," that is, it succeeds to vision in the sense of giving rise to new, culturally loaded and enhanced visual abilities (or "visualities," or "culturalities of vision"). What Davis here calls succession, and which he stresses must be a real, historical phenomenon, one that unfolds in the life of the species and also in the developmental life of the individual, is his language for the kind of looping that I have been describing. In my terms, pictures loop down and change how we think about what they display, just as writing loops down and changes how we talk. See Heinrich Wölfflin, *Principles of Art History: The Problem of the Development of Style in Later Art*, and Whitney Davis, *A General Theory of Visual Culture*.

Davis is admirably insistent that art historians (and visual studies scholars) are not entitled to *assume* that vision is cultural. This needs to be demonstrated. For Davis, this means that we need to investigate the "recursions of succession," that is, the mechanisms, both cultural and individual (as well as intra-individual), by which vision acquires cultural standing; that is, we need to study, in his peculiar and, to me anyway, inviting phraseology, the "relays, recursions, resistances, and reversions," whereby vision succeeds to visuality. Davis insists that "vision is not inherently a visuality" (p. 8). By this I take him to mean that vision is not inherently suffused with culture.

Now, this last point seems questionable. We can grant, as surely we must, that physiology is the ground of all human visual capacity, without supposing, therefore, that vision can operate, *as it does in the life of human beings* (and perhaps also other animals), in the absence of, if not full-blown pictoriality and full-blown language, then at least the full-blown precursors of these. And these precursors probably come in two basic forms. First, there is thought itself. I agree with John McDowell, and Immanuel Kant, that intuitions without concepts are blind, even if it is also true, as Kant admits (or insists) in *The Critique of Pure Reason*, that thoughts without intuitions are empty. Human (or animal) perceptual experience requires the exercise of understanding. Now, this exercise doesn't reduce to the operations of physiology. And moreover it is likely to be shared and cultural. We don't come at the world in thought alone. And so we don't come at the world in perception on our own, alone, either. Second, there is what I called, in the last chapter, the writerly attitude, or the pictorial attitude. These are species of the genus *normative attitude*, that is, the general standpoint in which we critically reflect on and evaluate not just how things are but also how we should think about, reflect on, look at, and describe how things are; this is the domain in which we concern ourselves with what is correct, right, normal, justified, in the ways we speak and in the ways we experience the world. If we allow that the writerly attitude is, really, a form of protowriting, then, we can say, with only seeming paradox, that there was writing in the era before writing, and there were pictures in the era before pictures, at least in this extended sense. The *actual* discovery of writing language and the actual development of picture-making practices didn't change anything or mark a new worldview. Not from one day to the next.

The upshot of these considerations is that, to use a phrase beloved of phenomenologists, we were *always already* cultural even in the exercise of biological faculties such as vision. In Davis's terms, vision has always been a visuality.

It may be that it is finally a mistake to think that the "succession to visuality" is a historical phenomenon. It is, if I am right, a prehistorical phenomenon. We need to go back to Eden to find a time when there was language that was not already shaped by writing or seeing that was not shaped by pictures. And so it is no historical accident that our visual lives are shaped by pictures as they are. Our concern should not be with an origins story but with an ontological one.

•

One art historian whose historical storytelling exhibits what I would describe as an ontological sensitivity to looping or recursion is Alexander Nagel. In *Medieval Modern: Art out of Time*, he discusses Gentile da Fabriano's *The Crippled and Sick Cured at the Tomb of Saint Nicholas*. This painting depicts the sick and the crippled praying, touching, giving thanks before the health-delivering sarcophagus set in the apse of a church on whose walls is a mosaic depicting *this very subject matter*. Now, in one sense there is no puzzle here. The actions of these pilgrims are the typical actions of pilgrims over centuries. The scene shown in the painted mosaic is not this exact scene, but one categorically like it, a different group of pilgrims visiting the chapel at an earlier date. But the painting does not only document the routine behavior of pilgrims; it also shows how actual pilgrim behavior models itself on that of earlier pilgrims by way of following the model set down in pictures; Gentile's pilgrims are shown fulfilling the model given in the (painted) apse mosaic. But the painting does something else as well, according to Nagel. It documents not only the routines of pilgrims but also the routines of art-makers. For the painting itself *enacts* the process whereby one picture (in this case that of Gentile) is a response to and in fact imitation of another (the depicted, imagined mosaic). Nagel writes (p. 79): "The main point is that the painting before us is more than a rendition of the scene in the mosaic apse. It offers a kind of document of routines of imitation occurring in the world, including the world of art-making. Artworks model themselves on earlier artworks, and pilgrims model themselves on earlier pilgrims. This painting shows us these processes at work and even interactions between the two processes."

Gentile's picture invites a sort of vertigo and regress. We see a picture of a church containing a picture of that very same church, and so on. Everyday perceptual life is not paradoxical in that very same manner. But something analogous goes on. When we see a real church, what we see is the execution of an idea or conception; it has its origin in a plan or a picture. It would be crazy to conclude that everything we see is in a picture in the way the pilgrims in the church are in the picture in the church. But it's not so crazy at all to conclude that our grip on what there is, especially our grip on what we see, is organized by pictures.

●

On pictures and culture: one of the central ideas of the chapter is that pictures are a technology that has altered the way we see in something like the way the technology of writing has changed how we talk. In chapters 12 and 13 I will argue that pictures are not truly optical phenomena; they are communication devices. They are tools for showing, and they are effective, they genuinely depict, only in a communicative setting. But they are, remarkably, tools for showing that alter the way we see. This makes seeing, and pictures, cultural, but not at the expense of their being natural. What I want to rule out by saying they are cultural is the possibility that pictures might operate neurologically, without any role for thought, communication, understanding, or meaning. So the account I develop is not consistent with the position developed by the British art historian John Onians (in his essay "Neuroarchaeology and the Origins of Representation in the Grotte de Chauvet"). Onians argues that pictures—even pictures of the sort of exquisite refinement of the cave art of Chauvet—might have arisen as the result of brute neurological events. "A naturalistic image," he writes, "might be produced completely sponta-neously, due to nothing more than the normal operation of the human neural make-up" (p. 314). Onians's account is ingenious. Roughly the idea is that seeing a bear's claw marks on the cave wall might spontaneously prompt us to do what the bear had done (thanks to "mirror neurons"). We might then take an immediate pleasure in the marks we ourselves have made and find ourselves disposed to repeat them as our visual neural networks plastically adapt to the effects of our own ac-tion. Add to this that we see on the surface of the cave walls natural images of things that matter to us and that provoke great feeling—predators and prey, for example—and, remembering the effects of our own accidental mark making, we might find ourselves drawn to enhance and elaborate what we see, with each ges-ture producing a stronger visual, emotional reaction that leads us to do more. "The continued activity is likely to have been fuelled by the brain's chemistry," Onians writes (p. 314), "with each enhancement of the correspondence causing the release in the brain of one of the neurotransmitters that drive all the actions that are vital for our survival." In this way, "an unconscious feedback process could thus lead to the production of a highly naturalistic representation without any teaching, guid-ing or other social stimulation."

Now what is striking in this account, and what lends it plausibility, is its ap-preciation of picture making as something that arises out of circuits of doing, under-going, seeing, feeling, responding, and more doing. And surely we can imagine individual processes such as this explaining the development, in the person or the animal, of all manner of skills or traits. It strikes me, for example, that it is plau-sible that a story along these lines would lead to the discovery of masturbation. One might stumble across an effect, like it, repeat it, like it more, and so on.

But I find it hard to believe that such an essentially reactive, felt, automatic kind of solo activity could give rise to pictures like those we find in Chauvet. If pictures are, in this way, stimuli we have learned to make as a result of neuro-logically grounded feedback processes, then wouldn't we expect to find scribbles and doodles, drafts and experiments? And why would we go into dark, out-of-the-way, hard-to-reach caves to make our pictures? Onians remarks that the caves, illuminated by torchlight, were surely visually stunning places. This presupposes, it seems to me, that the cave painters were observers, or aesthetes, who stood back and contemplated. But *that* attitude is already the pictorial attitude. The ability to look at the world and enjoy its appearance—contrasted with the engaged visual management of the environment as one hunts or climbs or spelunks—is the ex-pression of our interest in pictures, rather than a cause of our developing pictorial technologies.

The cave painters, I find it difficult to doubt, were thoughtful and interested; they were makers in the full sense of that term. They were experts. Onians seems to allow as much when he writes (p. 314), "the memory of what the hand could do is likely then to have primed the motor networks involved, and this in itself could have encouraged people to return to the cave later with their familiar tools, stones and sticks, ochre and charcoal, the neural networks controlling their hands primed to extend or complete an imagined shape." Talk of memory, here, and encouragement, and imagined shapes surely all suggests a view of thoughtful people making images knowledgeably and for reasons. No doubt neural systems are enabling the activity, but the activity is one that people rather than brains are carrying out. Against the idea that our ancestors made pictures to titillate, a kind of visual masturbation, my proposal is that we made pictures to show, or think about, that which we depict. We don't aim at brute resemblance; we aim at articulate communication. From this point of view, it should not be surprising that picture making happened in caves. Like cinemas, or auditoriums, or galleries, the caves were special places for a special kind of social event, one no less sophisticated than talking, and one that could not take place in the absence of language and intelligent communication.

•

On pictures and objects: Bruno Latour, speaking at a conference at MIT in September 2014—I was in the audience—observed that we think of the visible world on the model of the still life. This is exactly right. We—we philosophers, we cognitive scientists—think of seeing as something like the contemplation of a picture, and we think of what is seen, the visible world, on the model of the still life. What interests me is the fact that we cannot choose to see things differently. We cannot choose to free ourselves from the structures that organize us.

•

The idea that pictures exert a power over us is a theme in the work of Horst Bredekamp. His "*Bildakt*" (picture act) theory is premised on the idea that pictures have, or seem to have, a kind of agency and power; they act on us. Such a claim can seem unnecessarily anthropomorphizing or animistic. Pictures don't act on us; we use pictures, one might be tempted to respond. But in the text I converge on Bredekamp's idea. True, the picture is not an agent. But pictures, like language, are vested with meanings and qualities that exert an enormous influence on us. Pictures sometimes speak to us. This family of ideas is developed in Bredekamp's important book *Theorie des Bildakts*.

For Bredekamp, and indeed also for Whitney Davis, the power of pictures to organize and shape our thinking, their ability not only to show but also to loop down and change the way we think about what they show, makes pictures themselves strange tools, even pictures that are not, in my sense, works of art. This idea is also advanced by Joerg Fingerhut in his "Extended Imagery, Extended Access, or Something Else? Pictures and the Extended Mind Hypothesis."

In one sense I welcome this claim. It is precisely the consequence of the sort of mingling of level 1 and level 2 that I describe in the text and that finds support in the thinking of Bredekamp, Davis, Nagel, and others, that we can no longer, ever, entirely, take the art out of pictorial technology or the pictorial technology out of pictorial art. In a world with picture art—with *strange* pictures—every picture runs the risk of being strange. But we must not overstate the case. That picture of the politician in the newspaper *doesn't undertake* the work of a work of art. It just shows you something.

•

Pictures organize us. They transform. They alter seeing. These are themes of the chapter. But not only seeing. Pictures have also remade our sense of what there is to see. Pictures give us objects, a world of self-standing "still lifes." But if this is true, then, in some sense, pictures give us *physics*, for there would be no physics if not for the way of understanding the world as made up of detached, mind-independent, particular entities (objects).

Again I converge here on a central theme in Bredekamp's work. Bredekamp is keen to show how pictures and pictorial understanding permeate culture at large and that they are critical, in particular, for science. Science has never been just the science of words or mathematics; it has always rested on and made use of the practiced eye and the schooled hand of the artist. Nowhere is this clearer than in the case of Galileo, whose ability to make use of telescopic images and on their basis to draw pictures of the moon revolutionized our conception of the heavens. In his book on Galileo, Bredekamp argues that for Galileo, art gives the very model of philosophy (natural science, in Galileo's sense). To make sense of "the book of philosophy" or, indeed, "the book of nature," according to Galileo, you need to apply the standards of visual art. See Horst Bredekamp, *Galilei der Künstler: Der Mond, die Sonne, die Hand.*

•

For a clear and insightful exploration of evolution and art, see Stephen Davies's *The Artful Species: Aesthetics, Art, and Evolution.* See also my comment on his book, "Running up Against the Limits of Nature."

•

Ellen Dissanayake's writing on art, evolution, intimacy, and "making special" repays close attention. See, in particular, her *Homo Aestheticus: Where Art Comes From and Why.*

•

The phrase "transformational technologies" is from Aniruddh D. Patel, who gives fire as a paradigm example. The pervasiveness of such technologies throughout a culture can be explained without appeal to the idea of any kind of genetic encoding. Fire is so useful, and the rewards for mastering it so widespread and significant, that we can perfectly well understand its universality without supposing that there is, as it were, a "fire organ" or a "fire drive." See Patel's excellent *Music, Language, and the Brain.*

•

Daniel C. Dennett discusses the cultural origins of changes in human body size and the importance of selective pressures in the setting of cultural evolution in *Darwin's Dangerous Idea: Evolutions and the Meanings of Life*, especially chapter 12.

•

Ludwig Wittgenstein is said to have said, "In aesthetics the question is not 'Do you like it?' but 'Why do you like it?'" See *Wittgenstein's Lectures, Cambridge, 1932–35: From the Notes of Alice Ambrose and Margaret Macdonald* (p. 38).

•

See chapter 3 of *Homo Aestheticus* for Dissanayake's discussion of "making special," and its core function for art.

•

See Geoffrey Miller, *The Mating Mind: How Sexual Choice Shaped the Evolution of Human Nature*.

A far more plausible sexual-selection model has been advanced in recent work by Richard O. Prum (in "Coevolutionary Aesthetics in Human and Biotic Art-worlds"). This came to my attention too late to include the discussion it deserves here. A brief comment will have to suffice. In the more familiar story, art is like the peacock's tail; it signals fitness. As I note in the text, this account leaves anything distinctive about art, as distinct from other forms of fitness signals, out of the story. Prum corrects this by insisting that you can't eliminate pleasure from the story and by stressing that the pleasures we take in art are directly and specifically bound up with art. Not because art generates a special sort of aesthetic feeling or sensation, but because our responses to art—the pleasures we take in it—are bound up with art itself by processes of coevolution. Art is the result of a coevolutionary contest spanning evolutionary and cultural time scales. Art, as Prum puts it, is "a form of communication that has coevolved with its own evolution." One of the strengths of this view is that it can do justice to radical change in aesthetic evaluation. The works of an artist—think Andy Warhol, for example—can *become* beautiful; for these works can contribute to the changing of the very criteria of evaluation by which we aesthetically assess this work itself. Prum's account also does justice to the Kantian observation, made in the text, that it is one thing to like something and another to find it beautiful. Beauty isn't just a matter of liking. Prum can allow that our pleasures and preferences get refined through evolutionary recursion. Some pleasures—like that we might take in an elegant mathematical proof, for example, or in the late work of Beethoven—are available only to those who stand on the scaffolding of past communication and agreements.

This is a very powerful proposal. It brings out the distinctively *cognitive*, that is to say, *evaluative*, character of the pleasures that art affords. But the theory casts the net too wide: every artifact or social activity or technology is constrained by what we like (evaluative response) even as it offers the opportunity for us to change and update those responses (coevolution). But art is not merely an activity or technology even if it masquerades as such. Art always disrupts business as usual and puts the fact that we find ourselves carrying out business as usual on display. Put bluntly: the value of art does not consist in a (coevolving) fit (or dialogue) between what we make and what we like, but rather in the practice of investigating and questioning and challenging such processes.

•

The word "spandrel" was introduced into the evolutionary biological literature by Stephen Jay Gould and Richard C. Lewontin in "The Spandrels of San Marco and the Panglossian Paradigm: A Critique of the Adaptationist Programme." In architecture, a spandrel is a niche or space between arches. Architects don't make spandrels, they design arches, and spandrels come along for free as side effects. Gould and Lewontin argued that the same is true in evolution. Not every trait is an adaptation, for many traits are side effects of genuinely fitness-enhancing traits (adaptations). The existence of spandrels has a broader significance, at least for Gould and Lewontin. It shows that you can't think of the organism as a bundle or collection of traits each of which can be looked at as a self-standing solitary adaptation. Traits have significance only against the background, as it were, of the architectural plan of the whole organism. For a worthwhile critical response to Gould and Lewontin, see Daniel Dennett's chapter on this in *Darwin's Dangerous Idea*.

•

Three books that figure in my recollections of that walk to Washington Square are Edward O. Wilson's *Sociobiology: The New Synthesis*, Stephen Jay Gould's *The Mismeasure of Man*, and Thomas Nagel, *Mind and Cosmos: Why the Materialist Neo-Darwinian Conception of Nature Is Almost Certainly False*.

•

Thomas Nagel's *The View from Nowhere* articulates something like the scientific conception of reality. Bernard Williams uses the phrase "the absolute conception of reality" for this same idea in his *Descartes: The Project of Pure Enquiry* and also in his *Ethics and the Limits of Philosophy*. For a profound criticism of Williams's account of the absolute conception, see Hilary Putnam's *Renewing Philosophy*.

•

For Alvin Plantinga's criticism of naturalism, see his *Where the Conflict Really Lies: Science, Religion, and Naturalism*. My critical discussion of his ideas draws on my "Is There a Conflict Between Science and Religion?"

•

In connection with my discussion of scientism in this chapter, I would like to note a debt to the writings of the British philosopher of science John Dupré. In *Human Nature and the Limits of Science*, he offers a trenchant criticism of scientism (p. 1):

> One aspect of scientism is the idea that any question that can be answered at all can best be answered by science. This, in turn, is very often combined with a quite narrow conception of what it is for an answer, or a method of investigation, to be scientific. Specifically, it is supposed that canonical science must work by disclosing the physical or chemical mechanisms that generate phenomena. Together these ideas imply a narrow and homogeneous set of answers to the most diverse imaginable set of questions. Everywhere this implies a restriction of the powers of the human mind; but nowhere is this restriction more disastrous than in the mind's attempts to answer questions about itself.

•

Jesse Prinz, my former colleague at the Graduate Center of the City University of New York, argues that only strong emotions can explain the place of art in our lives. Prinz builds on the eighteenth-century Scottish philosopher David Hume's idea that reason never motivates or fixes our preferences. Hume wrote, in A *Treatise of Human Nature*, " 'Tis not contrary to reason to prefer the destruction of the whole world to the scratching of my finger. 'Tis not contrary to reason for me to chuse my total ruin, to prevent the least uneasiness of an *Indian* or person wholly unknown to me." Hume's point is that we need to look to feeling, not to reason, to understand why it would be outrageous to prefer the scratching of one's finger to the destruction of the world. Hume's argument is that only emotion, only feeling, can move us to act or shape our preferences. And so, in this spirit, Prinz argues that if we want to understand our positive attitude to art, if we want to understand why we like it as we do, why we seek to surround ourselves with it, why we pay good money to see it, we need to understand how art moves us emotionally. And since, for Prinz, as for Hume, the emotions are grounded on our human (and so our biological) nature, Prinz's approach seems to open up the possibility of framing something like a biological approach to art.

Crucially, Prinz does not make Dissanayake's mistakes. In particular, he doesn't suppose that for emotions to be authentic, for them to be biologically based, they need also to be, as it were, *a*cultural. Nor does he suppose that they need to be divorced from cognition or the capacity for rational thought. Indeed, he argues that the emotion that appears to be most closely bound up with aesthetic appreciation, and at whose activation art itself can be thought to aim, is wonder. Wonder is not a basic emotion like disgust. Moreover, it is highly cognitive. Wonder is tied to surprise and expectation and curiosity.

Nor does Prinz think that for wonder to be the key to art's importance, this must be because wonder itself is an evolutionary adaptation. He thinks that wonder is a spandrel; something we get for free given the rest of our cognitive and emotional makeup.

And truly, wonder, or the sense of awe, *is* a powerful emotion that in fact typically accompanies aesthetic encounters with artworks. The British monarch, upon visiting Christopher Wren's newly completed St. Paul's Cathedral for the first time, is said to have looked up at the enormous dome and remarked "it is aweful and artificial." With these words he expressed wonder, awe, astonishment in the face of art. (I heard this anecdote recounted by the philosopher John Rawls in 1990 in Philosophy 171, his famous Harvard lecture course on social and political philosophy.)

Nevertheless, I can't go so far as to endorse Prinz's theory. As I have argued throughout, art is not functional in the ways that normal, domesticated technologies are functional. Art cannot properly be said to aim at *any* effect, whether wonder or anything else. Wonder, or our disposition to respond with powerful feelings to what is beautiful or, to use the king's word, aweful, is art's raw material, grist for its mill; it is not something that art takes for granted but something that art investigates and puts into question. My point is not simply that art need not always produce wonder, although this seems likely to me. No, the point is that art isn't in the business of producing wonder or any other emotion. And even when it does, emotional effects cannot be the source of art's value.

See Prinz's "Wonder Works: Renovating Romanticism About Art," "How Wonder Works," and *Works of Wonder: The Psychology and Ontology of Art.*

6. A SHORT NOTE ON ECSTASY, SPORTS, AND HUMOR

Art releases us when we are trapped in modes of organization. This explains why art can occasion ecstasy. For ecstasy is precisely a name for this kind of engagement toward release. This chapter also contains a brief discussion of why sports are not art even though one can, in principle, make art out of sports.

•

I am indebted to Horst Bredekamp for suggesting to me the ways the theory developed here has the resources to make sense of ecstasy in our engagement with art.

•

Thanks to the television writer, author, and philosopher Eric Kaplan for illuminating conversation about the nature of jokes and "the funny." This forms the topic of the doctoral dissertation he is writing with me and Hubert Dreyfus at UC Berkeley.

•

"Wittgenstein once said that a serious and good philosophical work could be written that would consist entirely of *jokes* (without being facetious)." —Norman Malcolm, in *Ludwig Wittgenstein: A Memoir* (pp. 27–28)

•

In *In Praise of Athletic Beauty*, Hans Ulrich Gumbrecht defends the appropriateness of viewing sports as an aesthetic domain. My own view is that sports and art have nothing to do with each other. But that is no reason, given my general approach, for denying that we value sports in part because of their beauty or awe-inspiring quality. Aesthetic qualities such as these are not restricted to the domain of art.

7. PHILOSOPHICAL OBJECTS
In this chapter I turn attention to specific works of art. My aim is to illustrate the distinctively philosophical work that artworks undertake. Most of the short discussions are adapted from pieces I wrote for "13.7 Cosmos & Culture" on National Public Radio's website (www.npr.org/13.7) over the last five years. These include:

> "On Being Gay, Being Out and Being Art."
> "Lost and Found: The Art of Richard Serra."
> "An Object of Contention at the Venice Biennale."
> "There's Nothing to Do Here, and It's Perfect."
> "Unraveled Ravel Is a Revelation."
> "A Philosopher's View of *Rosemary's Baby*."

•

Geoff Dyer's book *Zona: A Book About a Film About a Journey to a Room* masterfully displays this DVD-commentary structure that I mention at the chapter's beginning. He simply begins at the beginning of the movie and rambles, amusingly, insightfully, freely, and seemingly in real time, until he reaches the movie's conclusion.

•

My first encounter with the works of Richard Serra was his *Torqued Ellipses* show at Dia Center for the Arts in New York in 1997. Since then I've seen numerous installations of his work—at his New York gallery, Gagosian; at the Geffen Contemporary at the Museum of Contemporary Art in Los Angeles; at Dia:Beacon; and at the Guggenheim in Bilbao as well as elsewhere. My comments here are written on the occasion of his 2013 show *New Sculpture* at the Gagosian in Chelsea.

•

Michael Fried on theatricality: I come back to Fried in the notes to the acknowledgments below. For now just this: Michael Fried, the brilliant art critic, poet, and philosopher, developed a criticism of what he called "theatrical" art in his famous essay "Art and Objecthood," published in 1967. Fried hasn't been much beloved of the world of theater ever since. But this turns on a misunderstanding. Fried isn't (wasn't) against theater, but rather, theatricality (a feature of bad theater). His concern in this paper is not with theatricality in the sense of artificiality, stiffness, or showiness (against which Diderot had warned). In later work—for example, *Courbet's Realism*—Fried does turn to theatricality in this sense as well. No, what is at stake here is a more psychological notion. What Fried is criticizing is the idea that a work's significance is tied to its psychological effect. A landscape might affect us movingly; it isn't thereby art. And likewise, it is a misunderstanding, for Fried, of the very project of art, to think of art as in the business of engineering or modulating effects.

In "Art and Objecthood," Fried targets Tony Smith as an example of a theatrical artist—someone who made objects that, in turn, simply affect us in ways we (may happen to) find interesting or valuable. In my judgment—I argued this in my first essay on art, "Experience and Experiment in Art"—this completely gets Tony Smith wrong (although it is a brilliant response to some things that Smith wrote about what he was doing; I return to this later). Smith's works are lyrical and constructed and formal; they are paradigmatic, investigating not mere things but ideas, problems, and puzzles.

But not so Richard Serra's. Serra really does what Fried criticizes "literalists" or "theatricalists" for doing: he makes things that mainline or shock or electrify; as my dad put it, he really gets under your skin and does something with your head. Hence my remark in the chapter that Serra's works may be theatrical in Fried's sense.

One way to bring out Serra's theatricality, and Smith's antitheatricality, is by thinking about scale. Smith's sculptures exist in different scales. A twelve-inch sculpture—*Cigarette*, for example, or *The Snake Is Out*—is *every bit* the equal of the fifteen-foot version. Whatever power and magic attach to the big one are there *in full* in the little one. It isn't about scale. It isn't about impact. It's more lyrical than that, and more thoughtful. This is not the case with Serra's works. At the big *Torqued Ellipses* show in LA in the late 1990s, they actually had lead mock-ups of the sculptures on display. They looked like little galvanized steel slop buckets. They were nothing. Whereas their thirteen-foot-high counterparts managed to become, as I explain in the chapter, worlds. Serra's is a work of psychological impact and, we might even say, neurological experiment.

But crucially, theatrical or not, it isn't confined by its theatricality. This is what I try to explain in the chapter.

•

Barnett Newman was a close friend of my father's. I was raised to take an interest in his work, although I don't believe that we owned any of it. In any case, my remarks here were written on the occasion of the *Abstract Expressionist New York* show that was put on at the Museum of Modern Art in New York in 2010–2011.

•

Tino Sehgal won the Golden Lion for his work at the 2013 Venice Biennale. I had the chance to spend a fair bit of time with his intriguing not-a-performance. I also participated in a workshop with him on art and neuroscience at the Biennale; I presented my thoughts about his piece to a small audience that included him. I am not sure what he made of it.

•

Robert Lazzarini is an American artist based in New York whose works are paradigm philosophical objects. I have written a catalog essay on his work: "Lost and Found: Working Back to the Meaning of Things in the Work of Robert Lazzarini."

•

Robert Irwin's *Scrim veil—Black rectangle—Natural light*, which I saw at the Whitney Museum in 2013, was a reprise of the work originally installed, in the same location, in 1977. James Turrell's exhibition at the Guggenheim (*James Turrell*) was open at the same time and made an interesting object of comparison.

•

Anri Sala's installation *Ravel Ravel Unravel* in the French Pavilion at the 55th Venice Biennale was a thrilling success. Thanks to Blake Gopnik for directing me to it.

•

See Noël Carroll's *The Philosophy of Horror, Or, Paradoxes of the Heart*. I also recommend his treatment of Buster Keaton, *Comedy Incarnate*. Another outstanding writer who explores the philosophy in film is Stephen Mulhall. I recommend his *On Film*. I explore some of Mulhall's ideas in connection with the Ridley Scott film *Blade Runner* in *Out of Our Heads*.

8. SEE ME IF YOU CAN!

This chapter marks, in some ways, a second introduction. I restate the basic ideas of the book—that art is linked to technology without being technology, that works of art are strange tools, that art is bound to philosophy. Every work of art, I argue, propositions you to see it, to comprehend it. In doing so it affords you an opportunity to reorganize, and also to catch yourself in the act.

•

The choreographer William Forsythe related to me that when a questioner at a postperformance talk ventured to offer his theory of art, Forsythe stopped him cold with exactly this reply: We don't want to know! Don't ruin it for us!

•

In this chapter I adapt some material from my short essay "Art and the Limits of Neuroscience."

•

Semir Zeki develops his approach to so-called neuroaesthetics in the book *Inner Vision: An Exploration of Art and the Brain*. He argues that a theory of art needs to be a theory of the brain because it is brains that make and brains that perceive art. The idea that brains make art, or that brains perceive it, is so wildly false that I think we must assume that he cannot be seriously proposing it. But what he does mean is not clear. If by "brain" he means something like "live human being" or, perhaps, "person," then I'd say he's right. But surely there's more to a theory of the person than a theory of the brain?

•

Francis Crick, who, with James Watson, won the Nobel Prize in 1962 for the discovery of the structure of DNA, develops the idea that you are your brain in *The Astonishing Hypothesis*. As I indicate in the chapter, this is not a hypothesis as much as a working assumption, and it isn't astonishing either way, since it is, in effect, the familiar traditional idea that the self is inside you. Crick offers a materialized Descartes. See my *Out of Our Heads* for an extended criticism of this view. It's bad philosophy and bad science.

•

I return to so-called neuroaesthetics. The neural approach to art has been championed by the psychologists Arthur P. Shimamura (*Experiencing Art: In the Brain of the Beholder*) and Vilayanur S. Ramachandran ("The Science of Art: A Neurological Theory of Aesthetic Experience"), by neuroscientists such as Anjan Chatterjee (*The Aesthetic Brain: How We Evolved to Desire Beauty and Enjoy Art*), Eric R. Kandel (*The Age of Insight: The Quest to Understand the Unconscious in Art, Mind, and Brain*), Margaret Livingstone (*Vision and Art: The Biology of Seeing*), and Semir Zeki (*Inner Vision*), by humanists such as the art historians John Onians (*Neuroarthistory: From Aristotle and Pliny to Baxandall and Zeki*) and David Freedberg, as well as the literary scholar G. Gabrielle Starr (*Feeling Beauty: The Neuroscience of Aesthetic Experience*).

•

For really sharp criticism of neuroaesthetics—criticism that has shaped my own thinking about these matters—see John Hyman's "Art and Neuroscience." I also admire Blake Gopnik's excellent essay on this topic: "Aesthetic Science and Artistic Knowledge." The idea that perceptual responses are not triggered events inside us but judgments is developed nicely by Gopnik. I am indebted to Hyman for the insight that so-called neuroaesthetics never quite succeeds in getting *art* as a phenomenon into focus.

•

John Dewey (*Art as Experience*) and James J. Gibson (*The Ecological Approach to Visual Perception*) offer alternatives to the idea that experience is a simple matter of events getting triggered in the head. Dewey and Gibson reject what Susan Hurley has called "the input-output picture," that is, the idea that perception is input from world to mind and action is output from mind to world, with *experience* or *thought* or *consciousness* being what goes on in the head causally mediating perception and action. This is a main theme of her important, and difficult, book *Consciousness in Action*. See also my own *Action in Perception* for more on an alternative to the orthodoxy that both Dewey and Gibson criticize, and also Hilary Putnam's *The Threefold Cord: Mind, Body, and World*.

•

It is impossible not to be struck at once by the fact that some animals make use of tools and implements, a famous case being the chimpanzee who carefully strips a branch to make a wand for the purpose of extracting insects from a mound. But it is also hard to ignore the fact that the tool using of human beings exhibits a thoughtfulness and flexibility unlike anything seen in the nonhuman world. Perhaps this has something to do with the fact that we don't use tools only to solve practical problems, we also use tools to think about ourselves, that is, to make art and philosophy.

•

See Larry Shiner's *The Invention of Art: A Cultural History* for the argument that art is a modern invention.

•

The paintings of Leonardo that I mention here—all but *Mona Lisa*—were on display at the exhibition *Leonardo da Vinci: Painter at the Court of Milan* at the National Gallery in London in the winter of 2011. I spent a long time looking at and thinking about them. The images are well known and can easily be found online. My remarks here draw loosely on a review I wrote of the exhibition for NPR: "The Hands of Leonardo."

•

Andrea Riccio's work was on display at the Frick in New York in the exhibition *Andrea Riccio: Renaissance Master of Bronze* (2008–2009). I draw here on Alexander Nagel's essay on the Riccio Moses that was published in the exhibition catalog and reprinted in his *The Controversy of Renaissance Art*. I also had a chance to hear Nagel present his argument in 2008 at the Wissenschaftskolleg in Berlin.

•

The story of Moses and the rock is told more than once in the Bible. Here, in the King James version, is the relevant passage from Numbers 20:

> And there was no water for the congregation: and they gathered themselves together against Moses and against Aaron.
>
> And the people chode with Moses, and spake, saying, Would God that we had died when our brethren died before the LORD!
>
> And why have ye brought up the congregation of the LORD into this wilderness, that we and our cattle should die there?
>
> And wherefore have ye made us to come up out of Egypt, to bring us in unto this evil place? it is no place of seed, or of figs, or of vines, or of pomegranates; neither is there any water to drink.
>
> And Moses and Aaron went from the presence of the assembly unto the door of the tabernacle of the congregation, and they fell upon their faces: and the glory of the LORD appeared unto them.
>
> And the LORD spake unto Moses, saying,
>
> Take the rod, and gather thou the assembly together, thou, and Aaron thy brother, and speak ye unto the rock before their eyes; and it shall give forth his water, and thou shalt bring forth to them water out of the rock: so thou shalt give the congregation and their beasts drink.
>
> And Moses took the rod from before the LORD, as he commanded him. And Moses and Aaron gathered the congregation together before the rock, and he said unto them, Hear now, ye rebels; must we fetch you water out of this rock?
>
> And Moses lifted up his hand, and with his rod he smote the rock twice: and the water came out abundantly, and the congregation drank, and their beasts also.
>
> And the LORD spake unto Moses and Aaron, Because ye believed me not, to sanctify me in the eyes of the children of Israel, therefore ye shall not bring this congregation into the land which I have given them.
>
> This is the water of Meribah; because the children of Israel strove with the LORD, and he was sanctified in them.

•

E. H. Gombrich discusses Masaccio's *Holy Trinity with the Virgin, Saint John and donors*, c. 1425–1428 (church of Santa Maria Novella, Florence) in *The Story of Art*. For Hyman's treatment of perspective and its significance for painting, see his *The Imitation of Nature*.

•

Chapters 12 through 14 focus on pictures. At this stage I want to note, simply, that as I use the word "picture," not every picture is a work of art (the picture of the chicken in the newspaper supplement, for instance), and not every artwork paint-ing is pictorial (Frank Stella's paintings, for example, are not depictions). My remarks in the text pertain to works of art (whether paintings or photographs) that are, as a matter of fact, pictures. Artwork pictures, in my sense, raise questions about the very nature of pictoriality that are usually, outside an art setting, ignored or left unasked. And this, I take it, is the sense of James Baldwin's words that art uncovers the questions that tend to be blocked from view by familiar answers. I am grateful to Lawrence Weschler for suggesting the quote to me. I have been unable, however, to find its exact source. The version I use as the epigraph to Part I is due to Weschler, and I offer it as "attributed to" Baldwin.

•

Robert Goodnough (1917–2010) was an American painter and sculptor. Sometimes called a second-generation Abstract Expressionist, and associated with that New York art circle, he was a close friend of my father's and I grew up around his work. The little sculpture I describe in the text is a valued possession.

•

The idea that art requires criticism has been suggested by different thinkers. The Italian philosopher Roberto Casati, who is based at the Institut Jean Nicod in Paris, argues that it is one of art's defining features that it serves as a topic for conversation. But the idea goes back farther, at least as far as Kant, who appreci-ated that our evaluation of art is the sort of thing we can and do and must argue about.

•

The German mathematician Gottlob Frege (1848–1925) wrote, "Without wishing to give a definition, I call a thought something for which the question of truth arises." See "The Thought" (or, as it is sometimes translated "Thoughts"), in his *Collected Papers on Mathematics, Logic, and Philosophy.*

•

Gombrich begins *The Story of Art* with these words: "There really is no such thing as art. There are only artists."

9. WHY IS ART SO BORING?
It is no accident that art can bore us. Indeed, it is a clue to art's nature that it can manage this feat.

•

Boredom has not often been the topic of theoretical investigation. One exception is Martin Heidegger, who discusses the topic in his lectures on *Fundamental Con-cepts of Metaphysics: World, Finitude, Solitude.*

•

John Dewey writes in *Art as Experience* (pp. 36–37):

> We have *an* experience when the material experienced runs its course to
> fulfillment. Then and only then is it integrated within and demarcated
> in the general stream of experience from other experiences. A piece of
> work is finished in a way that is satisfactory; a problem receives its solu-
> tion; a game is played through; a situation, whether that of eating a meal,
> playing a game of chess, carrying on a conversation, writing a book, or
> taking part in a political campaign, is so rounded out that its close is a
> consummation and not a cessation. Such an experience is a whole and
> carries with it its own individualizing quality and self-sufficiency. It is *an*
> experience.

•

The lectures of John Cage were the Charles Eliot Norton lectures given at Harvard
in 1988–1989, the year before I arrived there to study philosophy. My fellow graduate student, and dear friend, the philosopher Erin I. Kelly, attended the lectures
and my account here is based on her report. Cage published a book based on the
event: *I–VI*.

•

Jonathan Burrows's *A Choreographer's Handbook* is a beautiful book that can be
read as a work of philosophy. Drawing on his own artistic practice and his years as
a teacher, he illuminates choreography as a research practice.

•

I heard an interview with Jeffrey Deitch sometime after he'd resigned from his position as the director of the Museum of Contemporary Art in Los Angeles. Deitch's
directorship was controversial (by all reports) because of his commitment to moving the museum in the direction of popular forms of artistic expression.

10. ART AND THE LIMITS OF NEUROSCIENCE

In this chapter I argue that the empirical neuroscience of art has failed to bring its
subject matter—*art*—into focus for investigation.

•

In the text I refer to Francisco Varela and Antonio Damasio as neuroscientists
committed to a more holistic conception of the living human being or animal. See
the bibliography for references, as well as to work by me, Evan Thompson, J. Kevin
O'Regan, and Susan Hurley to which I refer.

•

David Marr's *Vision* famously argues that studying vision by looking at individual cells would be like trying to understand the flight of birds by studying the individual feathers. Vision, like other information-processing processes, according to Marr, needs to be investigated at different levels. We can ask: What is vision and what is it for? We can ask: How might one build a machine that could see? or How might a computer see? And finally we can ask: How, as a matter of fact, is vision implemented in the human brain? Marr's approach, which is really the application, to the problem of vision, of what is sometimes called the computational model of the mind, or functionalism, allows one to study vision without worrying about the messy, underlying biology.

•

David Hubel and Torsten Wiesel's papers have been collected in *Brain and Visual Perception: The Story of a 25-Year Collaboration*. See chapter 7 of my *Out of Our Heads* for an extended discussion of their research.

•

For Daniel C. Dennett's writings on the foundations of cognitive science, see his *Brainstorms* and *The Intentional Stance*. The murder in Trafalgar Square example is from his essay "Three Kinds of Intentional Psychology," in *The Intentional Stance*.

•

"Brain, body, and world make consciousness happen" is the central idea of Evan Thompson and Francisco Varela's article "Radical Embodiment: Neural Dynamics and Consciousness."

•

Dennett's reference to "vestigial Cartesian materialism" is from a discussion of "filling in" in chapter 11 of *Consciousness Explained*. It is known that there is a spot in each eye where there are no photoreceptors, the so-called blind spot. And yet we don't notice any gap or discontinuity in our visual field. Some thinkers suppose that this must be because the brain fills in the gap in subsequent representations. This is the assumption Dennett thinks is a giveaway of Cartesianism. Why should one suppose that there is any need for an act of filling in? If the brain already knows there is no gap, and so there is a need for filling in, for whose benefit is the actual filling in performed? It is as if we experience what is presented to the mind only in the Cartesian Theater. Dennett himself thinks there is an alternative to the idea that the brain fills in. The brain can just ignore the absence of a gap. See my "Is the Visual World a Grand Illusion?" for further discussion of this, as well as chapter 6 of *Out of Our Heads*. For a more technical treatment of the topic, and Dennett's view, see "Finding out About Filling-In: A Guide to Perceptual Completion for

Visual Science and the Philosophy of Perception," by Luiz Pessoa, Evan Thompson, and myself.

•

Marr argues that vision is the process of constructing a model of the environment on the basis of information encoded in the retina. The process has three steps. First, the generation of the retinal image as a result of light irradiating the nerves at the back of the eye. Second, the production of a "picture" of what is seen. This $2^1/_2$-D sketch shows things from a vantage point; this gives us the surfaces that we would see from that point of view, with no information about the partially hidden solid object. The final stage is the genuinely 3-D representation of the scene. What is distinctive of this stage is that objects are described in a way that is not limited by a particular point of view on them. The 3-D images show us not only how things look from here, but how they would look if we moved around. It is the intermediate level—the level of the $2^1/_2$-D sketch—that gives us visual consciousness. We don't visually experience the retinal image, or the world as it is in itself. What we see, really, as a matter of our pure experience, are pictures in the mind. This interpretation of Marr has been extended and defended by Jesse Prinz in *The Conscious Brain: How Attention Engenders Experience*.

•

See Patrick Cavanagh's "The Artist as Neuroscientist."

•

Ramachandran and Hirstein's discussion of the bronzes was published as "The Science of Art: A Neurological Theory of Aesthetic Experience" (p. 18):

> This leads us to our first aphorism: "All art is caricature." (This is not *literally* true, of course, but as we shall see, it is true surprisingly often.) And the same principle that applies for recognizing faces applies to all aspects of form recognition. It might seem a bit strange to regard caricatures as art but take a look at the Chola bronze—the accentuated hips and bust of the Goddess Parvati and you will see at once that what you have here is essentially a caricature of the female form. There may be neurons in the brain that represent sensuous, rotund feminine form as opposed to angular masculine form and the artist has chosen to amplify the "very essence" (the *rasa*) of being feminine by moving the image even further along toward the feminine end of the female/male spectrum. The result of these amplifications is a "super stimulus" in the domain of male/female differences. It is interesting, in this regard, that the earliest known forms of art are often caricatures of one sort or another; e.g. prehistoric cave art depicting animals like bison and mammoths, or the famous Venus "fertility" figures.

Ramachandran and Hirstein also observe (p. 16):

> In Western art, the "discovery" of non-representational abstract art had to await the arrival of Picasso. His nudes were also grotesquely distorted—both eyes on one side of the face for example. Yet when Picasso did it, the Western art critics heralded his attempts to "transcend perspective" as a profound new discovery—even though both Indian and African art had anticipated this style by several centuries!

Their immediate concern is to support the idea that all art aims at caricature and that the distortions Picasso introduced were in the direction of bringing out and amplifying essential features of the visible world. But the quoted passages are odd. For one thing, they suggest that artworks function out of time and culture. Picasso is thought to have discovered the very same trick that artists in India and Africa had used for centuries—the ability to amplify emotional response by making what are in effect caricatures. But surely Picasso's impact has just as much to do with the way his stylistic innovations refer to and differentiate himself from, and so comment on, the artistic tradition in which he finds himself, as any brute, direct, purely psychological effect his images might have on viewers (assuming, for the sake of argument, that there are such). This is a particularly blunt example of the neuroaestheticians' impulse to view the artwork exclusively as a trigger. (It's worth noticing, too, that the claim that abstraction in Western art begins with Picasso is untrue.)

See John Hyman's essay "Art and Neuroscience" for insightful criticism of Ramachandran and Hirstein.

•

Semir Zeki lays out his approach in *Inner Vision: An Exploration of Art and the Brain.*

•

For Gabrielle Starr's approach, see her *Feeling Beauty: The Neuroscience of Aesthetic Experience,* in which she draws on her work with Vessel and Rubin. See, in particular, E. A. Vessel, G. G. Starr, and N. Rubin, "The Brain on Art: Intense Aesthetic Experience Activates the Default Mode Network," and "Art Reaches Within: Aesthetic Experience, the Self and the Default Mode Network."

On the question of whether gender is hardwired, I draw here on "Gender Differences All in the Mind" by the Cambridge University philosophers John Dupré and Rae Langton, a letter to *The Guardian* in 2013. The reasoning they adduce applies to the case of aesthetic experience as well. The fact that there is or might be a neural correlate of aesthetic experience doesn't give us any reason for thinking we can learn what aesthetic experience is, or why we have it when we do, from facts about what's going on in the brain.

•

The whole topic of the so-called default mode network is controversial. I want to be clear that my main point in the text—that we shouldn't think of aesthetic experiences as events of the brain—is independent of the possibility that some neural system (e.g., the default mode network) is tied to the occurrence of the relevant kind of experience. That said, and as I indicate in the chapter, the very notion of a default mode network is in dispute. Some authors claim that "the default network is a specific, anatomically defined brain system preferentially active when individuals are not focused on the external environment" (Buckner, Andrews-Hanna, and Schacter, "The Brain's Default Network: Anatomy, Function, and Relevance to Disease"). Others argue that things are more complicated. According to Kalina Christoff, Diego Cosmelli, Dorothée Legrand, and Evan Thompson, for example, there is evidence that activation in the default mode network frequently occurs for a variety of world-directed activities such as movie viewing, speech perception, and planning ("Specifying the Self for Cognitive Neuroscience"). (They cite these studies: M. D. Greicius and V. Menon, "Default-Mode Activity During a Passive Sensory Task: Uncoupled from Deactivation but Impacting Activation"; Y. Golland et al., "Extrinsic and Intrinsic Systems in the Posterior Cortex of the Human Brain Revealed During Natural Sensory Stimulation"; S. M. Wilson et al., "Beyond Superior Temporal Cortex: Intersubject Correlations in Narrative Speech Comprehension"; and R. N. Spreng et al., "Default Network Activity, Coupled with the Frontoparietal Control Network, Supports Goal-Directed Cognition.")

But as I note in the text, Christoff and company make a conceptual point as well: even if it were true that the default mode network activates, or returns to baseline, when we turn away from the world, that doesn't mean that the default mode network serves to specify or model the self. The self as agent might be specified precisely by the fact of and manner of one's engagement with the environment.

•

Alexander Nehamas, in *Only a Promise of Happiness: The Place of Beauty in a World of Art,* places art, and our concern for beauty, in the setting of community. He frames his observations in a suggestively anti-Kantian spirit: far from demanding that our judgments be universal, he suggests it is precisely the differentiation in our aesthetic responses that marks off *our* community, or *mine,* from others, and that forms, if you like, the sinews of our shared values and commitments. But this insightful point is, by my lights at least, broadly Kantian: aesthetic response is not sensational or narrowly experiential; it is always potentially shared, possibly contentious, and in that sense open to all.

II. ART IS A PHILOSOPHICAL PRACTICE
AND PHILOSOPHY AN AESTHETIC ONE

In this chapter I argue that the similarities between art and philosophy run deep. Art and philosophy are not the same; they are, however, different species of a common genus.

•

Lawrence Weschler, writing in the online magazine Glasstire (glasstire.com), proposes that *Fountain*'s key art-becoming gesture was Duchamp's turning the urinal on its side. So oriented it presents, at least from the front, a kind of biomorphic triangular wedge. As Weschler writes, "Carl Van Vechten . . . enthused to Gertrude Stein, by letter, how 'the photographs make it look like anything from a Madonna to a Buddha.' Or, as I myself always thought, and, interestingly, found myself thinking again recently: a pietà."

•

"Method and result are one": actually, what Wittgenstein wrote (in the *Tractatus*, §6.1261) was: "In logic process and result are equivalent. (Therefore no surprises.)" The point is that the last line of a proof depends for its entire significance on the derivation that leads to it and has no self-standing interest or value. Logic doesn't accumulate results in the sense of bottom lines; it accumulates proofs, that is, routes to bottom lines. The point applies to philosophy as well, as Wittgenstein also certainly believed.

•

Dewey attacks "the museum conception of art" in *Art as Experience* (p. 2): "When artistic objects are separated from both conditions of origin and operation in experience, a wall is built around them that renders almost opaque their general significance, with which esthetic theory deals. Art is remitted to a separate realm, where it is cut off from that association with the materials and aims of every other form of human effort, undergoing, and achievement."

Plato's answer to the challenge that philosophy has no value: I take it that this is Plato's objective in *Meno*, which I read, following Gregory Vlastos, as a commentary on philosophical method (especially as this was practiced by Socrates). Plato's problem was that of explaining how philosophy can be a thing of value precisely when it does not yield positive knowledge.

•

The idea that art is philosophy, or that aesthetic problems are, in a way, philosophical in character, is implicit in Kant's treatment of the issue. He describes aesthetic disagreement in a way that brings this out. The disagreement is real and significant, but it does not admit of being settled once and for all; there are no rules for settling it. This idea is also explicit, and is developed with great brilliance, in

Stanley Cavell's masterpiece "On Aesthetic Problems of Modern Philosophy" in his collection *Must We Mean What We Say?*

12. MAKING PICTURES
The basic claim of this chapter is that pictures are artifacts; they are tools for putting things on display. I argue that they function only in the setting of communication. They have a rhetoric. They are not primarily optical.

•

In these opening paragraphs, I adapt material from my "The Producers: Are Pictures Detaching Us From Life?"

•

For an insightful treatment of the history of theories of vision, see David C. Lindberg's *Theories of Vision from Al-Kindi to Kepler*. I offer a sketch of this history in chapter 2 of *Action in Perception*.

•

The quotation from Steven Pinker is from his *How the Mind Works* (p. 217).

13. USING MODELS
Pictures, I argue in this chapter, are a special kind of *model*.

•

I first proposed the model theory of pictures developed here in "Presence in Pictures," chapter 5 of *Varieties of Presence*.

We use pictures, and other models, I argue, as substitutes, or stand-ins, for that which they depict. I here make use of a notion of substitution that was first developed by E. H. Gombrich. See "Meditations on a Hobby Horse," in his collection *Meditations on a Hobby Horse, and Other Essays on the Theory of Art*.

Alexander Nagel and Christopher S. Wood make different use of a closely related idea of substitution in their *Anachronic Renaissance*. Consider a church that has been rebuilt after a fire. Is it the same church, or a different one? It is remarkable that we are free to say that it is both new and old. We might insist on treating it as the ancient church and ascribing to it all the meanings attached to a long historical existence, even though we know perfectly well that it is a new building. We don't delude ourselves in a case such as this, nor do we deny the obvious, or act on the basis of superstition. It's rather that we understand that things, especially artworks, can participate in this way in different temporalities. And what makes this kind of "anachrony" possible is a principle of substitution: our willingness, or need, or ability to let something stand in for something else and so take on that thing's meanings. In a similar way, as Wittgenstein remarked, it isn't superstition on my part to kiss the photograph of my loved one.

•

For more on the theory of depiction and, in particular, the centrality of *resemblance* to any such account, see John Hyman's *The Objective Eye: Color, Form, and Reality in the Theory of Art*, as well as Robert Hopkins's *Picture, Image, Experience*.

•

Horst Bredekamp and John Michael Krois first put the objection to me that the account of depiction presented here makes pictures too mediated, too sophisticated, too beholden to understanding and knowledge and mastery of a background. Pictures, they insist, are more direct than that. You don't need to learn to see pictures. If you can see Mom, you can see Mom in a picture.

•

One might have thought the claim that you don't need to learn to see pictures would be pretty easy to test. But it turns out to be very difficult to tease apart the different kinds of skill and understanding that inform our handling of pictures. As I mention in the text, it is widely reported that some kids "reach into" pictures and try to take hold of things they see. This would seem to be evidence of a kind of pictorial recognition of depicted objects in the absence of a corresponding understanding of their pictorial status. But even assuming that these are not mere lapses on the part of some children, things may be more complicated. Perhaps what we have here is a form of imaginative play, comparable to other forms of pretend. Pretending to eat a nonexistent ice cream cone is not the same as being deluded into thinking that one is eating an ice cream when one is not. Or perhaps, as has been suggested by Judy DeLoache and her colleagues, maybe this kind of manual exploration of a picture is a way of achieving understanding of what pictures are and the fact that pictures are precisely a special class of objects. In any case, by the time kids are nineteen months of age, at least according to DeLoache et al., manual exploration is replaced by pointing. Pointing, it's worth noticing, is a quasi-linguistic communicative gesture. Understanding pictures, as opposed to mere pictorial recognition, seems to go with a kind of more general cognitive/communicative/perceptual savoir-faire.

It is noteworthy that, according to Dalila Bovet and Jacques Vauclair, "a clear case of a possible recognition of the difference between an object and its picture can be found with a linguistically trained chimpanzee . . . who showed an ability to refer to objects represented on pictures (by using a token) without confusing them with real objects." Even in a nonhuman animal, then, pictorial competence is bound up with symbolic communication.

All this is compatible with the admission that pictorial recognition is not learned. As I argue in the text, the fact that infants "see through" pictures is not evidence for the optical/psychological account of pictures that I reject. Gibson, in *The Ecological Approach to Visual Perception*, argues that kids don't need to learn to see pictures because the information is available in a picture in roughly the same way it is present at a point in the actual environment. My own view is that pictures are designed to be user-friendly: it isn't so much a reflection on our visual powers that we see into pictures without training; it reflects rather on the cleverness of pictorial engineering itself. Here I borrow an idea from Terrence Deacon (in *The Symbolic Species*), who made the same point about language: We find it easy to learn languages because we have made languages to conform to what we find learnable!

Pictures, like language, afford illusions of immediacy and naturalness. The fact that we don't need to learn to see pictures doesn't mean that pictures are natural or that our seeing them isn't an epistemic achievement.

14. PICTORIAL STRATEGIES

We use pictures to show things. But we show things for different reasons and in different settings. So we should expect that pictures come in different varieties. This is exactly what we find, as I explain in this chapter.

•

On Christian icons, see Henry Maguire's *Art and Eloquence in Byzantium*, Charles Barber's *Figure and Likeness: On the Limits of Representation in Byzantine Iconoclasm*, and Christoph Schönborn's *God's Human Face: The Christ-Icon*.

•

I close this chapter with the idea that Adolph Menzel makes pictures of the visual field. Commenting on Ernst Mach's famous but entirely unsuccessful attempt to give a visual representation of the visual field—drawn as it were with one eye closed, fixing a point straight ahead—Wittgenstein wrote, "No, you can't make a visual picture of our visual image" (*Philosophical Remarks*, p. 267). Wittgenstein was right that you can't depict the seeing. Menzel proves, though, that you can show the world as we visually experience it.

15. AIR GUITAR STYLES

In this chapter and the next I examine music. This chapter focuses on pop music. I am interested in understanding how pop music can be so vital and powerful as an art form, even though it is often not the scene of musical experiment and even though it tends to be governed by the market.

•

"Pink Cadillac" is in Dave Hickey's collection *Air Guitar: Essays on Art & Democracy*.

•

Roger Scruton's criticism of rock music, and Nirvana in particular, is to be found in his *The Aesthetics of Music*.

•

I attended a conference in Graz in 2009 on bodily expression and electronic music organized by Deniz Peters and Andreas Dorschel. I am indebted to them for my introduction to the whole topic of the acousmatic in music. Their book, *Bodily Expression in Electronic Music: Perspectives on Reclaiming Performativity*, is based on papers given at this conference.

•

I am indebted to the Cambridge, Massachusetts, blues guitarist Paul Rishell for opening my eyes and ears to Robert Johnson's artistic sophistication. At one time I read a lot about the blues and came to know a fair bit about it. I've forgotten most of what I read. One book that stands out in my memory, though, is Robert Palmer's *Deep Blues: A Musical and Cultural History, from the Mississippi Delta to Chicago's South Side to the World*.

•

Thanks to Alexander Nagel for much valuable conversation (and collaborative teaching) on the topic of style and its function enabling and disabling our perception.

•

On John Locke's account of the person, see his *An Essay Concerning Human Understanding*, chapter 27, "Of Identity and Diversity."

16. THE SOUND OF MUSIC

In this chapter I suggest that we experience music as an exploration of human action and modalities of its organization. Music is no more mere sound than is language.

•

I heard Peter Kivy, the noted philosopher of music, remark that the *main* problem in the philosophy of music is understanding how mere sound can be enthralling at a presentation he gave at the 2013 meetings of the American Philosophical Association in Baltimore.

•

The quote from Oliver Sacks is from his *Musicophilia! Tales of Music and the Brain*. The quote from Daniel Levitan comes from his *This Is Your Brain on Music: The Science of a Human Obsession* (New York: Dutton, 2006).

•

See *Action in Perception*, chapter 4, for a more detailed statement of my view of color.

•

See Chia-Jung Tsay, "Sight over Sound in the Judgment of Music Performance." I discuss her findings in "Seeing Music for What It Is."

17: A VERY ABBREVIATED AND HIGHLY OPINIONATED HISTORY OF AESTHETICS

For Plato's attack on the arts, see book X of the *Republic*, and also the dialogue *Ion*. In the *Republic*, he writes (600–601):

> Then must we not conclude that all writers of poetry, beginning with Homer, imitate phantoms of every subject about which they write, including virtue, and do not grasp the truth? In fact, as we were saying just now, will not the painter, without understanding anything about shoemaking, paint what will be taken for a shoemaker by those who are as ignorant on the subject as himself, and who judge by the colors and shapes? . . .
>
> . . . Then, Glaucon, whenever you meet with those who praise Homer, who tell you that he has educated Greece, and that he deserves to be taken up and studied with an eye to the administration and guidance of human affairs, and that a man ought to regulate his whole life by this poet's directions, it will be your duty to greet them affectionately as excellent men doing their best, and to admit that Homer is first and greatest among tragic poets; but you must not forget that, with the single exception of hymns to the gods and panegyrics on the good, no poetry ought to be admitted into a city. For if you determine to admit the highly-seasoned Muse of lyric or epic poetry, pleasure and pain will have sovereign power in your city, instead of law and reason, which is always thought in common to be the best.

•

Aristotle on tragedy versus history. In *Poetics* (1451a–b), Aristotle writes:

> From what we have said it will be seen that the poet's function is to describe, not the thing that has happened, but a kind of thing that might happen, i.e. what is possible as being probable or necessary. The distinction between historian and poet is not in the one writing prose and the other verse—you might put the work of Herodotus into verse, and it would still be a species of history; it consists really in this, that the one describes the thing that has been, and the other a kind of thing that might be.

Hence poetry is something philosophic and of graver import than history, since its statements are of the nature rather of universals, whereas those of history are singulars.

Aristotle defines tragedy thus (1449):

A tragedy, then, is the imitation of an action that is serious and also, as having magnitude, complete in itself; in language with pleasurable accessories, each kind brought in separately in the parts of the work; in a dramatic, not in a narrative form; with incidents arousing pity and fear, wherewith to accomplish its catharsis of such emotions.

What is noteworthy in this definition—and here the contrast with Plato is pronounced—is that it emphasizes how much you need to know or understand in order to make or comprehend a tragic drama. To be a playwright, you need to do metaphysics and psychology. Criticism, or in this case, *poetics*, is a window into human nature and human concerns.

•

Heidegger's philosophical writing is difficult. The theory of equipment is part of a larger theory of being that is presented in *Being and Time*. His lectures published under the title *The Basic Problems of Phenomenology* are bit easier to understand. There he writes (p. 163):

The *nearest things* that surround us we call *equipment*. There is always already a manifold of equipment: equipment for working, for traveling, for measuring, and in general things with which we have to do. What is given to us primarily is the unity of an *equipmental whole* . . . The *equipmental contexture* of things, for example, the contexture of things as they surround us here, stands in view, but not for the contemplator as though we were sitting here in order to describe the things . . . The view in which the equipmental contexture stands at first, completely unobtrusive and unthought, is the view and sight of practical *circumspection*, of practical everyday orientation.

It is in the remarkable "The Origin of the Work of Art" that Heidegger offers something like a theoretical account of art (pp. 34–35):

The equipmental quality of equipment was discovered. But how? Not by a description and explanation of a pair of shoes actually present; not by a report about the process of making shoes; and also not by the observation of the actual use of shoes occurring here and there; but only by bringing ourselves before Van Gogh's painting. The painting spoke. In

the vicinity of the work we were suddenly somewhere else than we usually tend to be.

This is a good articulation of Heidegger's thought that the artwork, in this case
the painting by Van Gogh, brings into view what is usually "unobtrusive and unthought," namely, the nature of equipment (that is to say: its equipmentality).

But he goes farther: the artwork first makes what it reveals—in this case, the
nature of equipment—actual; it brings it forth. I try to explain what this means in
the chapter. Heidegger himself writes (p. 35): "The art work lets us know what shoes
[a piece of equipment] are in truth . . . The work did not, as it might seem at first,
serve merely for a better visualizing of what a piece of equipment is. Rather, the
equipmentality of equipment first genuinely arrives at its appearance through the
work and only in the work."

•

Immanuel Kant's writings on aesthetics are developed in *The Critique of Judgment*
(¶212):

> With the agreeable [that is, with mere matters of liking], the axiom holds
> good: Every one has his own taste . . . The beautiful stands on quite a
> different footing. It would, on the contrary, be ridiculous if any one who
> plumed himself on his taste were to think of justifying himself by saying:
> This object (the building we see, the dress that person has on, the con-
> cert we hear, the poem submitted to our criticism) is beautiful *for me*. For
> if it merely pleases *him*, he must not call it *beautiful*. Many things may for
> him possess charm and agreeableness—no one cares about that; but when
> he puts a thing on a pedestal and calls it beautiful, he demands the same
> delight from others. He judges not merely for himself, but for all men, and
> then speaks of beauty as if it were a property of things. Thus he says the
> *thing* is beautiful; and it is not as if he counted on others agreeing in his
> judgement of liking owing to his having found them in such agreement
> on a number of occasions, but he *demands* this agreement of them. He
> blames them if they judge differently, and denies them taste, which he still
> requires of them as something they ought to have; and to this extent it is
> not open to men to say: Every one has his own taste. This would be equiv-
> alent to saying that there is no such thing at all as taste, i.e. no aesthetic
> judgement capable of making a rightful claim upon the assent of all men.

It is crucial to appreciate that Kant is not being dogmatic here. He is not simply
insisting on the objectivity of our judgments of beauty. No, his very starting point is
the recognition that when it comes to judgments of this sort we have in mind
something "whose determining ground cannot be other than subjective," a matter
of feeling. His aim, rather, is to give an account of what we might call *the phenom-*

enology of aesthetic judgment, that is, the way the aesthetic shows up for us. Kant recognizes that we care about aesthetic judgments; we take them seriously; we expect others, or demand of others that they try, to achieve agreement with us, *even though* the judgments in question are matters of subjective response. If you try to deny the claims to universality implied in our aesthetic judgments, then you lose a grip on the phenomenon itself. This is Kant's fundamental insight.

•

No contemporary writer has done more to bring out this vexing interplay of feeling and judgment, argument and response, claims to objectivity in the face of genuine disagreement, than Stanley Cavell. His remarkable essay "On Aesthetic Problems of Modern Philosophy" (published in *Must We Mean What We Say?*) also explores the marked kinship of aesthetic disagreement with *philosophical* disagreement and controversy. I am indebted to Cavell's investigations of this topic, which is so basic to the project of this book.

•

John Dewey's ideas are laid out in *Art as Experience.*

ACKNOWLEDGMENTS
My dad, Hans Noë, had been a painting student of the sculptor and architect Tony Smith at Cooper Union in New York in the early 1950s. He was with Smith, and two other students (Richard Schust and Tony Louvis), for what turned out to be, not only in their minds, a historic event, which Smith describes:

> When I was teaching at Cooper Union in the first year or two of the fifties, someone told me how I could get onto the unfinished New Jersey Turnpike. I took three students and drove from somewhere in the Meadows to New Brunswick. It was a dark night and there were no lights or shoulder markers, lines, railings, or anything at all except the dark pavement moving through the landscape of the flats, rimmed by hills in the distance, but punctuated by stacks, towers, fumes, and colored lights. This drive was a revealing experience. The road and much of the landscape was artificial, and yet it couldn't be called a work of art. On the other hand, it did something for me that art had never done. At first I didn't know what it was, but its effect was to liberate me from many of the views I had had about art. It seemed that there had been a reality there that had not had any expression in art.
>
> The experience on the road was something mapped out but not socially recognized. I thought to myself, it ought to be clear that's the end of art. Most painting looks pretty pictorial after that. There is no way you can frame it, you just have to experience it. Later I discovered some abandoned

airstrips in Europe—abandoned works, Surrealist landscapes, something that had nothing to do with any function, created worlds without tradition. Artificial landscape without cultural precedent began to dawn on me. There is a drill ground in Nuremberg large enough to accommodate two million men. The entire field is enclosed with high embankments and towers. The concrete approach is three sixteen-inch steps, one above the other, stretching for a mile or so.

The art critic and historian Michael Fried quotes this text in his "Art and Objecthood." For Fried, Smith's discovery of a reality that had not yet found expression in art is really a confused denial of art. For it belongs to art's essence, for Fried, to be pictorial, or articulate, to be a making, a framing. To reject pictoriality—or articulateness, or meaning—is, Fried thinks, to give up on art itself. In this book I have sought to frame a conception of art that vindicates Smith's discovery but without repudiating Fried's conviction that art happens in the domain of the meaningful. Art is always, in the first instance, an opportunity for this kind of transformative and revelatory experience.

•

Evan Thompson and I met in 1995, when I took up a postdoc at Tufts University, at Daniel Dennett's Center for Cognitive Studies, and Evan was working as an assistant professor at Boston University. I met Kevin O'Regan later that academic year. I list some of my work with these collaborators in the bibliography.

•

My essays "Tuning the Body" and "Making Worlds Available" were inspired by Lisa Nelson's ideas.

•

The choreographer, performer, and teacher Nicole Peisl and I jointly created, and performed, "What We Know Best" at Internationales Sommerlabor_2010: Play & Error in Frankfurt on August 27, 2010. A text drawn from this collaboration is reprinted in my *Varieties of Presence*.

•

Plato's so-called Socratic dialogues are thought to be his earliest work. These are true dialogues—that is, they are dramatic in style—and are widely supposed to be Plato's effort to record the ideas of his teacher, Socrates, who never committed his own thoughts to writing. The Socratic dialogues include, it is generally accepted, the *Euthyphro*, the *Laches*, the *Apology*, and the *Crito*. These dialogues exemplify what is known as Socratic elenchus, or Socrates' method of refutation. Interlocutors venture definitions of one or the other of the virtues; Socrates shows them that their definitions are inconsistent with what they, on reflection, already know to be the case. The dialogues end not in discovery of better definitions but in the confusion that comes of being unable to order our various bits of knowledge about the virtues. In the *Meno*, which is a later work, Plato, now in his own voice, examines this apparently negative Socratic philosophical method and asks how it can be, as he urges that it is, a thing of positive value.

Bibliography

Aristotle. *Nicomachean Ethics*. 2nd ed. Trans. Terence Irwin. Indianapolis: Hackett, 1999.

———. *Poetics*. Trans. Ingram Bywater. Oxford: Oxford University Press, 1920.

Arthur, W. Brian. *The Nature of Technology: What It Is and How It Evolves*. New York: Free Press, 2009.

Barber, Charles. *Figure and Likeness: On the Limits of Representation in Byzantine Iconoclasm*. Princeton, NJ: Princeton University Press, 2002.

Ballard, Dana H., Mary M. Hayahoe, Polly K. Pook, and Rajesh P. N. Rao. "Deictic Codes for the Embodiment of Cognition." *Behavioral and Brain Sciences* 20 (4) (1997): 723–42.

Bovet, Dalila, and Jacques Vauclair. "Picture Recognition in Animals and Humans." *Behavioral and Brain Research* 109 (2000): 143–65.

Bredekamp, Horst. *Galilei der Künstler: Der Mond, die Sonne, die Hand*. Berlin: Akademie Verlag, 2007.

———. *Theorie des Bildakts*. Berlin: Suhrkamp, 2010.

Buckner, Randy L., Jessica R. Andrews-Hanna, and Daniel Schacter. "The Brain's Default Network: Anatomy, Function, and Relevance to Disease." *Annals of the New York Academy of Sciences* 1124 (2008): 1–38.

Burrows, Jonathan. *A Choreographer's Handbook*. New York: Routledge, 2010.

Cage, John. *I–VI*. Cambridge, MA: Harvard University Press, 1990.

Cappella, J., and S. Planalp. "Talk and Silence Sequences in Informal Conversations III: Interspeaker Influence." *Human Communication Research* 7 (1981): 117–32.

Carroll, Noël. *Comedy Incarnate*. Malden, MA: Blackwell, 2007.

———. *The Philosophy of Horror, Or, Paradoxes of the Heart*. New York: Routledge, 1990.

Cavanagh, Patrick. "The Artist as Neuroscientist." *Nature* 434, no. 17 (March 2005): 301–307.

Cavell, Stanley. *Must We Mean What We Say?* New York: Scribner, 1969.

Chalmers, David J. "Perception and the Fall from Eden." In *Perceptual Experience*, edited by Tamar Szabó Gendler and John Hawthorne. New York: Oxford University Press, 2006.

Charlton, S. G. "Driving While Conversing: Cell Phones That Distract and Passengers Who React." *Accident Analysis and Prevention* 41, no. 1 (2009): 160–73.

Chatterjee, Anjan. *The Aesthetic Brain: How We Evolved to Desire Beauty and Enjoy Art.* New York: Oxford University Press, 2014.

Christoff, Kalina, Diego Cosmelli, Dorothée Legrand, and Evan Thompson. "Specifying the Self for Cognitive Neuroscience." *Trends in Cognitive Sciences* 15, no. 3 (2011): 104–12.

Clark, Andy. *Supersizing the Mind: Embodiment, Action, and Cognitive Extension.* New York: Oxford University Press, 2008.

Clark, Andy, and David J. Chalmers. "The Extended Mind." *Analysis* 58, no. 1 (1998): 7–19.

Condon, W. "An Analysis of Behavioral Organization." *Sign Language Studies* 13 (1976): 285–318.

Condon, W. S., and W. D. Ogston. "Sound Film Analysis of Normal and Pathological Behavior Patterns." *Journal of Nervous and Mental Diseases* 143 (1966): 338–47.

Crick, Francis. *The Astonishing Hypothesis: The Scientific Search for the Soul.* New York: Scribner, 1994.

Damasio, Antonio. *Descartes' Error: Emotion, Reason, and the Human Brain.* New York: Putnam, 1994.

———. *The Feeling of What Happens: Body and Emotion in the Making of Consciousness.* New York: Harcourt, 1999.

Davies, Stephen. *The Artful Species: Aesthetics, Art, and Evolution.* Oxford: Oxford University Press, 2012.

Davis, Whitney. *A General Theory of Visual Culture.* Princeton, NJ: Princeton University Press, 2011.

Deacon, Terrence. *The Symbolic Species.* New York: Norton, 1997.

DeLoache, Judy S., Sophia L. Pierroutsakos, David H. Uttal, Karl S. Rosengren, and Alma Gottlieb. "Grasping the Nature of Pictures." *Psychological Science* 9, no. 3 (May 1998): 205–10.

Dennett, Daniel C. *Brainstorms.* Cambridge, MA: MIT Press, 1978.

———. *Consciousness Explained.* Boston: Little, Brown, 1991.

———. *Content and Consciousness.* 2nd ed. Boston: Routledge, 1986.

———. *Darwin's Dangerous Idea: Evolutions and the Meanings of Life.* New York: Simon and Schuster, 1995.

———. *The Intentional Stance.* Cambridge, MA: MIT Press, 1987.

Dewey, John. *Art as Experience.* 1934; repr., New York: Penguin, 1980.

Dissanayake, Ellen. *Homo Aestheticus: Where Art Comes From and Why.* New York: Free Press, 1992.

Dupré, John. *Human Nature and the Limits of Science*. New York: Oxford University Press, 2001.

Dupré, John, and Rae Langton. "Gender Differences All in the Mind." Letter to the editor, *The Guardian*, December 5, 2013.

Dyer, Geoff. *Zona: A Book About a Film About a Journey to a Room*. New York: Pantheon, 2012.

Fine, Cordelia. *Delusions of Gender*. New York: Norton, 2010.

Fingerhut, Joerg. "Extended Imagery, Extended Access, or Something Else? Pictures and the Extended Mind Hypothesis." In *Bildakt at the Warburg Institute*, edited by S. Marienberg and J. Trabant, 33–50. Berlin: de Gruyter, 2014.

Frege, Gottlob. *Collected Papers on Mathematics, Logic, and Philosophy*. Trans. Max Black. New York: Blackwell, 1984.

Fried, Michael. "Art and Objecthood." *Artforum* 5 (June 1967): 12–23.

———. *Courbet's Realism*. Chicago: University of Chicago Press, 1990.

———. *Menzel's Realism: Art and Embodiment in Nineteenth-Century Berlin*. New Haven, CT: Yale University Press, 2002.

Gibson, James. *The Ecological Approach to Visual Perception*. Boston: Houghton Mifflin, 1979.

Giles, H. "Accent Mobility: A Model and Some Data." *Anthropological Linguistics* 15 (1973): 87–105.

Golland, Y., et al. "Extrinsic and Intrinsic Systems in the Posterior Cortex of the Human Brain Revealed During Natural Sensory Stimulation." *Cerebral Cortex* 17 (2007): 766–77.

Gombrich, E. H. *Meditations on a Hobby Horse and Other Essays on the Theory of Art*. London: Phaidon, 1963.

———. *The Story of Art*. New York: Phaidon, 1950.

Gopnik, Blake. "Aesthetic Science and Artistic Knowledge." In Shimamura and Palmer, *Aesthetic Science*, 129–60.

Gould, Stephen Jay. *The Mismeasure of Man*. New York: Norton, 1981.

Gould, Stephen Jay, and Richard C. Lewontin. "The Spandrels of San Marco and the Panglossian Paradigm: A Critique of the Adaptationist Programme." *Proceedings of the Royal Society of London*, series B, 25 (1979): 581–98.

Gregory, Richard L. *Eye and Brain: The Psychology of Seeing*. 5th ed. Princeton, NJ: Princeton University Press, 1997.

Greicius, M. D., and V. Menon, "Default-Mode Activity During a Passive Sensory Task: Uncoupled from Deactivation but Impacting Activation." *Journal of Cognitive Neuroscience* 16 (2004): 1484–92.

Gumbrecht, Hans Ulrich. *In Praise of Athletic Beauty*. Cambridge, MA: Harvard University Press, 2006.

Hacking, Ian. *The Social Construction of What?* Cambridge, MA: Harvard University Press, 1999.

Harris, Roy. *The Language-Makers*. Ithaca, NY: Cornell University Press, 1980.

———. *The Language Myth*. New York: St. Martin's Press, 1981.

———. *The Origin of Writing*. La Salle, IL: Open Court, 1986.

Havelock, Eric A. *Preface to Plato*. Cambridge, MA: Harvard University Press, 1963.

Heidegger, Martin. *The Basic Problems of Phenomenology*. Trans. Albert Hofstadter. Bloomington: Indiana University Press, 1982.

———. *Being and Time*. Trans. John Macquarrie and Edward Robinson. New York: Harper, 1962.

———. *Fundamental Concepts of Metaphysics: World, Finitude, Solitude*. Trans. William McNeill and Nicholas Walker. Bloomington: Indiana University Press, 1995.

———. "The Origin of the Work of Art." In *Poetry, Language, Thought*, translated by Albert Hofstadter, 15–86. New York: Harper, 1971.

Hickey, Dave. *Air Guitar: Essays on Art and Democracy*. Los Angeles: Art Issues Press, 1997.

Hollander, Anne. *Seeing Through Clothes*. New York: Viking, 1978.

Hopkins, Robert. *Picture, Image, Experience*. New York: Cambridge University Press, 1998.

Hubel, David H., and Torsten Wiesel. *Brain and Visual Perception: The Story of a 25-Year Collaboration*. New York: Oxford University Press, 2005.

Hume, David. *A Treatise of Human Nature*. 2nd ed. New York: Oxford University Press, 1978.

Hurley, S. L. *Consciousness in Action*. Cambridge, MA: Harvard University Press, 2002.

Hurley, Susan L., and Alva Noë. "Neural Plasticity and Consciousness." *Biology and Philosophy* 18 (2003): 131–68.

Hyman, John. "Art and Neuroscience." In *Beyond Mimesis and Convention*, edited by R. Frigg and M. C. Hunter, 245–61. Dordrecht, The Netherlands: Springer, 2010.

———. *The Imitation of Nature*. New York: Blackwell, 1989.

———. *The Objective Eye: Color, Form, and Reality in the Theory of Art*. Chicago: University of Chicago Press, 2006.

James, William. *Principles of Psychology*. Vol. 1. New York: Henry Holt, 1890.

Kandel, Eric R. *The Age of Insight: The Quest to Understand the Unconscious in Art, Mind, and Brain*. New York: Random House, 2012.

Kant, Immanuel. *The Critique of Judgment*. Trans. James Creed Meredith. New York: Oxford University Press, 1978.

———. *The Critique of Pure Reason*. Trans. Paul Guyer and Allen W. Wood. New York: Cambridge University Press, 1998.

Kaye, Kenneth. *The Mental and Social Life of Babies: How Parents Create Persons*. Chicago: University of Chicago Press, 1982.

Kelso, J. A. Scott. *Dynamic Patterns: The Self-Organization of Brain and Behavior*. Cambridge, MA: MIT Press, 1995.

Kendon, A. "Movement Coordination in Social Interaction: Some Examples Described." *Acta Psychologica* 32 (1970): 100–125.

Kittler, Ralf, Manfred Kayser, and Mark Stoneking. "Molecular Evolution of *Pediculus humanus* and the Origin of Clothing." *Current Biology* 13 (2003): 1414–17.

LaFrance, M. "Posture Mirroring and Rapport." In *Interaction Rhythms: Periodicity in Communicative Behavior*, edited by Martha Davis, 279–98. New York: Human Sciences Press, 1982.

Lindberg, David C. *Theories of Vision from Al-Kindi to Kepler*. Chicago: University of Chicago Press, 1976.

Livingstone, Margaret. *Vision and Art: The Biology of Seeing*. New York: Harry N. Abrams, 2013.

Locke, John. *An Essay Concerning Human Understanding*. Oxford: Clarendon Press, 1975.

Maguire, Henry. *Art and Eloquence in Byzantium*. Princeton, NJ: Princeton University Press, 1981.

Malcolm, Norman. *Ludwig Wittgenstein: A Memoir*. 2nd ed. New York: Oxford University Press, 1984.

Marr, David. *Vision*. San Francisco: W. H. Freeman, 1982.

Maturana, Humberto R., and Francisco J. Varela. *Autopoiesis and Cognition: The Realization of the Living*. Boston: Reidel, 1980.

McDowell, John. *Mind and World*. Cambridge, MA: Harvard University Press, 1994.

Merleau-Ponty, Maurice. *Phenomenology of Perception*. Trans. Donald A. Landes. 1945; repr., New York: Routledge, 2012.

Miller, Geoffrey. *The Mating Mind: How Sexual Choice Shaped the Evolution of Human Nature*. New York: Doubleday, 2000.

Montero, Barbara Gail. "The Myth of 'Just Do It.'" *The New York Times*, June 9, 2013.

Mulhall, Stephen. *On Film*. New York: Routledge, 2008.

Nagel, Alexander. *The Controversy of Renaissance Art*. Chicago: University of Chicago Press, 2011.

———. *Medieval Modern: Art out of Time*. New York: Thames and Hudson, 2012.

Nagel, Alexander, and Christopher S. Wood. *Anachronic Renaissance*. New York: Zone Books, 2010.

Nagel, Thomas. *Mind and Cosmos: Why the Materialist Neo-Darwinian Conception of Nature Is Almost Certainly False*. New York: Oxford University Press, 2012.

———. *The View from Nowhere*. New York: Oxford University Press, 1986.

Natale, M. "Convergence of Mean Vocal Intensity in Dyadic Communications as a Function of Social Desirability." *Journal of Personality and Social Psychology* 32 (1975): 790–804.

Nehamas, Alexander. *Only a Promise of Happiness: The Place of Beauty in a World of Art*. Princeton, NJ: Princeton University Press, 2007.

Noë, Alva. *Action in Perception*. Cambridge, MA: MIT Press, 2004.

———. "Art and the Limits of Neuroscience." *The New York Times*, "The Stone," December 4, 2011, http://opinionator.blogs.nytimes.com/2011/12/04/art-and-the-limits-of-neuroscience/.

————. "Experience and Experiment in Art." *Journal of Consciousness Studies* 7, nos. 8–9 (2000).

————. "Gender Is Dead! Long Live Gender." *13.7: Cosmos & Culture*, June 24, 2011, www.npr.org/13.7.

————. "The Hands of Leonardo." *13.7: Cosmos & Culture*, December 9, 2011, www.npr.org/13.7.

————. "Is There a Conflict Between Science and Religion?" *13.7: Cosmos & Culture*, March 2, 2012, www.npr.org/13.7.

————, ed. "Is the Visual World a Grand Illusion?" In *Is the Visual World a Grand Illusion?* Exeter, UK: Imprint Academic, 2002.

————. "Lost and Found: The Art of Richard Serra." *13.7: Cosmos & Culture*, October 21, 2011, www.npr.org/13.7.

————. "Lost and Found: Working Back to the Meaning of Things in the Work of Robert Lazzarini." In *Guns, Knives, Brass Knuckles*, edited by Robert Lazzarini, Judith Rodenbeck, Alva Noë, and Jonathan T. D. Neil. Los Angeles: Honor Fraser, 2012.

————. "Making Worlds Available." In *Knowledge in Motion: Perspectives of Artistic and Scientific Research in Dance*, edited by Sabine Gehm, Pirkko Husemann, and Katharina von Wilcke. Bielefeld: Transcript Verlag, 2007.

————. "An Object of Contention at the Venice Biennale." *13.7: Cosmos & Culture*, May 31, 2013, www.npr.org/13.7.

————. "On Being Gay, Being Out and Being Art." *13.7: Cosmos & Culture*, November 19, 2011, www.npr.org/13.7.

————. *Out of Our Heads.* New York: Hill and Wang, 2009.

————. "A Philosopher's View of *Rosemary's Baby*," *13.7: Cosmos & Culture*, June 7, 2014, www.npr.org/13.7.

————. "The Producers: Are Pictures Detaching Us From Life?" *13.7: Cosmos & Culture*, May 13, 2011, www.npr.org/13.7.

————. "Running up Against the Limits of Nature." *British Journal of Aesthetics* (forthcoming).

————. "Seeing Music for What It Is." *13.7: Cosmos & Culture*, August 25, 2013, www.npr.org/13.7.

————. "There's Nothing to Do Here, and It's Perfect." *13.7: Cosmos & Culture*, August 31, 2013, www.npr.org/13.7.

————. "Tuning the Body." *Ballettanz* (April 2006).

————. "Unraveled Ravel Is a Revelation." *13.7: Cosmos & Culture*, September 7, 2013, www.npr.org/13.7.

————. *Varieties of Presence.* Cambridge, MA: Harvard University Press, 2012.

————. "The World Looked Better Through Anne Hollander's Eyes." *13.7: Cosmos & Culture*, July 11, 2014, www.npr.org/13.7.

Noë, Alva, and Evan Thompson. "Are There Neural Correlates of Consciousness?" *Journal of Consciousness Studies* 11, no. 1 (2004): 3–28.

Ofek, Haim. *Second Nature: Economic Origins of Human Evolution.* New York: Cambridge University Press, 2001.

Ong, Walter J. *Orality and Literacy: The Technologizing of the Word*. New York: Methuen, 1982.

Onians, John. "Neuroarchaeology and the Origins of Representation in the Grotte de Chauvet." In *Image and Imagination: A Global Prehistory of Figurative Representation*, edited by Colin Renfrew and Iain Morley. Cambridge, UK: McDonald Institute for Archeological Research, University of Cambridge, 2007.

————. *Neuroarthistory: From Aristotle and Pliny to Baxandall and Zeki*. New Haven, CT: Yale University Press, 2007.

O'Regan, J. Kevin. *Why Red Doesn't Sound Like a Bell: Understanding the Feel of Consciousness*. New York: Oxford University Press, 2011.

O'Regan, J. Kevin, and Alva Noë. "A Sensorimotor Account of Vision and Visual Consciousness." *Behavioral and Brain Sciences* 24, no. 5 (2001): 939–73.

Palmer, Robert. *Deep Blues: A Musical and Cultural History of the Mississippi Delta*. New York: Penguin, 1982.

Patel, Aniruddh D. *Music, Language, and the Brain*. New York: Oxford University Press, 2008.

Pessoa, L., E. Thompson, and A. Noë. "Finding out About Filling-in: A Guide to Perceptual Completion for Visual Science and the Philosophy of Perception." *The Behavioral and Brain Sciences* 21, no. 6 (1998): 723–48.

Peters, Deniz, Gerhard Eckel, and Andreas Dorschel. *Bodily Expression in Electronic Music: Perspectives on Reclaiming Performativity*. London: Routledge, 2012.

Pinker, Steven. *How the Mind Works*. New York: Norton, 1997.

Plantinga, Alvin. *Where the Conflict Really Lies: Science, Religion, and Naturalism*. New York: Oxford University Press, 2011.

Plato. *Five Dialogues: Euthyphro, Apology, Crito, Meno, Phaedo*. Translated by G.M.A. Grube. Indianapolis: Hackett, 1981.

————. *Republic*. Trans. Paul Shorey. 2 vols. Cambridge, MA: Harvard University Press, 1953, 1956.

Prinz, Jesse. *The Conscious Brain: How Attention Engenders Experience*. New York: Oxford University Press, 2012.

————. "How Wonder Works." *Aeon Magazine*, June 21, 2013, http://aeon.co/magazine/psychology/why-wonder-is-the-most-human-of-all-emotions/.

————. "Wonder Works: Renovating Romanticism About Art." *Aesthetics for Birds*, August 5, 2013, www.aestheticsforbirds.com/2013/08/wonder-works-renovating-romanticism.html.

————. *Works of Wonder: The Psychology and Ontology of Art*. Oxford: Oxford University Press (forthcoming).

Prum, Richard O. "Coevolutionary Aesthetics in Human and Biotic Artworlds." *Biology and Philosophy* 28 (2013): 811–32.

Putnam, Hilary. *Renewing Philosophy*. Cambridge, MA: Harvard University Press, 1992.

————. *The Threefold Cord: Mind, Body, and World*. New York: Columbia University Press, 1999.

Radford, Andrew. *Transformational Syntax: A Student's Guide to Chomsky's Extended Standard Theory*. Cambridge, UK: Cambridge University Press, 1981.

Ramachandran, Vilayanur S., and William Hirstein. "The Science of Art: A Neurological Theory of Aesthetic Experience." *Journal of Consciousness Studies* 6, no. 6–7 (1999): 15–51.

Ridley, Matt. *The Rational Optimist: How Prosperity Evolves*. New York: Harper, 2010.

Rodríguez-Vidal, Joaquín, et al. "A Rock Engraving Made by Neanderthals in Gibraltar." *Proceedings of the National Academy of Sciences* 111, no. 37 (2014): 13301–306.

Sacks, Oliver. *Musicophilia: Tales of Music and the Brain*. Rev ed. New York: Vintage, 2008.

Scholl, Brian J., Nicholaus S. Noles, Vanya Pasheva, and Rachel Sussman. "Talking on a Cellular Telephone Dramatically Increases 'Sustained Inattentional Blindness.'" *Journal of Vision* 3, no. 9 (October 22, 2003), article 156.

Schönborn, Christoph. *God's Human Face: The Christ-Icon*. Trans. Lothar Krauth. San Francisco: Ignatius Press, 1994.

Scruton, Roger. *The Aesthetics of Music*. Oxford: Oxford University Press, 1999.

Shimamura, Arthur P. *Experiencing Art: In the Brain of the Beholder*. New York: Oxford University Press, 2013.

Shimamura, Arthur P., and Stephen E. Palmer, eds. *Aesthetic Science: Connecting Minds, Brains and Experience*. New York: Oxford University Press, 2014.

Shiner, Larry. *The Invention of Art: A Cultural History*. Chicago: University of Chicago Press, 2001.

Shockley, K., D. C. Richardson, and R. Dale. "Conversation and Coordinative Structures." *Topics in Cognitive Science* 1 (2009): 305–19.

Shockley, K., M. V. Santana, and C. A. Fowler. "Mutual Interpersonal Postural Constraints Are Involved in Cooperative Conversation." *Journal of Experimental Psychology: Human Perception and Performance* 29 (2003): 326–32.

Spreng, R. N., et al. "Default Network Activity, Coupled with the Frontoparietal Control Network, Supports Goal-Directed Cognition." *Neuroimage* 53 (2010): 303–17.

Starr, G. Gabrielle. *Feeling Beauty: The Neuroscience of Aesthetic Experience*. Cambridge, MA: MIT Press, 2013.

Street, R. L. "Speech Convergence and Speech Evaluation in Fact-Finding Interviews." *Human Communication Research* 11 (1984): 139–69.

Thompson, Evan. *Colour Vision*. New York: Routledge, 1995.

———. *Mind in Life: Biology, Phenomenology, and the Sciences of Mind*. Cambridge, MA: Harvard University Press, 2007.

Thompson, Evan, and Francisco J. Varela. "Radical Embodiment: Neural Dynamics and Consciousness." *Trends in Cognitive Sciences* 10, no. 5 (2010): 418–25.

Tsay, Chia-Jung. "Sight Over Sound in the Judgment of Music Performance." *Proceedings of the National Academy of Science* 110, no. 36 (2013), 14580–85.

Varela, Francisco J., Evan Thompson, and Eleanor Rosch. *The Embodied Mind: Cognitive Science and Human Experience.* Cambridge, MA: MIT Press, 1991.

Vessel, E. A., G. G. Starr, and N. Rubin. "Art Reaches Within: Aesthetic Experience, the Self and the Default Mode Network." *Frontiers in Human Neuroscience* 7 (2013): 258.

———. "The Brain on Art: Intense Aesthetic Experience Activates the Default Mode Network. *Frontiers in Human Neuroscience* 6 (2012): 66.

Wade, Nicholas. *Before the Dawn: Recovering the Lost History of Our Ancestors.* New York: Penguin Press, 2006.

———. "What a Story Lice Can Tell." *The New York Times*, October 5, 2004, F1.

Weschler, Lawrence. "Variations of a Theme by Duchamp." *Glasstire*, June 1, 2014.

Williams, Bernard. *Descartes: The Project of Pure Enquiry.* Atlantic Highlands, NJ: Humanities Press, 1978.

———. *Ethics and the Limits of Philosophy.* Cambridge, MA: Harvard University Press, 1985.

Wilson, Edward O., *Sociobiology: The New Synthesis.* Cambridge, MA: Harvard University Press, 1975.

Wilson, S. M., et al. "Beyond Superior Temporal Cortex: Intersubject Correlations in Narrative Speech Comprehension." *Cerebral Cortex* 18 (2008): 230–42.

Wittgenstein, Ludwig. *The Blue and Brown Books.* New York: Harper, 1958.

———. *Philosophical Investigations.* Trans. G. E. M. Anscombe. Oxford: Blackwell, 1954.

———. *Philosophical Remarks.* Trans. Raymond Hargreaves and Roger White. Chicago: University of Chicago Press, 1980.

———. *Tractatus Logico-Philosophicus.* Trans. C. K. Ogden. New York: Routledge, 1990.

———. *Wittgenstein's Lectures, Cambridge, 1932–1935: From the Notes of Alice Ambrose and Margaret Macdonald.* Chicago: University of Chicago Press, 1982.

Wölfflin, Heinrich. *Principles of Art History: The Problem of the Development of Style in Later Art.* Trans. M. D. Hottinger. New York: Dover, 1950.

Zeki, Semir. *Inner Vision: An Exploration of Art and the Brain.* New York: Oxford University Press, 1999.

Index

A NOTE ABOUT THE AUTHOR

Alva Noë is a professor of philosophy at the University of California, Berkeley, where he also serves as a member of the Institute for Cognitive and Brain Sciences. A graduate of Columbia University, he holds a B.Phil. from the University of Oxford and a Ph.D. from Harvard University. Noë is the recipient of a 2012 Guggenheim fellowship and is a weekly contributor to NPR's science blog *13.7: Cosmos & Culture*. Visit his website at www.alvanoe.com.